4/4/01

HOLMES
AND
WATSON

HOLMES
AND
WATSON

JUNE THOMSON

CARROLL & GRAF PUBLISHERS, INC.
NEW YORK

First Carroll & Graf edition 2001

Carroll & Graf Publishers, Inc.
A Division of Avalon Publishing Group
19 West 21st Street
New York, NY 10010-6805

Library of Congress Cataloging-in-Publication Data is available.
ISBN: 0-7867-0827-1

Manufactured in the United States of America

For Andrew, Lee, Frances and John Paul

ACKNOWLEDGEMENTS

I should like to thank the following people for their generous help with the research for this book: H. M. Brodie, Archivist of Blackheath Football Club; Catherine Cooke, Curator of the Sherlock Holmes' Collection at Marylebone Library who also read the manuscript and gave invaluable advice; Julia Sheppard, Archivist of the Contemporary Archives Centre at the Wellcome Institute for the History of Medicine; and Geoffrey Yeo, former head of the Archives Department at St Bartholomew's Hospital.

I also thank Professor B. J. Rahn for her very special assistance, and Rita and Malcolm de Selincourt for their help with the binomial theorem.

Finally, I should like to pay tribute to the memory of the late Sir Arthur Conan Doyle, author of the canon and creator of those two immortal characters, Sherlock Holmes and Dr John H. Watson MD, without whom this book could not have been written.

PROLOGUE

Any attempt to write a biography of Holmes and Watson is fraught with problems. Not only is the canon itself immense, amounting approximately to 700,000 words, but Sherlockian commentators have, over the years, written many thousand more words about it and around it, their contributions ranging from suppositions regarding Holmes' astronomical sign – was he a Scorpio or a Virgo? – to a full-length novel by Cay Van Ash, *Ten Years Beyond Baker Street*, in which Holmes, having brought about the downfall of Professor Moriarty, takes on no less a protagonist than Dr Fu Manchu.

It is impossible to refer to all these writings in detail within the scope of this biography. I have therefore chosen only those which tend to affect the chronology of the subjects' lives. Rather than hold up the narrative by including these in the main part of the book, I have placed the references to them in two appendices, in which those readers interested in particular areas of Sherlockian research, such as the dating of some of Watson's accounts or the location of 221B Baker Street, will find the relevant theories set out in condensed form.

Wherever possible, I have kept to the facts given by Holmes and Watson in the canon and, where there are gaps, have used other sources of information to supply the missing data. When that has been impossible and I have been forced to speculate, I have made this quite clear.

Because readers might find it tedious, I have also limited the number of attributions to the places in the canon where direct quotations can be found and, with some of the less important data, have given no references at all. However, where any detail is stated as fact, readers may be assured that this is based on given information. Nor have I supplied, except in a few cases, potted accounts of the inquiries in which Holmes and Watson were involved. I have assumed that the readers are already acquainted with the narratives or would prefer to read them for themselves.

In the course of this biography, I have also put forward some theories of my own, for example, those regarding the identities of the king of Bohemia and the second Mrs Watson, both of which, as far as I know, are original. Some Sherlockian commentators may find these unacceptable, as they may find much else that is in the book.

But the biography is not intended for the experts. It was written with a very different reader in mind: the ordinary man or woman who, like me, has found much pleasure in Watson's chronicles of his adventures with Holmes and would like a more detailed account of their lives as well as background information about the period in which they lived.

My main concern, however, as the title suggests, is to celebrate the friendship between Holmes and Watson, arguably one of the most famous ever recorded, and to chronicle its progress, including the setbacks from which it inevitably suffered.

It was not, I believe, homosexual although some evidence in the canon might suggest, on first reading, a homoerotic relationship, such as the fact that Holmes and Watson share a double bedroom during the Man with the Twisted Lip inquiry or that Holmes bundles Watson out of sight in the Dying Detective case with the words 'Quick, man, if you love me!' Although on occasions he might have been naif, Watson possessed a great deal of common sense and, knowing, as he must have done, the penalties of social ostracism should sexual deviation be suspected, or imprisonment should he be found engaging in homosexual activities, he would hardly have risked rousing suspicion by publishing these admissions unless he knew his own and Holmes' sexual behaviour was beyond reproach.

Watson also married twice, on both occasions for love. No one who has read his account of his courtship of Mary Morstan and his description of his feelings for her can doubt they are anything other than genuine. Nevertheless, Rohase Piercy in his book *My Dearest Holmes* has claimed that Watson, who was in love with

Holmes, married Mary for convenience only, in order to appear respectable and to cloak his own homosexual practices.

I consider this a quite erroneous interpretation of his relationships both with Holmes and Mary Morstan. Watson, one of whose most endearing qualities was an inability to lie convincingly, was incapable of carrying through such a sustained deception on his readers.

His relationship with Holmes was therefore exactly as he describes it: a close friendship and an example of male bonding which, though not unusual in itself, especially in an age of single-sex schools and gentlemen's clubs, is unique because of the detailed account of it which Watson has given us and also for its strength of endurance, despite the many strains to which it was subjected. It was a friendship which was to last for at least forty-six years.

CHAPTER ONE

HOLMES AND WATSON

Beginnings

'My dear fellow, life is infinitely stranger than anything
which the mind of man could invent.'

Holmes to Watson: *A Case of Identity.*

Holmes and Watson: their names are inextricably linked while
their friendship is known throughout the world, a fame which is
largely attributable to Watson who, as Holmes' chronicler, was to
write over half a million words about their relationship and their
adventures together. These accounts, which have never been out
of print, were later translated into most languages and used as
the basis for numerous films and plays as well as television and
radio programmes which have assured their continuing
popularity.

And yet remarkably little is known about their early lives
before their celebrated meeting in 1881. Not even their dates of
birth can be established with any certainty.

It is not altogether surprising. Holmes was deliberately
reticent about his past for reasons which will be examined in
more detail later in the chapter. As for Watson, he was more
concerned with recording Holmes' exploits and publicizing his
friend's unique skills as a private consulting detective than with
thrusting his own personal reminiscences upon his readers.
However, there are clues within the canon and, where evidence
is lacking, some of the gaps can be filled from other sources of
information.

Holmes was probably born in 1854.* In *His Last Bow: The War Service of Sherlock Holmes*, dated August 1914, Holmes is described as a man of sixty. Therefore, he was, like Watson, a Victorian, born within the reign of Queen Victoria, who succeeded to the throne in 1837. The month of his birth is unknown; so, too, is the place although some commentators have put forward various theories about both.*

Little is known either about his immediate family apart from the fact that he had one brother, Mycroft, who was seven years his senior. However, his background was what his fellow Victorians, with their fine distinctions over such matters of social status, would have defined as upper middle-class. Holmes himself has provided some information about his antecedents. His ancestors, he tells Watson in *The Adventure of the Greek Interpreter*, were country squires 'who appear to have led much the same life as is natural to their class'. In other words, they were more concerned with running their estates and following such leisure activities as hunting, shooting and fishing than in scholarly or artistic pursuits.

Holmes ascribes his own and his brother's quite different interests to his grandmother, the sister of Vernet, the French painter, from whom both had inherited their less conventional natures.

As Holmes remarks, 'Art in the blood is liable to take the strangest forms.'

Holmes does not say whether this Mlle Vernet was a paternal or maternal grandmother nor which Vernet was her brother. There were several Vernets, all artists, but the most likely candidate, as many commentators agree, is Horace Vernet (1789–1863), the son of Carle Vernet (1758–1836), who was awarded the Légion d'Honneur by Napoleon for his painting, *Morning of Austerlitz*. Horace Vernet was himself a distinguished artist. Holmes' grandmother was most probably a daughter of this same Carle Vernet and was therefore Horace Vernet's sister. The dates agree and there is further confirmation in a comment made by the composer Felix Mendelssohn on Horace Vernet's extraordinary memory, which he compared to a well-stocked

* See Appendix One

14

bureau. 'He had but to open a drawer in it to find what was needed,' he is quoted as saying.

This gift was inherited by both the Holmes brothers, by Mycroft with his capacity for storing and correlating facts which he was to put to good use in his future career, and by Sherlock in his ability to recall information at will, a talent which is remarkably similar to that of his great-uncle Horace Vernet.

'I hold a vast store of out-of-the-way knowledge, without scientific system, but very available for the needs of my work,' he was later to say of himself.

Some commentators have expressed surprise that Mycroft Holmes had apparently not inherited the family estates. But Holmes makes it quite clear that it was his *ancestors* who were the country squires, possibly as far back as a great grandfather or even a great-great grandfather. If he and Mycroft were descended from a younger son, they would have belonged to the cadet branch of the family and therefore Mycroft would not have been a direct heir. Or they may have descended through the female line, in which case 'Holmes' would not have been the ancestral surname.

Holmes may have inherited more from his French grandmother than his unusual talents. His mercurial temperament suggests the influence of his Gallic genes rather than those of his more stolid and conventional Anglo-Saxon antecedents. Indeed, the extreme swings of mood from which he suffered in his early manhood, and presumably also in childhood and adolescence, suggest some of the symptoms of manic depression without its psychotic features, although whether this should be entirely blamed on his French blood is questionable. He could have inherited this tendency from one of his English fox-hunting forebears. But, whatever its source, this cyclothymic temperament is undoubtedly part of his personality which may have been exacerbated by his upbringing.

Holmes says nothing at all about his parents. However, his 'strong aversion to women', as Watson was later to report, is significant. From various comments Holmes made on the subject, it is possible to form a clear idea of his attitude towards them. They are inscrutable, trivial, illogical and vain. They vacillate, are subject to emotional outbursts and are naturally secretive.

15

'Woman are never to be entirely trusted – not even the best of them,' he states in one particularly revealing remark. However, he was always polite to them, the mark of a gentleman, and, when he wished, could have a 'peculiarly ingratiating way' with them.

This mistrust can only have been formed from personal experience and the most likely cause, as many psychiatrists would agree, is found in the mother/child relationship.

Given Holmes' remarks, it is possible to build up a credible, if speculative, picture of his mother. She was a vain, shallow and self-centred woman, more interested in her own pleasures than in forming a close and loving bond with her children, whom she handed over to the care of servants, as was usual at that time among women of her class.

To a small child, who may well have inherited a tendency towards manic depression, such lack of maternal affection would have had serious effects on his subsequent psychological development. At the very least, it would have given rise to anxiety and tension, evident, in Holmes' case, in such nervous mannerisms as nail-biting, pacing restlessly about, twisting his fingers together or drumming them on the table.

Even his dislike of chess* may be traced back to those early childhood experiences. As a game, it has all the intellectual and logical challenges which should have appealed to him. However, it is significant that the most dominant piece in chess is the queen, which alone has the ability to move freely about the board, an obvious symbol of the all-powerful mother.

Such symbolism may also be reflected in Holmes' interest in later life in bee-keeping, an activity in which a queen again plays an important role. However, in this instance, though forming the nucleus of the hive, she is an inert, passive creature whose only function is to lay eggs. In short, although a sex object, she is rendered harmless. He was to write a *Practical Handbook of Bee Culture, with Some Observations upon the Segregation of the Queen.*

---

* In *The Adventure of the Retired Colourman* Holmes states that Amberley's proficiency at chess was the mark of a 'scheming mind'. As William S. Baring-Gould has pointed out, most Sherlockian students believe Holmes was not himself a chess-player although he used chess terms and expressions in his conversation.

Although Holmes himself may have been unaware of the significance of this title, readers will not need to have their attention drawn to it.

A child who is deprived of his mother's love may also find difficulty in forming close relationships. This, too, is true of Holmes who, as a protective shell against further rejection, could have deliberately developed that coldness of temperament which Watson was to criticize on several occasions, unaware that this lack of emotional warmth was a consequence of Holmes' upbringing.

Such suppression of the feelings could also have encouraged Holmes to regard logical and rational thought as superior to the emotions, leading in turn to his interest in science, in particular to chemistry with its emphasis on precise analysis. This analytical turn of mind combined with his undoubted intelligence and an unwillingness to suffer fools gladly made him insensitive to other people's feelings. He was far too quick to see others' weaknesses and too frank in pointing them out, an outspokenness which led Watson to accuse him, not without justification, of egotism.

Watson tempered this criticism by adding that, although callous, Holmes was never cruel. Certainly, there were occasions when he was downright rude and his behaviour hurtful, although it should be said in his defence that he was also capable of great kindness.

Holmes never married and he almost certainly remained celibate all his life. In Victorian times, the opportunities for sex outside marriage were limited either to casual encounters with prostitutes or a more permanent liaison with a mistress. Holmes was too fastidious for the former type of relationship and too wary of women to commit himself to the latter, although he was not entirely asexual. Later, he was to be attracted to one woman in particular and, had events not prevented it, might have married her or at least had an affair with her. But she was exceptional and he was never again to meet anyone who measured up to her beauty, intelligence and strength of personality. Holmes was too much of a perfectionist to settle for second-best. Instead, his sexual energy was channelled into other outlets, principally into an overwhelming need for achievement, the roots of which may also be traced back to his childhood.

An emotionally deprived child may suffer from low self-esteem, a feeling that, if he is not given love, then it is because he is unworthy of it. This, too, can lead to depression or, as the child grows older, to a strong urge for success in order to prove to himself and other people that he is indeed worthy. He may also look for admiration as a means of boosting his self-esteem. Holmes was certainly ambitious and susceptible to flattery, as Watson was to discover, while Watson's unfailing admiration was an important factor in maintaining their friendship.

Another consequence of early emotional deprivation is hostility, even hatred, towards the mother for withholding that affection for which the child naturally craves. Unable to cope with the guilt such violent feelings arouse, the child may sublimate the aggression into more acceptable forms. Holmes' interest in sensational literature, his knowledge of which Watson says was immense, probably originated in childhood. This type of reading matter, with its emphasis on violence and murder, could well have acted as an outlet for the hidden hostility Holmes felt towards his mother. It was to lead eventually to his specialization in the study and investigation of crime.

These aggressive urges were later to find a more direct expression in Holmes' study of anatomy. In the dissecting room at St Bartholomew's Hospital, it was more or less acceptable for a student, in the name of forensic research, to beat dead bodies with a stick in order to discover to what extent bruises are produced after death. However, even Stamford, Watson's former dresser, who, as a member of the hospital staff, was surely not over-squeamish, considered such behaviour bizarre and extreme, as indeed it was. Holmes carried out similar research on a dead pig which he stabbed furiously with a huge, barb-headed spear in an attempt to prove that it could not be transfixed with a single blow. Significantly, he returned from this experiment much invigorated and with a hearty appetite.

This same transferred aggression is seen in his choice of sporting activities: boxing, fencing, singlestick play and baritsu, the latter a Japanese form of self-defence. All are combative sports carried out against one individual opponent, not as part of a team.

Some sufferers learn to cope with their recurrent bouts of depression by immersing themselves in activity so that their minds are stimulated and fully occupied. This is also true of Holmes. He was to become a workaholic, frequently staying up all night and sometimes working for days at a stretch without proper food or rest. On two occasions, he drove himself to the point of physical and mental breakdown. It was only when he was idle that he became prone to depression, when he would lie on the sofa, hardly speaking or moving, staring vacantly up at the ceiling.

As well as work, Holmes became dependent on other stimulants in later life: tobacco, strong black coffee and cocaine, which itself can exacerbate the symptoms of manic depression, causing 'high' and 'low' states of mind. On occasions, he used morphine as well.

His manic-depressive tendencies could also account for the complexities and apparent contradictions in his character, those light and dark sides to his nature. The brighter, more optimistic qualities found expression in his zest for life, his undoubted charm and energy, his enthusiasm and sprightly conversation, and even in more minor traits such as his enjoyment of good food and wine. The darker side to his character gave rise to pessimism, to feelings that nothing in life was worthwhile and to an ascetic, almost monk-like disregard for his creature comforts. Even his sense of humour had its darker element when the wit turned to sarcasm.

Another contradiction is seen in his personal habits, in his extreme untidiness with his possessions compared with his 'cat-like love of personal cleanliness' shown in his care over his clothes and appearance.

Holmes says nothing at all about his father, not even obliquely. The impression conveyed by this complete silence is one of absence, either through early death or physical withdrawal. His parents may have lived apart or his father's profession, which Holmes does not specify, may have taken him away from home for long periods. Or, if present, he may have shown little interest in his sons. As they grew up, Mycroft, as the older brother, seems to have acted in some respects as a surrogate father, giving

Holmes advice and taking on responsibilities on his behalf. His habit of addressing Holmes as 'my dear boy' has a paternal ring to it.

Mycroft was also affected by his upbringing and the same lack of maternal love. Like Holmes, he never married and, while not showing his brother's manic-depressive tendencies, was even more unsociable than Holmes. He had no close friends at all and his later life was restricted to his office, his club and his bachelor apartment. He also lacked Holmes' driving ambition. In this respect, he appears to have inherited more of the phlegmatic qualities of his English forebears.

It is not known where Holmes was educated, whether at a public school, where boys of his class would normally be sent, or at home with a private tutor, as some commentators have claimed. Certainly his sporting interests do not suggest a conventional school, where at that time only team games would have been encouraged. Superficially, his education appeared erratic. After their first meeting, Watson was to draw up a list in which he tried to rate Holmes' knowledge of various subjects, giving him a zero mark for literature, philosophy and astronomy.

In fact, Holmes was better educated than Watson's list might suggest. He evidently spoke French like a native for later he was able to pass himself off as a French workman. He may have learned the language in France when visiting his French relations. He may also have been able to speak German, which he considered unmusical although 'the most expressive of all languages'. He had certainly read Goethe, could quote from his works in the original and he knew 'Rache' was the German for 'revenge'. His interest in languages was to persist all his life. For example, he formed the theory that ancient Cornish was similar to Chaldean and may have derived from the Phoenician-speaking tin-merchants who had traded with Cornwall in the past.

His reading included the Bible, Shakespeare, Meredith, Carlyle, Poe, Boileau and Flaubert as well as the works of Darwin, Thoreau and the German philosopher Richter.

As for astronomy, which Watson marked 'nil', Holmes had studied it in sufficient depth to discuss 'the change in the obliquity of the ecliptic' or, in layman's terms, the alteration to the angle at which the sun's circuit stood in relation to the equator. It is doubtful if Watson was as well informed about the subject.

He studied Latin, a prerequisite in those days for boys of his class, and was familiar with such authors as Horace and Tacitus. He may also have learned Italian. In later life, he once carried a copy of Petrarch in his pocket on a train journey.

His ability to play the violin is well attested by Watson, who also states that he composed as well as performed. His interest in music was almost certainly formed in his childhood and reflects the more creative and intuitive side of his nature. He may also as a child have begun to develop those many other hobbies and interests which Watson mentions and which are too numerous to list in full. They included Buddhism, ancient documents, antiquarian books, miracle plays, guns, golf clubs and the effects of heredity, the latter possibly arising from his own family background. Other interests, such as in codes and cyphers and in tracking footprints, both human and animal, which were to prove useful in his later career as a private consulting detective, may also have begun as boyhood hobbies.

The picture which emerges of Holmes when young is of a highly intelligent but solitary child, the age gap of seven years between himself and Mycroft being then too wide to make them close playmates. Lively and energetic, he could at times be moody and withdrawn, apparently preferring his own company while secretly longing for affection and admiration. He may already have learnt to cope with the pain of his mother's lack of interest in him by throwing himself into a variety of sports and hobbies and by avoiding any close contacts with others for fear of further rejection. It is therefore not surprising that, as an adult, he would shun any discussion about his family and childhood, preferring to keep those old emotional scars hidden even from Watson, his close friend and confidant. His Victorian upbringing, with its emphasis on keeping a stiff upper lip, would have further inhibited him from revealing his emotions.

Watson's date of birth is less easily established. For reasons which will be fully explained in Chapter Three where Watson's medical training is more closely examined, he was probably born either in 1852 or 1853 which would have made him a year or two older than Holmes.

Little is known about his family background but it was apparently fairly well-to-do middle-class. Although his profession is not stated, Watson's father was wealthy enough to own a fifty-guinea watch, the only fact known about him. Like Holmes, Watson had an older brother, whose name is not given although his first name began with an H. He was later to become the black sheep of the family, much to Watson's deep embarrassment. This reaction suggests a conventional, respectable upbringing.

Watson appears to have had a normal childhood for he suffered from none of the effects of psychological damage which characterize Holmes' personality. His reticence about his family background and early life is due more to a natural modesty and to his self-appointed role as Holmes' chronicler, not as his own, than to a desire to repress unhappy memories.

Dorothy L. Sayers has suggested he may have had Scottish connections.* Whether or not this theory is correct, Watson was clearly educated at an English school, possibly a boarding school although this is not firmly established. Another commentator has suggested that, because of Watson's skill at rugby, he may have been a pupil at Rugby, the well-known public school where the game was first introduced in 1823. This, however, is unlikely. One of Watson's fellow pupils was Percy Phelps, the nephew of Lord Holdhurst,† the Conservative politician. Watson and the other boys bullied Phelps because of this 'gaudy relationship', as Watson terms it. Pupils at Rugby, or at any other of the famous public schools such as Eton and Harrow, where boys from an aristocratic background were the norm rather than the exception, would not have ragged Phelps about his noble connections. The attitude of Watson and his friends suggests the school was a minor establishment.

The passage in which Watson reminisces about Percy Phelps is also revealing about other aspects of Watson's schooldays. 'Tadpole' Phelps was an intimate friend of Watson, indicating that, unlike Holmes, Watson was capable of making close relationships. He was also apparently on good terms with the other

* See Appendix One.
† Like most personal names in the canon, this is a pseudonym, devised by Watson to hide the individual's identity. Many places and addresses are also similarly disguised, including the location of 221B Baker Street.

boys, joining in the ragging of the unfortunate 'Tadpole'. Phelps seems not to have borne Watson any grudge and later was to appeal for his help in persuading Holmes to investigate the case of the Naval Treaty.

In addition, the passage shows that, although about the same age as Watson, Phelps, a brilliant scholar who was to win all the school prizes, was two classes ahead of him, suggesting Watson was a pupil of average intelligence and attainment, an assessment which will be more fully examined in Chapter Three.

Watson's love of rugby, a team game, is also significant, indicating an ability to co-operate with others as well as to enjoy the rough and tumble of a highly physical sport. It also bears out his own statement about himself that he was 'reckoned fleet of foot.'

As an adult, he also prided himself on his common sense while admitting to extreme laziness, a judgement which shows a clear insight into his own personality, although in the latter estimation Watson was being a little hard on himself. Although he shows none of Holmes' ambitious drive, when given the right incentive he was capable of aspirations and was willing to work hard to achieve them.

Despite his criticisms of Holmes' accomplishments, Watson was less widely read or educated than Holmes and his interests and hobbies were much more limited, being restricted in later years to billiards and horse-racing. His taste in books extended little further than the sea stories of William Clark Russell. This preference for an exciting yarn was probably established in boyhood and may well have bred in him a love of travel and adventure. It was a part of his personality which, as will be seen later, was to influence his subsequent career as well as form an essential factor in his friendship with Holmes. It was also to contribute to his later success as a writer. In *The Hound of the Baskervilles*, Watson was to say of himself, 'The promise of adventure had always a fascination for me.'

Quite apart from his talent as a writer, an attribute which will also be examined in more detail later, Watson showed this creative side to his personality in other ways. Although not a performer himself, he enjoyed listening to music, in particular to Mendelssohn, a romantic composer. He also possessed a deep love cf the English countryside, which is frequently expressed in his writing, and a sympathy for other people, especially for women, in which that romantic quality is again seen.

His attitude to women was normal. He was chivalrous towards them, admired them and enjoyed their company. He was to marry twice,* the first time very happily. His second marriage, about which Watson says nothing, will be dealt with in more detail at the appropriate time.

As well as a romantic, Watson was an idealist. Of the few personal possessions he contributed to the shared Baker Street sitting-room two were portraits, one of General Gordon, the hero of Khartoum, the other of Henry Ward Beecher, the American preacher and supporter of Negro rights during the American Civil War. His choice could well reflect a boyhood admiration for men of courage, distinguished, in Gordon's case, for physical bravery, in Beecher's for the moral stand he took in the name of freedom and care for the oppressed. This tendency towards hero-worship was to play a significant role in his friendship with Holmes.

The sympathetic, idealistic side to Watson's nature, with its concern for the underprivileged, may have prompted him to choose medicine as his future career, while his love of adventure would have drawn him towards the army with its promise of excitement and action.

His upbringing, though stable, may however have been strict, with an emphasis on such middle-class virtues as good manners, modesty, loyalty, honesty and kindness towards others. Certainly Watson shows all these traits as well as the guilt which often results from such an upbringing when the child falls short of such high moral standards. As a result, Watson was to grow up to be a thoroughly nice man.

If this sounds a little too dull and worthy, he could on occasions be short-tempered, impatient and forthright, prepared to stand up for himself and to express his opinions quite forcibly when the need arose. As he himself admits, he also had a tendency at times towards self-importance.

Unlike Holmes, he was also willing to express his feelings

* See Appendix One.

openly and references to his emotional reactions are found throughout the canon, whether to the sympathy he felt towards some of Holmes' clients, particularly the women, or his exasperation towards Holmes himself, as well as the horror, excitement or occasional fear his experiences roused in him.

The impression one receives of Watson as a child is of a sturdy, sensible, nicely brought-up little boy, from a stable if conventional background, who was generally on good terms with other children. Although not scholastically brilliant, he was capable of average academic success when he put his mind to it. He may already have shown in childhood that more romantic and idealistic side to his nature in a tendency towards day-dreaming of exciting adventures in exotic places and, as he grew older, of aspirations towards making a positive contribution to the good of mankind.

Much less complex than Holmes, Watson nevertheless possesses far more depth of character than he is sometimes credited with, even by Holmes himself who, in one rather backhanded compliment, suggests that he lacked luminosity.

'It may be that you are not yourself luminous,' he tells Watson, 'but you are a conductor of light. Some people without possessing genius have a remarkable power of stimulating it.'

Characteristically, rather than being offended, Watson was delighted by the remark.

As a personality, Watson may indeed not glitter quite as brightly as Holmes but nevertheless there is a warm, steady glow about him which was to illuminate their friendship as much as Holmes' more pyrotechnic brilliance. Without it, it is doubtful if their relationship would have survived intact for all those years.

CHAPTER TWO

HOLMES

Oxford and Montague Street
1872–1880

'It is my business to know things. Perhaps I have trained myself to see what others overlook'.

Holmes: *A Case of Identity*

Holmes is more forthcoming about his life after his schooldays. Even so, there are gaps and apparent discrepancies in the information he confided to Watson, largely because it was given in a piecemeal fashion during the course of conversations and not as a straightforward autobiographical account. Watson himself has further confused the issue by his carelessness in recording some of the facts.

However, it is possible to gather up the references and from them to piece together a fairly coherent account of Holmes' life and career before 1881.

He went to university, either Oxford or Cambridge. At that time, an upper middle-class family would not have considered sending its son anywhere else and the fact that Reginald Musgrave, the heir to one of the oldest families in the country, was one of Holmes' fellow students puts the matter beyond doubt.

Although Dorothy L. Sayers has opted for Cambridge,* the weight of evidence favours Oxford as the more likely choice, based largely on the references in *The Adventure of the Three*

* See Appendix One.

Students, a case which Holmes investigated in 1895 and which is clearly set in Oxford. Both Holmes and Watson speak of 'quadrangles', a term never applied to Cambridge where the equivalent reference is 'court'. It is also quite evident that Holmes was familiar with the place. He knew, for example, that there were four stationers of any importance in the town and was acquainted with Mr Hilton Soames, a tutor and lecturer at St Luke's College. As there is no evidence to suggest that Soames was ever one of Holmes' clients, they must have met during their time together at university. St Luke's is a pseudonym. Watson admits that he has deliberately altered the details so that the college cannot be identified. It may also conceal the name of Holmes' own college, although this cannot be proved.

The whole subject of Holmes' university career is fraught with problems, especially over the dating, and all theories regarding it are therefore speculative. It is not even known when Holmes entered university but, assuming he went up at eighteen, the usual age, he would have begun his undergraduate studies in October 1872.* It is not known, either, what he read, but in view of his subsequent knowledge of chemistry, which Watson says was profound, it was probably this subject. With his own medical training, Watson was in a good position to judge Holmes' expertise.

It is likely that Holmes was introduced to cocaine and morphine while he was at university. Both were rich man's drugs, unlike opium which was considered a working-class indulgence. It should be pointed out that Holmes, in taking drugs, was not breaking the law. Until the Dangerous Drugs Acts of 1965 and 1967†, it was not illegal to possess or even to deal in such substances. Holmes was eventually to become an addict, regularly injecting himself three times a day with a 7 per cent solution of cocaine, or 'mainlining' to use the modern jargon. Its effect is to create a sense of euphoria followed by a relaxed drowsiness, the 'high' and 'low' states already referred to in Chapter One. He also occasionally used morphine, a narcotic and analgesic. It was

* See Appendix One.
† These acts were later repealed and replaced by the Misuse of Drugs Act 1971.

to take Watson several years before he finally persuaded Holmes to give up the habit.

Holmes gives the impression he found little satisfaction in his time at university, not even in his studies. Throughout his life he preferred to follow his own individual interests rather than to keep to a formal course of education, a tendency already seen in his childhood reading of sensational literature, certainly not part of any school curriculum or recommended reading list.

As he acknowledges, when he went up to university he was already deeply immersed in his ideas about crime and its detection which, over the next few years, he was to expand into his theories of scientific deduction and analysis, based on careful observation of material evidence and its logical interpretation, not on mere speculation. However, this theory did not entirely rule out the application of intuition and 'scientific use of the imagination'. He was later to criticize the police for their lack of 'imaginative intuition'.

He admits he rarely mixed socially with the other students, preferring to remain in his rooms, mulling over these ideas, although he must have discussed them with his acquaintances because he tells Watson that his methods had already begun to gain him a reputation among the other undergraduates. These contacts were to prove useful to him after he left Oxford.

Despite his unsociable habits, he made two friends, one of whom was particularly close. This was Victor Trevor, whose bull terrier bit him on the ankle as Holmes went to chapel one morning, incidentally the only occasion recorded in the canon of Holmes attending a church service. As he was laid up for ten days, Trevor used to call to see how he was, visits which led to their friendship. The other was Reginald Musgrave who was a fellow student at Holmes' college. Although he was never more than a slight acquaintance, he became interested in Holmes' theories. Both were later to introduce him to two of his earliest cases.

There were, however, diversions. Holmes spent some time fencing and boxing, the only sports he indulged in during his time at university. He excelled in the latter sport and, according to Watson, was one of the best boxers of his weight he had ever seen, a claim supported by the professional prizefighter

28

McMurdo with whom Holmes was to fight four rounds at the former's benefit night and who maintained Holmes could have turned professional. Holmes does not state if he boxed or fenced for either his college or the university and there is no evidence to suggest he gained a 'Blue' for either of these sports.

Holmes apparently left university after only two years, instead of the more usual three, without sitting his final examinations and therefore without taking a degree. There is, however, confusion over even this fact. Holmes refers on one occasion to 'the two years I was at college' and on another to 'my last years at university', implying he was there for at least three years. It is possible Watson either misheard or misquoted Holmes and the latter remark should read 'my last year at university'. If that is the case, then Holmes went down in 1874 at the age of twenty.*

One reason for his early departure could have been that dissatisfaction, already mentioned. Another was possible financial problems. Neither Holmes nor his brother Mycroft appears to have inherited much money for both were obliged to earn their own livings. In fact, it was shortage of funds which was later to compel Holmes to share lodgings with Watson. A family financial crisis at this point in Holmes' university career could have meant that there was no longer enough money to support him or pay his fees.

For whatever reason, Holmes left Oxford for London, where he found rooms, presumably the same lodgings in Montague Street which he was still occupying at the end of 1880. If the dates are correct, he was to remain there for the next five and a half years. It was a convenient address, handy for the British Museum and its Reading Room where Holmes no doubt studied the many subjects in which he was interested. The rents, too, were reasonable, a single room costing £1 10s a week (£1.50p), two rooms £3. This would have included food and cleaning. As Holmes speaks of 'rooms', he presumably had two, a bedroom and a sitting-room where, once he had established himself professionally, he interviewed his clients.

Montague Street, which runs along the side of the British

* See Appendix One.

Museum towards Russell Square, is still lined with the same terraces of flat-fronted, four-storeyed houses, built of brick and stucco, with basement areas and iron balconies on the first floors. Since Holmes' time, several of them have been converted into hotels.

On first coming down from university, Holmes had no idea what profession to follow for at that stage in his life he regarded his interest in detection as 'the merest hobby'. It was a chance remark that was to decide his future for him.

That same summer of 1874* he was invited by Victor Trevor to stay for a month at his family home in Donnithorpe, Norfolk. At the time, Holmes was working on an experiment in organic chemistry, suggesting that soon after coming down from university he had already set up the equipment he would need to continue his chemical studies which might indicate that he had considered a career as an experimental chemist.

While at Donnithorpe, Holmes was unwittingly drawn into a situation which was to lead to the *Gloria Scott* inquiry, the first, he told Watson, that he was asked to investigate. Strictly speaking, this is not accurate. Holmes' involvement was limited to deciphering a cryptic letter sent by one of the participants in an old crime which had taken place thirty years earlier on board a convict ship.* Apart from this, he merely acted as an observer of the events, taking no active role in their solution. But the case was important for the part it played in Holmes' decision to become a private consulting detective: the only one in the world, as later he was proudly to inform Watson.

On meeting Trevor's father, Holmes impressed him by deducing several facts about his background so correctly that he caused his host to have a heart attack, much to Holmes' and young Trevor's consternation. On recovering, Trevor senior made a remark which was to have significant consequences. Detection, he announced categorically, was Holmes' 'line in life'. He backed up this assertion by adding, 'You may take the word of a man who has seen something of the world.'

It was the first time it had occurred to Holmes that he might turn his hobby into a profession.

* See Appendix One.

It is not known what his second case involved. He may have been asked to investigate it by another of his varsity acquaintances. Holmes told Watson that the few cases which came his way during his early years in Montague Street were mainly from this source. But the third of these inquiries was undoubtedly the Musgrave Ritual case. He was introduced to it by Reginald Musgrave, his former fellow student at St Luke's College, who travelled especially to London to ask for Holmes' help, suggesting that word of his growing expertise was spreading among the varsity set.

Holmes says that it was four years since he had last seen Musgrave. Assuming June 1874 is the correct date for Holmes' departure from Oxford, the case therefore occurred either in 1878 or 1879, depending on how precise Holmes was over the matter of the time gap.* That being so, Holmes had undertaken only three cases during those four years. They were lean times indeed and Holmes' comment about his 'all too abundant leisure time' was fully justified.

Although Holmes does not say as much, he may have charged Musgrave a fee for his services. When Musgrave arrived, Holmes told him, 'I have taken to living by my wits.' It is possibly a hint that he had turned professional and expected to be paid. This would accord with a statement Watson was to make many years later. In the opening sentence of *The Adventure of the Veiled Lodger*, Watson states quite categorically that Holmes was in active practice for twenty-three years and that 'during seventeen of these I was allowed to co-operate with him'. Although Watson is notoriously unreliable about facts and figures, it seems that on this occasion at least his arithmetic was partly correct, according to this dating scheme.

It is generally accepted by most commentators that Holmes retired in 1903. After discounting the three years of the Great Hiatus, the period in which Holmes disappeared and was thought dead, we arrive at 1877, possibly the same year in which Holmes undertook his second case, as the date when he also began his 'active practice', a term which probably implies his decision to turn professional and charge fees. The second part of

* See Appendix One.

Watson's statement, that he co-operated with Holmes during seventeen of these years, will be examined in more detail in a later chapter.

It is not known how Holmes supported himself financially during the two and half years from the summer of 1874 when he left university until 1877 when he may have begun charging his clients. Presumably he had a little money of his own or his family may have paid him a small allowance, to which his brother Mycroft may also have contributed. By that time, it is likely Mycroft was established in his career as a Civil Service auditor and was living in London in his own bachelor lodgings. Certainly he took an active interest in his younger brother's career, for he introduced Holmes 'again and again' to cases, amongst which were some of the most interesting he was to undertake.

We are on safer ground when we come to consider how Holmes spent that 'all too abundant leisure time' during those early years. He used it to study 'all those branches of science' in which he needed to become an expert before turning professional. In short, he was perfecting his tradecraft, to use one of John le Carré's terms.

One method of achieving this goal was to join the anatomy and chemistry classes at St Bartholomew's Hospital in West Smithfield, near St Paul's Cathedral. These courses were open to members of the general public who, while not intending to become doctors, were interested in medical subjects. Holmes could have found out about these classes from the registrar of the University of London, which had its offices in Malet Street, only a few minutes' walk from Montague Street.

It is possible Holmes chose Bart's in preference to other London hospitals because it was then one of the largest, with 676 beds, and because of its reputation. Its staff included Sir James Paget,* the distinguished consulting surgeon who lectured on anatomy, one of the subjects Holmes elected to study. Bart's ran four separate courses of anatomy lectures as well as two demonstration classes. It is not known which of these Holmes chose to

---

* At the age of twenty-one, while still a medical student, James Paget, who was later knighted, discovered *trichenella spiralis*, the minute intestinal worm which infested humans and some animals.

32

attend but he almost certainly enrolled for the demonstration class in Morbid Anatomy under Dr Gee. He also joined at least one of the chemistry courses, possibly the one on Practical Chemistry, taught by Dr Russell. The fees varied from ten guineas for an unlimited course in anatomy to three for practical chemistry.

During this period, Watson was himself a medical student at Bart's and he was probably present at some of the classes which Holmes attended, although they never became acquainted. However, they may well have passed each other on the stairs leading up to the chemistry laboratory or watched the same anatomy demonstrations. They may even, without knowing it, have sat together reading in the library or examining the jars of specimens in the Pathological Museum.

Apart from these courses at Bart's, Holmes' time was taken up with conducting his own chemical experiments at his lodgings, where he had presumably set up a work-bench similar to the one he was later to install at 221B Baker Street. He was also perfecting his skills in other areas.

Throughout his professional life, Holmes stressed the importance to a detective of a knowledge of the history of crime. 'Everything comes in circles,' he was to tell Inspector MacDonald, whom he advised to shut himself up for 'three months and read twelve hours a day' into the subject. No doubt, this advice was based on personal experience of his time at Montague Street before his practice was established and he had the leisure for such sustained reading.

'All knowledge comes useful to a detective,' was another of his maxims, and it was probably also during these years that he made a serious study of tobacco on which he wrote a monograph: *Upon the Distinction between the Ashes of the Various Tobaccos.* This may have been published while he was still at Montague Street. It was certainly in print by March 1881, the date of the Study in Scarlet case. Two other articles published in the *Anthropological Journal* on the subject of ears may also belong to this period. If not, Holmes would have carried out the research while a student at Bart's.

Over the years, he was to publish other articles and monographs on codes and cyphers in which he analysed 160 different types, on tattoos, on the influence of a man's trade on his hands, and on footprints, a special interest of his which, as has already been suggested, may have stemmed from a boyhood hobby.

'There is no branch of detective science which is so important and so much neglected as the art of tracing footprints,' he was to inform Watson.

From such prints he was able to tell not only the type of footwear a suspect was wearing but also his height from the length of his stride. Holmes was to put this skill to use in numerous cases and, in his monograph on the subject, was to add some remarks about the use of plaster of Paris in taking impressions of the prints.

Other specialized subjects in which he took a professional interest and which no doubt he studied during these years were the dating of documents, watermarks in paper, the analysis of handwriting and perfumes, and the study of different makes of bicycle tyres. He also made himself familiar with the types used by newspaper printers and, at one stage, he considered writing monographs on typewriters and their own distinctive print as well as the use of dogs in detection.

His writing activities were not confined only to the subject of crime. Several years later, in November 1895, when in the middle of the inquiry into the theft of the Bruce-Partington plans, a case of national importance, he was working on a monograph on the polyphonic motets of Orlandus Lassus, the sixteenth-century German composer, which was published privately and was considered by the experts to be the last word on the subject.

But, above all, he studied his fellow human beings, a subject on which he was to publish a magazine article entitled 'The Book of Life' in which he asserted that a man's whole history, as well as his trade or profession, could be deduced from his appearance. It was a skill which, as we have seen, he had already demonstrated to Victor Trevor's father with such unfortunate results. As Watson read the article soon after meeting Holmes, it was almost certainly written and probably published while Holmes was still living in Montague Street.

Some at least of these early monographs were later translated into French by François le Villard, a French detective who also consulted Holmes about a case involving a will. As M. le Villard corresponded with Holmes in French, this is further proof of Holmes' familiarity with the language.

This exchange of ideas was not just in one direction. Holmes was to become an enthusiastic admirer of the Bertillon system for identifying criminals. Devised by Alphonse Bertillon, who was Chief of Criminal Investigation with the Paris police force from 1880, it was based on detailed descriptions, photographs and precise bodily measurements. It was eventually superseded by fingerprinting.

The use of disguise was another aspect of detection which Holmes must have studied during this period. He was a natural actor, capable of taking on a role so convincingly that Watson was later to state that 'his very soul seemed to vary with each fresh part he assumed'. Even old Baron Dowson, for whose arrest Holmes was responsible, said of him on the night before he was hanged that 'what the law had gained the stage had lost'. Among the many disguises Holmes was to adopt during his career were those of a plumber, an elderly Italian priest, a sailor and an old woman.

William S. Baring-Gould has suggested that between 1879 and 1880 Holmes was touring the United States of America as an actor with the Sasanoff Shakespearean Company. There is no evidence in the canon to support the theory. On the contrary, all the available information tends to show that Holmes was fully occupied and living in Montague Street during these years. Nor was there any need for him to take to the professional stage to learn the art of disguise. There were plenty of retired or out-of-work actors in London who could have taught him how to fix on a wig or false moustaches and to apply greasepaint.

But it wasn't all work and study. London offered plenty of opportunities for diversion and amusement in the way of plays, operas, concerts and music-hall entertainments. Although there is no evidence in the canon to suggest he ever went to the theatre or music hall, he certainly attended operas and concerts. He was familiar with St James's Hall in Westminster for he was to discuss its acoustics with Watson. It was there that he heard Wilhelmine Norman-Néruda play the violin at concerts given by Sir Charles Hallé, whom she later married. Holmes admired her bowing technique and the vigour of her perform-ances. However, other concert-goers must have found his habit of beating time to the music with one hand annoying although, as Holmes kept his eyes shut, he was probably quite unaware of their reaction.

And if the price of a concert or opera ticket was beyond his means while he was struggling to establish himself pro-fessionally, there were plenty of other ways he could amuse himself for nothing.

Holmes enjoyed walking and it was during his time in Montague Street that he began the habit of taking long walks about the capital, familiarizing himself with its streets, particu-larly the slum areas of the East End with its docks and with the gin shops and opium dens of Limehouse.

He also became acquainted with the second-hand shops in and around Tottenham Court Road for it was here that he bought his Stradivarius violin, worth at least five hundred guineas, for fifty-five shillings (£2.75p) from a Jewish broker. Today it would be worth many more times this amount.

For a man interested in antiquarian books, there were the booksellers as well, although at this stage in his career Holmes may not yet have been able to afford to indulge his hobby of collecting unless he was lucky enough to find a bargain, such as the little brown-backed volume of *De Jure Inter Gentes*, published in Liége in 1642, which he found on a stall selling second-hand books and which he later showed to Watson.

But business was picking up. Between 1878 and the last months of 1880, at least eight more cases came his way. As he was later to tell Watson that his practice became 'considerable', there were undoubtedly more which he failed to mention. Those he listed were the Tarleton murders and the case of Vamberry, the wine merchant, as well as the inquiries involving an old Russian woman, the club-footed Ricoletti and his abominable wife, and a particularly curious investigation which concerned an aluminium crutch. Unfortunately, Holmes has given no further details about these cases.

Other clients included a Mrs Farintosh who consulted him about an opal tiara and a Mr Mortimer Maberley whom Holmes was able to help over a 'trifling matter' and whose widow later requested his advice over the sale of her house, the Three Gables. A Mrs Cecil Forrester also asked for his assistance. Although her case was straightforward, involving only a minor domestic complication, Mrs Forrester was to play an important part in Watson's future for it was through her that Miss Mary Morstan heard of Holmes and several years later came to consult him about a much more complex problem of her own. Some of these cases came, as he told Watson, from private detective agents who turned to him for help when they found themselves in difficulties and whom Holmes charged for his services.

It is clear from even the limited list he gave Watson that Holmes' reputation as a private consulting detective was spreading far outside the circle of his former varsity acquaintances and that he was considered expert enough to be consulted, presumably by the police, over such serious crimes as murder.

It is not known when Scotland Yard first asked Holmes for his assistance, but it was before the end of 1880, by which date he was already acquainted with Inspector Lestrade and was helping him with a forgery case. This investigation, which lasted into the early part of 1881, was probably one of the last Holmes undertook while at the Montague Street lodgings. His attitude towards what he called the 'Scotland Yarders' was contemptuous and shows all the arrogance of a young man aware of his own superior intelligence. As he grew older and more mature, he was to moderate his opinions. At the time he considered Lestrade and Gregson, whom he also met during this period, 'the pick of a bad lot', quick and energetic but shockingly conventional in their methods. He was exasperated, too, by their professional jealousy and their habit of claiming all the credit when a case was successfully solved.

Watson, with his gift for sketching people in a few vivid words, has given us descriptions of them. Lestrade was a 'little sallow, rat-faced, dark-eyed fellow' in contrast to Gregson who was a 'tall, white-faced, flaxen-haired man'.

During these years, Holmes may also have made the acquaintance of Athelney Jones,* another Scotland Yard detective, a

* Presumably Athelney Jones is the same detective as Peter Jones, the inspector who was officially engaged on the Red-Headed League inquiry.

'very stout, portly man', as Watson describes him. If Holmes met him before the end of 1880, then he was also involved in the Bishopgate jewel case, on which he lectured Jones and his colleagues on its causes, inferences and effects – an occasion which clearly rankled and led Jones several years later to refer to Holmes sneeringly as 'the theorist'. His comment may well sum up the general attitude of the police at that time towards Holmes and his methods.

Holmes' disdain was not entirely unjustified. At that time, senior police officers came up through the ranks and their standard of education was not high, compared with Holmes'. Nevertheless, one can appreciate how Lestrade, an officer of twenty years' experience, must have felt when taught his business by a young man who was himself only in his twenties. Watson was right in thinking that at times Holmes was bumptious.

Watson has given us many descriptions of Holmes, the most detailed the one he drew of him soon after their first meeting. He was, Watson writes, rather above six feet in height and 'so excessively lean that he seemed to be considerably taller'. His eyes were 'sharp and piercing . . . and his thin, hawk-like nose gave his whole expression an air of alertness and decision. His chin, too, had the prominence and squareness which mark the man of determination'.

Over the years, Watson was to add further touches to this description, referring to Holmes' deep-set, grey eyes; his narrow features; his dark, heavy eyebrows; his black hair, thin lips and his high, quick and 'somewhat strident voice'.

Physically, Holmes was strong, especially in the hands, although, when necessary, he had 'an extraordinary delicacy of touch'. Watson also states that Holmes' senses were 'remarkably acute'. Holmes had trained himself to see in the dark and was capable of hearing even the slightest sounds.

Towards the end of 1880 Holmes decided to look for other lodgings. He does not say what prompted this decision. Perhaps, now that his clientele was expanding, he needed more space. Or there may have been difficulties with his landlord or landlady or with other lodgers. He may even have been asked to leave. Many years later, Holmes was to tease Watson on this very subject when they were lodging in one of the university towns.*

'What with your eternal tobacco, Watson, and your irregularity at meals, I expect that you will get notice to quit, and that I shall share in your downfall.'

This could be a wryly humorous reference to his own experience.

He cannot have been an easy tenant, with clients coming and going, quite apart from his own eccentric life-style which included playing the violin at all hours and conducting chemical experiments in his sitting-room. As Watson was to discover, the stench from these could at times be offencive.

The need to move must have come at an inconvenient time. Not only was the number of clients increasing but Holmes was busy working at the chemistry laboratory at Bart's on an experiment which, if successful, would be 'the most practical medico-legal discovery for years'. This was a new method for testing the presence of blood in even a highly diluted form.†

Nevertheless, he decided to look for new lodgings at a reasonable rent, bearing out his own statement that although his practice was by this time considerable, it was 'not very lucrative'. As someone who preferred his own company, he would certainly, given the choice, have rather lived alone. But, as he was to discover, finding the right accommodation at a price he could afford was not to prove easy.

* Probably Oxford; see The Adventure of the Three Students.
† Christine L. Huber has suggested that Holmes' method involved the use of sodium hydroxide and a saturated solution of ammonium sulphate. When these are added to distilled water containing only a drop of blood, a brownish dust is precipitated, denoting the presence of haemoglobin.

CHAPTER THREE

WATSON

Bart's and Afghanistan
1872–1880

'Watson has some remarkable characteristics of his own,
to which in his modesty he has given small attention
amid his exaggerated estimates of my own performances.'

Holmes: *The Adventure of the Blanched Soldier*

'In the year 1878 I took my Degree of Doctor of Medicine of the
University of London, and proceeded to Netley to go through
the course prescribed for surgeons in the army,' Watson states in
the opening sentence of *A Study in Scarlet*.

It all seems perfectly straightforward. But for the sake of
brevity, Watson has telescoped the information, leaving out
certain important facts about his medical training. He has said
nothing either about his life immediately preceding his entry to
London University as a student. Apart from two oblique references elsewhere in the canon, he hardly touches on this period
at all. As they are crucial in establishing Watson's date of birth, it
is necessary to examine them in some detail.

In *The Sign of Four* (1888) Watson remarks, on noticing the
heaps of earth dug up by the Sholtos in the grounds of Pondicherry Lodge: 'I have seen something of the sort in the side of a
hill near Ballarat, where the prospectors have been at work.'

This is a reference to the gold-prospecting town of Ballarat in
Victoria, south-east Australia. It is quite clear Watson has been

there. But when? Some commentators have suggested he was taken to Australia as a child. This, however, is unlikely.

Also in *The Sign of Four*, Watson, who regarded himself as something of a ladies' man, makes another revealing comment. He states that his 'experience of women' extended over 'three separate continents', by which he must mean Europe (England), Asia (India) and Australia, the only parts of the world of which at that time, 1888, he had any personal knowledge. It is unlikely he is referring to a childhood experience of women. As the remark is made on his first meeting with Miss Mary Morstan, to whom he was strongly attracted, it is clear from the context that this experience was gained when he was of an age to appreciate the charms of the opposite sex. The only period in his life before 1888 when such a trip to Australia was feasible was in the years between his leaving school at seventeen or eighteen and enrolling as a medical student. He would then have been old enough to admire a pretty face although, at that stage, his 'experience' may not have extended much beyond an adolescent longing or a mild flirtation. Watson was always a little prone to exaggeration.

As we have already seen, Watson had a love of adventure and it was no doubt this urge which prompted him to set off for Australia on leaving school. He may even have been attracted by the possibilities of becoming a gold prospector himself, which would explain why he visited Ballarat. Whether or not this was the case, he may, like many other school-leavers, have wanted to travel abroad before settling down to further studies.

In *The Sign of Four*, Holmes remarks that Watson's father had been dead for many years. If he died about 1870, the approximate date of this Australian adventure, Watson may have inherited enough money from his father to finance the trip. The time gap of eighteen years accords with Holmes' remark.

The question of Watson's date of birth hinges on this visit to Australia. The voyage took about two months by sea: four if one counts the return trip. Watson must therefore have been away for at least a year, possibly two, otherwise the trip was hardly worth the time and expense. If Watson left England at the age of seventeen or eighteen, he was aged between eighteen and twenty when he returned to England and began his medical studies.

As we shall see later in the chapter, Watson spent at least six years before qualifying as a doctor in 1878. This would place his date of birth between 1852 and 1854, the more likely being either the year 1852 or 1853.* He gives the impression of being a year or two older than Holmes, although this is an entirely subjective judgement.

We shall assume therefore that Watson entered medical school in 1872 at the age of nineteen or twenty.

The Medical Act of 1858 prohibited anyone from using the title of physician, surgeon, doctor or apothecary without holding a licence from one of the appropriate corporations: the Royal College of Surgeons, the Royal College of Physicians or the Society of Apothecaries. As Watson later practised both as a surgeon and a general practitioner, he must, at the very least, have qualified as a Member of the Royal College of Surgeons (MRCS) and, in order to prescribe medicines for his patients as a GP, must also have passed as a Licentiate of the Society of Apothecaries (LSA), in addition to holding a medical degree (MD). It is less likely that he was also a Member of the Royal College of Physicians (MRCP). Most GPs at that time held only two licences, the minimum required. This agrees with the rather unkind comment Holmes makes in *The Adventure of the Dying Detective* on Watson's medical qualifications, which he describes as 'mediocre'.

Watson would have had to sit an entrance examination before being accepted as a student at London University and, having passed, would have registered both with the university and also with the General Medical Council. Once these formalities were completed, he was then free to attend the medical school of his choice, in his case St Bartholomew's Hospital.

Bart's, as it is affectionately known, is one of the oldest hospitals in the world. Founded in 1123 by Rahere, an attendant at the court of Henry I†, it still occupies its original site in West Smithfield where it was established as a hospital for the poor. In Watson's time it retained its charitable status, relying on donations from wealthy sponsors.

Although much has changed since the day when Watson first

---

* Most commentators accept 1852 as the year of Watson's birth.
† According to tradition, Rahere was Henry I's jester.

entered its gates, he would still recognize parts of it – as would Holmes, too, for that matter – in particular the church of St Bartholomew the Less and the square with its trees and central fountain. He could well have strolled here between lectures, enjoying a quiet cigar. But the old chemistry laboratory has gone: so, too, has the original Pathological Museum where Watson studied the anatomical specimens and perhaps shared a table with Holmes.

At that time, the basic course for an MD was four years, ten months of which had to be spent on the wards. In addition, students spent further time preparing for the examinations which would qualify them for membership of the professional medical corporations.

The early career of Frederick Treves, the doctor who later befriended Joseph Merrick, the Elephant Man,* demonstrates this clearly. Although he studied at the London Hospital, his training would have been similar to Watson's. Having taken his MD in 1873, Treves then sat for the licence of the Society of Apothecaries in 1874 and, in the following year, on passing the examination, became an MRCS. As he practised as a GP as well as a surgeon, we can see how closely his career parallels Watson's[†]. Like Treves, Watson almost certainly took his MD first, in his case in 1876, before going on to qualify as an LSA and an MRCS, a fact which, in his abbreviated account of his medical training, he has failed to make clear, lumping all his qualifications together under the general title of MD. It was probably in 1878 that he was accepted by the General Medical Council as a fully qualified doctor, licensed to practise.

The first part of Watson's course at Bart's consisted of lectures given by the hospital's physicians and surgeons, and anatomy demonstrations in the dissecting room. As we have seen, Holmes may well have attended some of these classes, which was when their paths could have first crossed.

* Joseph Merrick was the subject of the film, *The Elephant Man* (1980), starring John Hurt.

† Frederick Treves, who went on to qualify as a Fellow of the Royal College of Surgeons, later became a consulting surgeon at the London Hospital as well as a distinguished and highly-paid private practitioner. He was knighted in 1901.

Once the introductory courses were completed, the student then went on to study medicine and surgery, observing operations and accompanying the consultants on their rounds of the hospital wards.

Students were required to pass an interim examination in anatomy, physiology, botany and *materia medica*.* The final examination in their fourth year covered advanced studies in these subjects as well as the principles and practice of medicine and surgery.

In order to qualify as an LSA and an MRCS, students had then to take further courses in chemistry, including practical chemistry, forensic medicine, the theory and practice of medicine and surgery, midwifery and hospital practice. Holmes may also have enrolled for some of these classes, in particular those on chemistry and anatomy, subjects in which he had a special interest.

Like Holmes, Watson's time was not spent entirely on study. There were diversions; in Watson's case, rugby. Although it is not known in which position he played, he was good enough at the game to be accepted by Blackheath Football Club, the oldest open rugby club in the world. In Watson's time, the club had no ground of its own and matches were played on the heath, with the spectators occasionally encroaching on the field. Watson almost certainly played under the captaincy of Lennard Stokes, considered by some the best drop-kick in rugby football. Stokes, who won twelve international caps, was studying medicine at Guy's Hospital and several other players were, like Watson, medical students.

Watson's physique suited him for the game. According to a subsequent description, unwittingly passed on by Inspector Lestrade when Watson was mistaken for an escaping burglar, he was a 'middle-sized, strongly-built man' with a 'square jaw' and a 'thick neck'. At the time of this description, he also sported a small moustache although this may be a later addition to his appearance.

Watson may have had lodgings at Blackheath. If so, it would explain an otherwise puzzling remark he makes in *The Sign of Four* regarding his own 'limited knowledge of London'. Consid-

* The substances from which medicines are compounded.

ering that at the time he had spent at least seven years in London at Bart's Hospital, the admission seems strange unless he had lived somewhere on the outskirts and travelled into town every day. This was perfectly possible even from as far away as Blackheath. There was a regular train service from there to London Bridge station, from where he could have caught a dark green Bayswater omnibus which ran close to Bart's.

In his last year as a medical student, Watson was required to serve at least three months as a dresser to one of the hospital surgeons, treating patients on the wards under the consultant's supervision.

Watson's career at Bart's seems to have been average. He apparently won none of the prizes offered to the more promising students, unlike Dr Percy Trevelyan (*The Adventure of the Resident Patient*), also a former London University man, who was awarded the Bruce Pinkerton medal for his monograph on nervous lesions while at King's College Hospital's medical school. Nevertheless, Watson passed his examinations and was offered a post as house surgeon at Bart's. House surgeons usually served for a year only, six months as a junior, six as a senior. Again, Watson makes no reference to this part of his career but the fact that he had his own dresser, Stamford, puts it beyond doubt.

The post of house surgeon was a lowly one with long hours and poor pay. Dr James Mortimer (*The Hound of the Baskervilles*), himself a 'humble MRCS', as he terms it, had served as a house surgeon at Charing Cross Hospital and as such was 'little more than a senior student', to use Holmes' rather dismissive comment.

At the end of his year's service as house surgeon, Watson was faced with a crucial decision about his future career: what should he do next? In order to set up in private practice, he needed capital which he did not possess, a dilemma also faced by Dr Percy Trevelyan, although he was lucky enough to find a wealthy backer.

On the other hand, he could remain in hospital service although this had its own disadvantages. Hospitals then employed only four consulting surgeons and, as a consequence, promotion was slow. Watson might have to wait until he was in his forties before a senior post became vacant. He would also be required to qualify as a Fellow of the Royal College of Surgeons (FRCS). Watson may have realized that, as he was no academic high-flyer, he had better turn his sights elsewhere.

To a medical man, a military career offered several advantages. An army assistant surgeon earned £200 a year, with his keep and living quarters provided. After ten years' service, he could retire on half pay with enough money saved to set himself up in private practice. As C. B. Keetley pointed out in *The Students' and Practitioners' Guide to the Medical Profession* (1885), the army offered 'a serviceable if not brilliant career' for a man of 'fairly good abilities' but 'with no chance of doing great things as a town practitioner or consultant'. The advice might have been written with Watson in mind.

Above all, though, from Watson's point of view, the army, unlike the surgical wards at Bart's, held out the promise of travel and adventure as well as better opportunities for promotion. After all, he was still young, only twenty-five or twenty-six. Consequently, he decided to sit for the entrance examination to the Army Medical School at Netley in Hampshire.

The school, later called the Royal Army Medical School, was first established at Fort Pitt, Chatham, in 1860 and was moved to Netley three years later when the military hospital, the Royal Victoria, was opened. One of the wards was converted into a classroom while laboratories as well as quarters and mess facilities for the students were housed in separate buildings behind the main hospital block.

The site of the Royal Victoria Hospital was superb.* Set in 210 acres of parkland, it overlooked Southampton Water, where a special jetty was later built to receive casualties from the Boer War and First World War who were brought there by boat. It was a vast building, with beds for 1,400 patients in wards which opened off corridors a quarter of a mile in length. Florence Nightingale, who advocated the pavilion-style hospital with smaller units, was horrified when she was shown the plans. But it was too late; the foundations were already begun. Neverthe-

* The Royal Victoria Military Hospital was demolished in 1966/7. The site is now a public park.

less, she played an active part in the setting up of the Army Medical School, helping to draw up the regulations and to nominate the teaching staff.

There were two courses a year at Netley, each lasting five months, the first beginning in April, the second in October. It is not known exactly when Watson entered but in the light of subsequent events, he was probably accepted for the October course in 1879, after having served as a house surgeon at Bart's for a year.*

The course, which was divided into two parts, covered such subjects as hygiene, including the burial of the dead, as well as military surgery and pathology. Field exercises were also organized during which the candidates were expected to choose suitable sites for latrines, kitchens and dressing-stations. The training, however, was limited. Tropical medicine was not taught and there was no training in emergency surgery on the battlefield nor into the trauma of transporting the wounded.

During their time at Netley, the candidates were expected to obey army discipline, which included the wearing of uniform and attendance at parades. Their duties also entailed caring for patients in the wards. Special emphasis was laid on military red tape such as the correct procedures for filling in forms, requisitions and chitties.

A final examination was held and these marks were added to those already gained at the entrance examination and at practical tests in chemistry and pathology. These combined marks decided the order in which the candidates' names appeared in the Army Gazette and consequently their place in the list of Lieutenants. From Watson's previous record both at school and at Bart's, he probably came somewhere in the middle.

But he passed and in February 1880, if the suggested chronology is correct, he became Lieutenant John H. Watson, a rank he never referred to after he returned to civilian life. His memories of his military career were too bitter for him to wish to be reminded of it, although he did keep two mementoes, his service revolver, a Webley No. 2, and a tin dispatch-box, possibly army

* See Appendix One.

47

issue, with John H. Watson MD and the words 'Late Indian Army' painted on the lid.*

International events now overtook him which, in the short term, were to prove disastrous.

The Second Afghan War had broken out in 1878, not for economic reasons, for Afghanistan had no commercial interest for the British. It was a wild and desolate region of high mountains and barren plains, inhabited by fiercely independent Muslim tribes who were skilled in guerilla warfare as the Russians found to their cost when they invaded the country in 1979.

Strategically, however, the area was of immense importance for it acted as a buffer state between tsarist Russia to the north and imperial India to the south. Anyone who controlled Afghanistan also controlled the mountain passes across the north-west frontier. It was fear of Russian influence which had led to the First Afghan War of 1839–42 and to Britain's subsequent and humiliating defeat at the hands of the Afghan tribesmen.

In 1869 the Russians, under Tsar Alexander II, again began to show an interest in Central Asia, invading first Samarkand and then Khokund. Afraid they might move on to take Baluchistan and then Afghanistan, the British prime minister, Benjamin Disraeli, and Lord Lytton, Viceroy of India, decided to invade Afghanistan for the second time and, by seizing the passes, secure the frontier. Kabul, the Afghan capital, was captured and occupied in May 1879 but the tribesmen soon struck back and overran the city, killing the garrison and the British Resident. It was reoccupied by the British four months later after a pitched battle.

This was the situation in October 1879, the same month in which Watson entered the Army Medical School at Netley.

It is impossible to establish an exact chronology of the events which followed. Watson hasn't given us enough facts. But it would seem that soon after qualifying as an assistant army surgeon, he was posted to India to join his regiment, the Fifth Northumberland Fusiliers, which was already serving there.

* Strictly speaking, Watson was never a member of the Indian Army but of the British Army serving in India.

Assuming he embarked in March 1880, he arrived in Bombay in April, after a sea voyage lasting a month. Here he received his first setback.

Watson states that he was 'removed' from his brigade. It is a strange word to use, the more usual term being 'transferred' or 'seconded' and it suggests that the decision was taken against his wishes. However, Dr Zeisler's theory that it was made because Watson was suffering from gonorrhea seems improbable. A more likely explanation is that the Berkshire regiment to which he was attached was short of medical staff and Watson was selected to make up the numbers. Although Watson fails to make this clear, the transfer must have happened soon after his arrival in India. He was then sent to Kandahar (Watson spells it Candahar) to join his new regiment along with other recently-arrived officers.

Kandahar was a strategically important Afghan town situated 155 miles inside the frontier. It had been taken by the British earlier in the war and was defended by a garrison of both British regular soldiers and Indian sepoys, drawn from several regiments, including the 1st Bombay Native Infantry, Jacob's Horse and Watson's own regiment, the 66th Berkshire Regiment of Foot, later renamed the Royal Berkshire Regiment.

Professor Richard D. Lesh has traced the probable route Watson took on his journey to Kandahar. After travelling from Bombay to Karachi by steamer, he then went by rail to Sibi and from there by horse and camel caravan across the mountains to Kandahar, encamping at night. Although Watson does not refer to this part of his Indian experiences, it was probably during this journey that an incident occurred which he was later to recall. A tiger cub looked into his tent one night and he fired a musket at it. He may also at this time have made the acquaintance of Colonel Hayter to whom he gave medical treatment and who became a close friend. The going was hard and it was common for men to collapse with sunstroke in temperatures of over 100 degrees Fahrenheit. Colonel Hayter may have been one of the victims. Watson and Hayter were to keep in touch after both had left the army and the Colonel was later to feature in an episode in Watson's life as a civilian.

Up to this point, Watson appears to have enjoyed his army

49

experience. Later he was to refer to his 'adventures in Afghanistan' and speak of himself as an 'old campaigner', a slight exaggeration as at most he served only nine months in India. And he was evidently hoping for 'honours and promotion' which, in the event, were denied him. But, had all gone well, he might have remained in the army and made it his career.

In the meantime, the war had been gathering momentum. Despite their defeat at Kabul, the Afghans were by no means beaten. To the south, a large army of tribesmen, led by Ayub Khan, the son of the former emir, was advancing towards Kandahar. Their numbers, estimated between 9,000 and 25,000, consisted of horsemen and foot soldiers, some armed with British Enfield rifles. They were also equipped with artillery, which included modern 14-pounder Armstrong guns, far heavier than anything the British garrison, numbering only 2,500 men, possessed.

Although outgunned and outnumbered, the British troops, led by Brigadier General George Burrows, moved forward to the attack, among them the 66th Berkshire Regiment of Foot, accompanied by its medical team, which included Watson and his orderly, Murray. The two forces met at the village of Maiwand, fifty miles to the north-west of Kandahar, in the early morning of 27th July 1880 on a hot, dusty plain dissected by dry water courses. For the Afghans, it was a jihad or holy war against the infidels.

Taking advantage of the terrain, they moved their artillery forward and pounded the British rear, where casualties were as heavy as those in the front lines. Altogether, the British lost 934 men killed and 175 wounded or missing, nearly half the total force. The fighting was so fierce that at times the stretcher bearers dared not break cover to collect the wounded.

Watson was later to speak of seeing his comrades hacked to death in battle, a possible reference to the gallant rearguard action which was fought by the survivors of two companies of the 66th who stood back to back, fighting off the advancing tribesmen until all were killed.

Two men were later to receive Victoria Crosses for their bravery in the battle. Even a dog, a small mongrel named Bobbie belonging to Sergeant Kelly of the 66th, was later awarded with the Afghan Medal by Queen Victoria herself. Although his master was killed and Bobbie was wounded, he managed to escape safely back to the British lines.*

All Watson received was a bullet in his left shoulder fired from a jezail rifle, one of the Afghan long-barrelled guns, which shattered the bone, presumably his collar-bone, and grazed the subclavian artery. He was also struck in the leg although at the time the wound seemed less serious. The bullet may have passed through the fleshy part of the calf missing the bone but injuring the nerves or the muscles. Although Watson himself is not specific, Holmes later refers to his damaged Achilles tendon. This leg wound was to have more long-lasting effects than the injury to his shoulder.

Watson's life was undoubtedly saved by the prompt action of Murray, his orderly, when, in mid-afternoon, Ayub Khan decided to mount an all-out attack. Led by white-robed ghazis, fanatical warriors armed with long knives, the Afghans over-ran the British lines. In the face of the fierce onslaught, the defences broke and what remained of the British forces turned and fled, including the medical staff of a field hospital who abandoned their patients, leaving them lying on stretchers.

It was an overwhelming defeat†, saved only from turning into a total massacre by the failure of the Afghans to follow up their advantage. Instead, they remained behind to loot the baggage and dismember all those found on the battlefield, both the living and the dead, assisted by their womenfolk.

Rudyard Kipling has this chilling advice for a young British soldier who found himself in this situation:

'When you're wounded and left on Afghanistan's plains,
An' the women come out to cut up what remains,
Jest roll to your rifle and blow out your brains
An' go to your Gawd like a soldier.'

---

* Bobbie was subsequently run over and killed by a hansom cab in Gosport. He can be seen, stuffed and mounted in a glass case and still proudly wearing the Afghan Medal round his neck, in the Royal Berkshire Regiment's museum in Salisbury.

† Despite their defeat, the Royal Berkshire Regiment still carries 'Maiwand' as one of its battle honours.

Murray threw Watson over the back of a pack-horse and joined the retreat to Kandahar. It was itself an ordeal. Exhausted men and horses, suffering from heat and thirst and sniped at by Afghans as they passed their villages, straggled back along the fifty-mile desert tract to Kandahar, the gun-carriages loaded with those dead and wounded they had managed to save from the ghazis' knives.

Kandahar was a walled town and Lieutenant-General James Primrose, in charge of the garrison, decided to defend the whole perimeter. Breaches in the walls were repaired, gun emplacements set up and every Afghan man of fighting age, 13,000 in all, was expelled from the town as the British prepared for the coming siege. Food was not short and there were fresh-water wells. But morale was low and the garrison too small to hold off the Afghan forces whose casualties, compared to the British losses, had been light.

Watson says nothing about the siege, merely stating that he was taken safely to the British lines. For this reason, some commentators have assumed he was not at Kandahar. But there was nowhere else Murray could have taken him. Watson's intention was to give only an abbreviated account of this period in his life, not a full autobiography, and anyway he was too seriously wounded to take much notice of what was happening around him at the time. He must have received medical treatment, however, during which it is possible not enough attention was paid to the wound in his leg.

On 5th August an advance guard of Ayub Khan's army arrived at Kandahar to be joined two days later by the main Afghan force which set up camp outside the town. The siege had begun. It lasted for twenty-four days and was lifted on 31st August when Major General Frederick 'Bobs' Roberts, after a march of 320 miles across the mountains from Kabul, arrived with a relieving army of 10,000 and attacked Ayub Khan's camp, killing thousands of his men and putting the rest to flight. British losses were 58 men killed and 192 wounded.

These casualties, together with those from the battle of Maiwand, Watson among them, were transferred to the base hospital at Peshawar, the capital of the British north-west Indian possessions. Here Watson began to recover from his wounds and was eventually fit enough to walk about the wards and sunbathe on the verandah. It was then, when he was convalescent, that he received a further setback. He was struck down by enteric, or typhoid fever, an infectious disease which causes a high temperature and debility and can, in its more serious form, lead to pneumonia and thrombosis.

There is no doubt Watson was gravely ill but his statement that 'for months my life was despaired of' is again a little exaggerated. Typhoid fever usually lasts about five weeks and the time scale will not allow for a protracted illness. No doubt the weeks he suffered seemed like months to him. In fact, he was in the Peshawar hospital for less than two months for by the end of October he was back in Bombay, having in the meantime been examined by a medical board, which decided that in view of his 'weak and emaciated condition' he should be repatriated to England straightaway. In addition, he had to make the 1,600 mile journey south by train and boat in time to embark on the troopship SS *Orontes* which sailed from Bombay on 31st October 1880.

Thanks to the researches of Mr Metcalfe, the ship's movements have been exactly established. Having left Bombay, she called at Malta on 16th November and finally arrived at Portsmouth on the afternoon of Friday 26th November, 'bringing home the first troops from Afghanistan, including eighteen invalids.' All of them were transferred to the Royal Victoria Hospital at Netley, Watson presumably among them.

We are given a few clues to Watson's state of mind on returning to the place from which, less than a year before, he had set out with such high hopes of a successful future in the army. He was certainly bitter. His health, as he himself states, was 'irretrievably ruined' and the prospects of beginning a new career in civilian life seemed bleak. Even his rugby-playing days were over. From the symptoms of which he was later to complain, including sleeplessness, depression, irritability and nervous tension, he was probably suffering from the effects of post-traumatic stress disorder, a condition for which today he would receive treatment.

There was no one to whom he could turn. He had neither 'kith nor kin' living in England, which suggests both his parents were dead by this time, as well as his elder brother who, although his prospects had been good, had died in poverty after taking to drink, leaving Watson the gold watch which belonged to their father. Consequently, on his discharge from Netley, Watson made his way to London, which at least was familiar to him from his student days at Bart's, and booked himself into an hotel off the Strand. He also acquired a bull pup, company for him in the lonely days which lay ahead.* It was a 'comfortless, meaningless existence', made worse by the additional burden of money worries.

On being invalided out of the army, he had been awarded a pension of 11s 6d a day (about 57 pence), which should have been enough to keep him in moderate comfort. It was, in fact, more than his officer's pay of £200 a year. But he now had to find the money for food and accommodation and London could be costly, especially as Watson's tastes ran to the more expensive places in which to drink. It is doubtful if, during his short army career, he had managed to save much. If he had, it was soon gone and he was faced with the unpleasant choice of either moving out of London altogether or finding cheaper accommodation.

It was at this low point in his life that Watson's luck began to turn. For just over a mile away, in Montague Street, Sherlock Holmes, who had been flat-hunting on his own account and had found a set of rooms which seemed suitable, was turning over in his mind the possibility of finding a fellow-tenant who would go halves with him on the rent.

* In *The Encyclopaedia Sherlockiana*, Jack Tracy suggests that the phrase 'to keep a bull pup' was Anglo-Indian slang meaning 'to have a quick temper'. However, most commentators seem to agree that the dog really existed.

CHAPTER FOUR

MEETING

1st January 1881

'He (Holmes) is a little queer in his ideas – an enthusiast
in some branches of science. As far as I know, he is a
decent fellow enough.'

Stamford: *A Study in Scarlet*.

Faced by the choice, Watson decided to find somewhere cheaper
to live rather than move out of London. By a lucky coincidence,
it was on the very same day he came to this conclusion that
circumstances contrived to bring about a meeting which was to
become as famous in its own way as that between Stanley and
Livingstone.

Although we know exactly what Holmes and Watson were
doing that day, Watson has failed to record the date when the
introduction took place. The suggestion that it occurred on 1st
January and was the result of a New Year's resolution on
Watson's part to opt for less expensive accommodation seems
plausible. This date is accepted by many students of the canon.

Holmes had set off from his rooms in Montague Street for the
chemistry laboratory at St Bartholomew's Hospital to continue
his experiments into finding a more effective test for haemoglobin, research which has already been referred to in Chapter Two.
During the morning, he spoke to Stamford, Watson's former
dresser at Bart's,* and in course of the conversation happened

---

* Stamford must have been a qualified doctor at this date, having served as
a dresser, like Watson, during his final year as a medical student. He would

to mention that he was looking for someone with whom he could share lodgings he had found.

That same morning, Watson left his hotel off the Strand and, no doubt feeling at a loose end as usual, found his way to the bar of the Criterion Hotel in Piccadilly Circus, then called Regent Circus, much smaller than it is today and lacking the central statue of Eros which was not erected until 1890.

It was a large hotel, built in 1873, and was well-known for its restaurant but most particularly for its American or Long Bar. Sumptuously decorated with marble-clad walls and a ceiling inlaid with gold mosaic and semi-precious stones, it was a popular meeting-place although its prices were not cheap. It is still standing on the south side of Piccadilly, its ornamental white stone facade recently cleaned. Part of it houses the Criterion Restaurant, the original American Bar, its interior restored to the magnificence that Watson would have known.*

By great good fortune, Stamford also chose to call at the 'Cri' that same morning on his way home from Bart's and recognized the figure standing at the bar as Dr Watson, although much thinner and browner than in the days when they had walked the hospital wards together. Going up to him, Stamford clapped him on the shoulder.

For his part, Watson was pleased to meet him again for, although they had never been close, he was delighted to see one friendly and familiar face among the teeming multitude of four million strangers which then made up London's population.

He promptly invited him to lunch at the Holborn Restaurant[†] in Little Queen Street, since widened and now forming part of Kingsway, regaling Stamford on the journey there by cab with an account of his adventures since they had last met. One has

---

appear to have held the post as a house surgeon at St Bartholomew's, a post Watson also held before leaving hospital service to join the army.

* When the American or Long Bar was converted into a cafeteria in the 1960s, the walls and ceiling were covered over with formica which, when removed during renovation in 1984, revealed the original decorations. The Criterion Restaurant was opened in 1992.

† The Holborn Restaurant has since been demolished.

the impression that Watson was grateful for the opportunity to talk to someone, another measure of his loneliness.

Holborn is greatly changed since that lunch-time over a hundred years ago when the two of them rattled through it in their hansom and it is doubtful if Watson would recognize parts of it. In 1881 Little Queen Street was still lined with old houses, some of which dated to before the Great Fire of London of 1666. It led into Clare Market, a slum area of narrow streets and historic buildings, all of which were demolished in the late nineteenth and early twentieth centuries when Aldwych and Kingsway were developed, proving that urban vandalism is not confined to our own times.

Like the Criterion, the Holborn Restaurant was not cheap. Luncheon cost 3s 6d (about 33 pence) per person and presumably, as Watson had issued the invitation, he paid for Stamford as well. Wine was drunk with the meal and taking this into account, together with the hansom fare and a tip for the waiter, the total bill probably cost Watson more than a day's pension, as Michael Harrison has pointed out in *In the Footsteps of Sherlock Holmes*.

But the expense was worth it for, over the meal, when Watson confided in Stamford his need to find somewhere cheaper to live, Stamford remembered a similar conversation he had held with Holmes that very morning, and passed the information on to Watson that a man he knew had found lodgings but needed someone with whom he could go halves with the rent. Watson treated the news with enthusiasm. More sociable than Holmes, he welcomed the opportunity of sharing rooms rather than living alone, despite Stamford's warning that Holmes, while seeming a decent enough fellow, might not make an ideal companion. He was, Stamford, who seemed to be having second thoughts about mentioning Holmes, explained, eccentric, uncommunicative and a little too cold-blooded for his own tastes. Furthermore, Stamford had no idea what career Holmes proposed taking up for, although he was a first-class chemist, he was not a medical student.

Not at all deterred, Watson, assuming from Stamford's remarks that Holmes was a man of quiet and studious habits and would therefore suit him as a fellow-lodger, suggested a meeting, which Stamford proposed could take place that same afternoon at Bart's, although he refused to take any responsibility for the outcome of the introduction.

On finishing luncheon, they therefore took another cab to St Bartholomew's Hospital, familiar ground to Watson who needed no help in finding his way up a stone staircase and down a long, whitewashed corridor to the chemistry laboratory. It was here in the high-ceilinged room among the broad benches, littered with bottles, retorts and bunsen burners, and empty apart from Holmes, that the famous meeting took place.

The timing was dramatic, for at the very moment Stamford and Watson entered Holmes found the reagent which was precipitated by haemoglobin and nothing else, a discovery which he greeted with the exultant cry of 'I have found it!', as triumphant as Archimedes' shout of 'Eureka!'

After the formal introductions, Holmes astonished Watson, probably intentionally, by announcing as he shook him firmly by the hand, 'You have been in Afghanistan, I perceive.' There was no time for Watson to ask how Holmes knew this. In his eagerness, Holmes had seized him by the sleeve and dragged him to the bench where his experiment was set up, digging a bodkin into his own finger and drawing off a drop of blood which he used to demonstrate the efficacy of his new test for haemoglobin.

It is clear from his excitable behaviour that Holmes was going through one of his manic periods and it is not surprising that Watson, unused then to his companion's swings of mood, was much taken aback, although a few minutes later, in an exchange of mutual confidences regarding their personal shortcomings, Holmes confessed, 'I get in the dumps at times. You must not think me sulky when I do that. Just let me alone, and I'll soon be all right.'

He was careful at this early stage of his acquaintance with Watson to make no reference to another habit of his, that of regularly injecting himself with cocaine. Both admitted they were smokers, so that was all right. In his turn, Watson confessed to his own drawbacks: his ownership of the bull pup; his laziness; his habit of getting up at ungodly hours. However, his admission that he had another set of vices when he was in good health is puzzling. To what vices can he possibly be referring? One suspects that Watson, suffering from low self-esteem, a symptom of depression, and conscious of Holmes' intelligence and brilliant eccentricity, wished to present himself in a more interesting light.

Watson's last confession that, because of his shattered nerves, he disliked 'row', caused Holmes some anxiety. Did this, he asked, extend to violin-playing? Watson, not knowing Holmes' musical proficiency, hedged a little. It depended on the player, he replied, adding rather sententiously, 'A well-played violin is a treat for the gods – a badly played one . . .'

Holmes, who clearly considered his talent belonged to the former category, brushed aside any further objections with 'a merry laugh' and, treating the matter as settled, made arrangements for Watson to call for him at the laboratory at noon the following day so that he might accompany Watson on an inspection of the rooms.

The next day, probably 2nd January, they therefore met again as arranged and set off for Baker Street.*

Despite bombing during the war and redevelopment, many of the original brick-built houses of four or five storeys, with their plain façades and tiers of sash windows, remain relatively unaltered. Until the early 1860's, it was a fashionable area but, with the coming of the Metropolitan railway and the construction of Baker Street station, its character changed and it became more commercialized. However, it still remained a respectable, middle-class address.

By 1881 many of the houses were used as business premises, including the waxwork museum of Madame Tussaud and Son which was at numbers 57 to 58. Not far away were the popular Portman Rooms and the Baker Street Bazaar. Other smaller commercial entrepreneurs included dressmakers, music and

* Baker Street was developed in the eighteenth century by the Dorsetshire businessman Edward Berkely Portman (1771–1823), who named it after a friend of his, Sir Edward Baker. Portman's son and grandson, the first and second Viscounts Portman, continued to own the land. The properties were therefore leasehold, the land on which they stood part of the Portman estate to which the leaseholders paid ground rent.

dance teachers, dentists and milliners. As he frequently sent telegrams, Holmes would have found the presence of a post and telegraph office at number 66 particularly useful.

In many other ways, Baker Street was a convenient address. Baker Street station lay only a short distance away in Marylebone Road, although there is only one instance recorded in the canon of Holmes and Watson using the underground railway when they travelled to Aldersgate on their way to Saxe-Coburg Square (*The Adventure of the Red-Headed League*), while Cadogan West's body was found on the rails near Aldgate Station (*The Adventure of the Bruce-Partington Plans*). The trains were drawn by steam engines and although parts of the line ran above ground, passengers suffered the inconvenience of smoke and coal smuts accumulating in the tunnels.

There were also omnibus routes nearby, among them that of the green 'Atlas' which ran via Baker Street or, if Holmes and Watson chose to walk through Portman Square into Oxford Street, with its excellent shopping facilities, they had a choice of no less than seven omnibus companies. However, there is no reference in the canon to either of them using this cheap form of transport.

They generally preferred cabs, usually a hansom which seated two, or, if more people needed to be accommodated, a four-wheeler, also known as a 'growler'. There was a cab-rank outside Baker Street station or a passing cab could be hailed in the street or summoned by blowing a whistle, one blast for a four-wheeler, two for a hansom. Many Londoners carried a cab whistle on them for this purpose.

But where exactly was 221B Baker Street?

Apart from the matter of dating, this is one of the most vexed questions facing the Sherlockian scholar and several different sites have been claimed as its location. The problem is compounded by two factors: the renaming of part of Baker Street since Holmes' and Watson's time, and the renumbering of the houses.

The present-day Baker Street crosses Marylebone Road at right angles, running from Portman Square in the south to Clarence Gate, Regent's Park, in the north, where it swings west and becomes Park Road. In 1881 this northern section was known as

Upper Baker Street. It is in this more recently named extension that the present 221 Baker Street is situated. The site is now occupied by the Abbey National Building Society which has offices at numbers 215 to 229.* A few doors away is the Sherlock Holmes Museum, opened in 1990, which claims to be 221B Baker Street, although its correct postal address is 239.

When Holmes and Watson arrived to inspect the lodgings, Baker Street was much shorter than it is today and extended only from Portman Square to the intersection of Paddington Street and Cranford Street. The section north to Marylebone Road was known as York Place. The numbering ran north from number 1 at the Portman Square end as far as number 42 at York Place on the east side before continuing south on the west side from number 44 to number 85. There was therefore no number 43. Nor, more significantly for students of the canon, was there a 221.

Watson has therefore clearly changed the number in order that the house should not be identified in the same way as he changed Mrs Hudson's[†] name, as no such person figures as a householder in any of the street directories of the period. However, he has given several clues which might help identify 221B Baker Street, although care should be taken over these. If Watson changed the number of the house and the name of his landlady, he may well have deliberately altered other details as well in order that the house should not be recognized. After his accounts were published and the address became well known, it would have been embarrassing to Holmes' clients, some of whom were eminent men and women, if sight-seers had gathered on the pavement to stare up at the windows.

Readers are referred to Appendix Two for a more detailed account of the clues within the canon which might point to the

* The Abbey National Building Society still receives on average twenty letters a week from all over the world, some asking for Sherlock Holmes' help with specific problems.

† In *A Scandal in Bohemia*, Holmes refers to a Mrs Turner who had 'brought in the tray' containing 'the simple fare our landlady had supplied'. Although Watson gives no explanation for her presence in 221B Baker Street, she could either be the maid who brought up the tray prepared by Mrs Hudson, the landlady, from the kitchen, or a temporary replacement for Mrs Hudson, who may have been ill or absent for some reason.

possible siting of 221B Baker Street and of some of the theories put forward by Sherlockian scholars. Incidentally, the B of 221B refers to Bis, the French word meaning 'twice', signifying a subsidiary address, in this case the set of rooms occupied by Holmes and Watson.

But wherever 221B was situated, certain facts can be established, particularly concerning the interior of the house about which Watson had less reason to fabricate.

There was a basement, where the kitchen, scullery and pantries were housed and where the servants, in this case a maid and possibly also a daily cleaning woman, would have taken their meals. Photographs of the period show areas with iron railings and steps leading down to a basement entrance. Billy the page-boy, whom Holmes later introduced into the household, would have eaten his meals here as well. These basement areas have since been paved over. The kitchen would have been equipped with a cast-iron, coal-burning stove, which needed daily black-leading, and almost certainly a deal kitchen table for the preparation of food, and a range of wooden dressers and cupboards.

The front door opened into a passage from where the staircase rose to the upper floors and a narrower set of steps led down to the basement.

The ground floor (American first floor) consisted of two main rooms, the original front and back parlours. As we shall see later in the chapter, Mrs Hudson probably received between £208 to £260 a year from letting off the three upper rooms, not a large income to cover household expenses which included grocery bills, the wages of at least one servant and the payment of ground rent, and she may have augmented this sum by letting out the front room to a commercial tenant, such as a dressmaker. If she did so, there is no reference to one in the canon. However, it would seem that she kept the back parlour for her own use as a sitting-room, which she also made available as a waiting-room for Holmes' clients. There are several references to such a room and, according to the occupation of the rest the house, it was the only one which would have been free for such a purpose.

It is unlikely there were any other private tenants. Watson never refers to any and the general impression he gives is of Holmes and himself being the only lodgers.

From the hall, seventeen steps led up to the first or drawing-room floor which, like the ground floor, consisted of two rooms, a large one at the front and a smaller back room opening from it. When the houses were first built in the eighteenth century, these two rooms were connected by a pair of folding doors which, when opened back, would have made one large L-shaped area. When Holmes and Watson moved into the lodgings, these doors had already been removed, the opening bricked up and plastered over, and a single door put in their place.

Watson describes the sitting-room as being 'light and airy and illuminated by two broad windows'. The use of the word 'broad' is a little confusing. As we have seen, the windows were sash and were long and narrow rather than of broad proportions. Watson may have been referring to the fact that they were larger than those on the bedroom floors above. Readers are again referred to Appendix Two in which the vexed matter of the bow window, to which Watson also refers, is examined.

Watson also remarks that the sitting-room was 'cheerfully furnished'. From references scattered throughout the canon, it is possible to establish what this furniture comprised. Although individual items may have been changed over the years, it is unlikely that Mrs Hudson went to the expense of refurnishing the lodgings entirely. After he had left Baker Street, Watson writes fondly of returning to the familiar rooms as if delighted at finding them exactly as he had left them.

We know that there was a sofa, two armchairs and a basket chair, which probably had loose cushions for extra comfort. As well as a mahogany sideboard, the room also contained a table and upright chairs for it was used as a dining- as well as a sitting-room. Both Holmes and Watson had their own desks, Holmes' fitted out with pigeon-holes and probably also a roll-top lid. It may have been his own property. In addition, Holmes had a deal bench on which he conducted his chemical experiments and which Watson sometimes refers to as a table. Gas was laid on so there was no problem in connecting up a bunsen burner, although water must have been brought to the room in jugs or buckets from elsewhere in the house, presumably from the kitchen. Holmes' microscope stood on this bench among the test-tubes, retorts and other paraphernalia.

There was a fireplace with a mirror hanging above it, possibly part of an elaborate wooden overmantel. A coal-scuttle, where Holmes kept his cigars, stood in the fender and bookcases filled the chimney alcoves containing Watson's modest collection of medical books and Holmes' more extensive library of reference volumes. These included a copy of the current Bradshaw which contained railway timetables, an *Almanach de Gotha*, listing the genealogies of all the European royal families, a *Whitaker's Almanac* and his own, personally-compiled commonplace books of newspaper cuttings as well as his encyclopaedias in which he collected any facts which he considered interesting or relevant. Near at hand were Holmes' pipe-rack and the Persian slipper he used as a tobacco pouch.

The windows were fitted with blinds and also with curtains, probably two sets, one of lace and a heavier pair made of velvet or some other thick material to exclude draughts.

Readers who wish to see what the room may have looked like are recommended to visit the Sherlock Holmes public house in Northumberland Street to the south of Trafalger Square where a reconstruction of it is on display upstairs. The pub itself has a strong Sherlockian connection for it was formerly the Northumberland Hotel, where, it is believed by some commentators, among them William S. Baring-Gould,* Sir Henry Baskerville stayed before travelling to Dartmoor and where two of his boots so mysteriously disappeared.

Or if such a visit is not possible, readers may picture it for themselves on, say, the wild, tempestuous evening in late November 1894 when Inspector Hopkins called on Holmes and Watson at the beginning of the Golden Pince-Nez inquiry. The wind is howling down Baker Street and the rain is beating against the windows but inside all is warm and cheerful, with a bright coal-fire burning in the grate and the gas jets lit, as well as the oil lamps for extra illumination, their yellow glow falling on the room strewn with Holmes' and Watson's possessions; mainly Holmes', it must be admitted. They consist mostly of documents

* Other commentators suggest the Grand Hotel in Trafalgar Square or the Hotel Metropole in Northumberland Avenue as the most likely candidate for the hotel where Sir Henry stayed.

connected with his cases and they lie everywhere, piled up in every corner of the room. He had a horror of destroying papers and over the months they would accumulate until Holmes found the time and energy to docket them and put them away.

Newspapers add to the general untidiness. Holmes was an avid reader of the daily press, particularly the personal advertisements or 'agony' columns, as well as the reports on criminal cases. There are references to at least eight London dailies which Holmes regularly studied, including *The Times* and the *Daily Telegraph*, and seven evening papers, among them the *Echo* and the *Evening News*. Mixed up with the documents and newspapers are relics of the cases he had worked on which, Watson remarks, with a touch of humorous exaggeration, got everywhere, even into the butter-dish.

Apart from the books and possibly also one of the desks, Holmes and Watson introduced other items of their own over the years into the sitting-room, including a gasogene, a curious Victorian invention consisting of two glass globes which produced aerated or soda water; a safe for more confidential papers, and a spirit case or tantalus for bottles of whisky, brandy and so on. Holmes was later to buy a gramophone which he put to good use in recovering the Mazarin stone. By 1898, the date of the case involving the retired colourman, he had had the telephone installed; quite late as the telephone was introduced into London in 1876 and Bow Street police station was equipped with one by 1889. Perhaps he preferred his privacy to remain undisturbed.

Watson's contribution was the two pictures of General Gordon and Henry Ward Beecher, referred to in Chapter One.

A door in the interior wall of the sitting-room led to Holmes' bedroom which was at the back of the house, while another door in the bedroom itself gave direct access to the landing. The only description Watson gives of Holmes' bedroom is in *The Adventure of the Dying Detective*, a case which occurred much later in November 1890, but the room probably had much the same appearance during this earlier period. Every wall, Watson writes, was adorned with pictures of celebrated criminals, while the mantelpiece was covered with 'a litter of pipes, tobacco-pouches, syringes, pen-knives, revolver cartridges, and other debris'.

Apart from the bed, which had a headboard high enough for

Watson to conceal himself behind it (*The Adventure of the Dying Detective*), the room must also have contained a chest of drawers and a wardrobe in which Holmes kept his clothes as well as his store of many disguises which he adopted when the need arose.

Later on, Holmes was to make use of the two lumber rooms, presumably in the attic, as extra storage space for newspapers and some of these disguises, for in *The Adventure of the Beryl Coronet*, Watson writes of Holmes coming down the stairs after having changed his appearance. Over the years, he also acquired the use of at least five small refuges in different parts of London where he could adopt a disguise without the need to return to Baker Street, as Watson reports in *The Adventure of Black Peter*.

While on this subject of apparel, it is worth pausing here to consider what clothes Holmes – and Watson, also – would have possessed.

Conventions of the period demanded that a gentleman dressed according to the occasion. For formal day-wear in town, a frock-coat worn with a topper and a stiff shirt with a wing-collar was considered *de rigueur*. For less formal occasions, a short jacket and a bowler or Homburg hat were acceptable. A dinner or theatre engagement called for full evening dress of tails, starched shirt and silk hat, worn either with a cloak or a dress overcoat. Tweed suits or jackets and plus-fours were acceptable in the country. Holmes would have worn his famous deer-stalker hat and cape only when travelling or out of town, never in London. Other clothing would have included a smoking-jacket, blazer and flannels and, of course, a dressing-gown, which features in so many of Watson's accounts. Over the years, Holmes owned at least three, a grey or mouse-coloured one, a blue one and a purple.

Despite his untidiness over papers, Holmes was neat in his personal appearance and Watson refers to his 'quiet primness of dress'.

Watson's bedroom was on the second floor (American third) at the back of the house and would have been furnished in a similar fashion to Holmes' room. There are several references to his coming downstairs to the sitting-room and in *The Problem of Thor Bridge*, he describes the back yard and its single plane tree, which he could see from his window.

There may not have been gas laid on in the upper floors for in *The Adventure of the Solitary Cyclist*, Watson mentions lighting a candle when woken by Holmes in the early hours of the morning. But this may have been easier and quicker than fumbling his way in the dark across the room to light the gas jets which were usually placed on the wall over the fireplace.

Mrs Hudson almost certainly occupied the front bedroom on this floor, while the servant slept on the floor above. In *A Study in Scarlet* Watson writes of hearing her and the maid passing the sitting-room door on their way upstairs to bed.

There is no reference to a bathroom although Watson twice mentions taking a bath, but he could have done so in a hip-bath in his bedroom. All the bedrooms would have been equipped with a marble-topped wash-hand stand, complete with a large china bowl and jug. Hot water would have been carried up from the kitchen. Nor is there any reference to a lavatory although, after the cholera epidemic of 1849, a sewer system was installed in the 1860s and by 1881 many houses were connected to the main drainage.

Strangely, for Watson gives detailed accounts of the women he encounters, there is no description anywhere in the canon of Mrs Hudson, apart from one reference to her 'stately tread', suggesting she was a dignified, well-built lady. As there is no reference either to a Mr Hudson, William S. Baring-Gould is probably correct in suggesting she was the widow of a prosperous shopkeeper who had invested the money he left her in buying the leasehold of 221 Baker Street with the intention of taking in lodgers, thus providing herself with a steady income.

Certainly, whatever her antecedents, she was a woman of amazing tolerance, putting up with Holmes' untidiness and irregular life-style although even her good nature must have been sorely tried when, in one of his 'queer humours' as Watson describes them, presumably a manic phase, he carried out revolver practice in the sitting-room, neatly picking out the letters V. R., for Victoria Regina, in bullet holes in the plaster of one of the walls. One wonders what the neighbours thought of the noise. His habit of keeping the old plugs and dottles from his pipes on one corner of the mantelpiece for his first smoke of the morning or of skewering his unanswered correspondence to the centre of the mantelshelf with a jack-knife cannot have been very endearing either.

One has the impression that Holmes and Watson were Mrs Hudson's first tenants and that she had not become case-hardened by a succession of lodgers and their peculiar ways. She was to grow very fond of both her gentlemen, especially Holmes, who knew how to charm women when he put his mind to it. When she thought he was seriously ill (*The Adventure of the Dying Detective*), she was genuinely distressed. In later years when he became successful, Holmes was to reward her by increasing the rent he paid to a sum Watson regarded as princely.

It is not known exactly what rent she charged for the set of rooms. In Pascoe's *London Guide and Directory for American Travellers*, the recommended prices in Baker Street were £1 10s (£1.50p) a week for a single room to £5 for two. As Watson describes the rent as 'moderate', she probably charged between £4 and £5 for the three rooms, that is £2 to £2 10s (£2.50p) each, amounting to £208 to £260 a year. This would have included food, cleaning, and possibly also laundry and lighting as well although they may have had to pay extra for coal. At the end of the week, Watson would have still been left with £1 17s 6d (about £1.87p) or £1 10s 6d (about £1.52p) for clothes, tobacco, travelling expenses and entertainment. It was not a large sum considering Watson's rather extravagant habits but, once he had settled down into the lodgings, there was less need for him to go looking for company in such places as the American bar at the Criterion.

Mrs Hudson was a good, plain cook of the Scottish style, as Holmes describes her, which probably meant she provided large helpings of nourishing food but nothing fancy. When he wished to entertain guests, such as Lord St Simon, more lavishly, he sent out for an 'epicurean little cold supper' consisting of a brace of cold woodcock, a pheasant, a *pâté de foie gras* pie and bottles of vintage wine. The dinner of oysters and a brace of grouse, served with 'something a little choice in white wines', to which he invited Inspector Athelney Jones at the end of the Sign of Four case was probably also supplied by an outside caterer.

Having inspected the rooms, Holmes and Watson decided then and there to take them, Watson moving his possessions in that very same evening, taking with him his tin dispatch box but not apparently the bull pup as there is no further reference to it. As Watson was a kindly soul, one assumes he found it a good home. As she herself owned an elderly and ailing terrier, Mrs Hudson may have put her foot down about allowing another dog into the house. With her permission, Holmes was later to put it out of its misery by giving it one of the pills containing an alkaloid poison he had found in Joseph Stangerson's room. It was a quick and merciful death.

Holmes arrived the following morning with several boxes and portmanteaus, including the large tin trunk containing papers and mementoes relating to those cases he had already undertaken during the five and a half years he had spent at Montague Street.

And so they took possession of the apartment which was to be Watson's home for the next eight years, Holmes's for the next twenty-two and which was eventually to become one of the most famous addresses in London.

CHAPTER FIVE

A STUDY IN SCARLET

4th March 1881–7th March 1881

'There's the scarlet thread of murder running through the colourless skein of life, and our duty is to unravel it, and isolate it, and expose every inch of it.'

Holmes: *A Study in Scarlet*

For the first few weeks of their shared tenancy of 221B Baker Street, Holmes was on his best behaviour and proved to be a model companion and lodger. He was, Watson reports, quiet in his ways and regular in his habits. Usually in bed by ten o'clock at night, he was up early in the mornings and had breakfasted and left the house before Watson had come downstairs. As far as Watson could discover, his days were spent either at Bart's in the chemistry laboratory or the dissecting room, or in long solitary walks which took him to the seedier parts of London. On his return, Holmes, with his delight in deliberately mystifying others, at times quite unnecessarily, would show Watson the mud stains on his trousers and explain how, by their colour and consistency, it was possible to tell exactly where he had acquired them, although to what purpose he failed to make clear.

It was during these excursions that Holmes must have set about recruiting the six ragged little street urchins who were to form the Baker Street division of the detective police force, as Holmes at first called them, or the Baker Street Irregulars, their subsequent and best remembered title.

Led by Wiggins, they were to assist Holmes in at least two

inquiries, the Study in Scarlet case in March of that year, and the Sign of Four affair seven years later in September 1888 when their number was increased to twelve. It is possible that the same Wiggins acted as leader on both occasions. If he were first recruited at the age of ten or eleven, he would have been only seventeen or eighteen at the time of the Sign of Four inquiry. Watson writes of him then as being 'taller and older' than the others while the adjective 'little' applied to him in the same passage may refer to his lack of inches compared to better-nourished youths of the same age. On the other hand, 'Wiggins' may be a generic name used by Holmes to apply to any of the lads appointed as group-lieutenant and spokesman. One of the 'Baker Street boys' was to mount guard on Henry Wood's lodgings in Aldershot during the Crooked Man inquiry in 1889.*

There was no shortage of such urchins to choose from, as Dr Barnardo[†] had discovered through his work among them in the East End. London teemed with them. Some were orphans or had run away from violent homes but many were turned out into the streets by parents too poor to feed them. They earned a few coppers as crossing sweepers or by running errands. When these legitimate methods failed, they survived by pilfering from coster-mongers' barrows or living off the discarded fruit and vegetables they found in the gutters.

From among their number, Holmes was careful to pick the most intelligent and streetwise. As he was to point out to Watson, they were invaluable as assistants as they were able to go anywhere and hear everything, unlike a more official investigator to whom some people would hesitate to speak openly. All they needed was organization. The sums of sixpence or a shilling each which Holmes paid a day for their services must have seemed a fortune.

Wiggins must have had a permanent address for in the Sign of Four inquiry Holmes sent him a wire, instructing him to report

* The Baker Street Irregulars may also have assisted Holmes during the Lady Frances Carfax inquiry. As well as the official police, Holmes used his 'own small, but very efficient, organization' in an attempt to discover the whereabouts of the missing lady.

† Thomas John Barnardo (1845–1905) founded more than ninety homes for destitute children, the first for boys in 1870, for girls in 1876.

with his gang to him at Baker Street. Evidently none of them lived in the immediate area for Holmes had to reimburse Wiggins the 3s 6d (approximately 17p) it had cost him in fares for the twelve of them to travel there for the appointment. Holmes may have employed a similar group of street urchins during his time in Montague Street although there is no evidence in the canon to prove this.

He was also careful not to introduce them into 221B Baker Street until he had established himself in Mrs Hudson's good books as a model lodger. Even so, the sight of six little ragamuffins invading her house *en masse* was too much for even that good lady's tolerance and her exclamations of disgust led Holmes to warn Wiggins that in future only he must report directly. The others were to wait outside on the pavement. These instructions evidently went unheeded, for in the Sign of Four case all twelve came rushing upstairs into the sitting-room and Holmes had to repeat the warning.

These first few weeks were a honeymoon period in Holmes' and Watson's relationship as fellow-lodgers although there were some doubts and minor irritations on Watson's part. While Watson enjoyed Holmes' playing of Mendelssohn's Lieder and other of his favourite pieces on his violin, he found his companion's habit of laying the instrument across his knees and scraping out a succession of desultory chords, some melancholy, some cheerful, extremely trying at times. Aware of Watson's impatience, Holmes was careful to round off these exasperating solos with a performance of those musical items which Watson enjoyed.

As a doctor, Watson was also concerned by the occasions when Holmes' energy seemed to desert him and he would lie for days on end on the sofa, hardly speaking or moving, a vacant expression in his eyes. Under any other circumstances, Watson would have suspected Holmes of taking narcotic drugs had not his temperate habits ruled this out of the question. It was only later that Watson discovered how wrong he had been in this assumption. Presumably, Holmes injected himself in the privacy of his bedroom and took care to keep the evidence of his drug addiction concealed from Watson and Mrs Hudson.

Watson was naturally curious about his fellow-lodger. With no friends to visit and little to occupy either his time or his mind, he had the leisure to watch his co-tenant closely and to speculate about him. The wound to his leg, which he had received at the battle of Maiwand and which had seemed a minor injury, was painful, especially in cold or damp conditions, and prevented him from going out except when the weather was mild. During those winter months of early 1881, he must have been confined to the house for days at a stretch. As he makes no reference to the wound in his shoulder, this must have healed satisfactorily and gave him no further trouble.

In particular, it was Holmes' occupation which mystified Watson. He was evidently not a medical student. Stamford had made this clear and Holmes had confirmed this fact when Watson questioned him directly. But his studies, however eccentric and haphazard, seemed to suggest he was preparing himself for some profession. But which? It was all very confusing.

Watson has left no record of their conversations during these first few weeks at Baker Street but, given Watson's curiosity and the contents of the list he was soon to draw up enumerating Holmes' limitations, it is obvious that whenever he had the opportunity, he quizzed him in some detail, and probably not very subtly, about his interests, hobbies and attitudes.

At the same time, Holmes was quietly studying Watson and his observations led him to conclude that his fellow-lodger was rather a dull dog although Watson, to give him his due, was far from being at his best. His low state of health, both physical and mental, cannot have made him a very stimulating companion. To Holmes, he must have seemed worthy enough but stolid, literal-minded and, frankly, something of a bore. He was therefore ripe for teasing. Watson was later to comment on Holmes' sense of humour as being 'peculiar and at times offensive'.

Faced with Watson's ill-disguised curiosity, Holmes amused himself by giving tongue-in-cheek answers to his questions, designed to shock the good doctor by his apparent ignorance of, for example, Thomas Carlyle and even the Copernican theory. The irony was lost on Watson, who took it all much too seriously to the extent of explaining to Holmes that the world went round the sun and not the other way round. His earnestness must have afforded Holmes a great deal of quiet entertainment.

Holmes's explanation for his apparent ignorance was reasonable. The human brain, he declared, was like an empty attic which each individual stocked according to choice. It was a wise man who threw away the lumber and retained only that knowledge which was useful. As we have seen in Chapter One, Holmes had the capacity for storing information which he could recall when he needed it.

It was after this conversation that Watson drew up his list in an attempt to get to grips with the puzzling anomalies in Holmes' education and to come to some conclusion on what, if anything, he did for a living.

It read as follows:

SHERLOCK HOLMES – his limits

1. Knowledge of Literature. – Nil.
2.   "   " Philosophy. – Nil.
3.   "   " Astronomy. – Nil.
4.   "   " Politics. – Feeble.
5.   "   " Botany. – Variable. Well up in belladonna, opium, and poisons generally. Knows nothing of practical gardening.
6.   "   " Geology. – Practical, but limited. Tells at glance different soils from each other. After walks has shown me splashes upon his trousers, and told me by their colour and consistency in what part of London he had received them.
7.   "   " Chemistry. – Profound.
8.   "   " Anatomy. – Accurate, but unsystematic.
9.   "   " Sensational Literature. – Immense. He appears to know every detail of every horror perpetrated in the century.
10. Plays the violin well.
11. Is an expert singlestick player, boxer and swordsman.
12. Has a good practical knowledge of British law.

Knowing the full extent of, for example, Holmes' knowledge of literature and astronomy, we can see how far Watson was deceived and even he realized the list was worthless for he tore it up and threw it into the fire. The exact nature of Holmes' profession, if indeed he had one, continued to mystify him and Holmes was careful to keep him in the dark.

For the first few weeks, Holmes had no visitors and one suspects that he had deliberately told no one of his change of address in order to give himself time to settle into his new lodgings. Once he was established and felt that his relationships with Watson and, in particular, with Mrs Hudson were on a firm footing, he let his new address be known and visitors began to arrive in a steady stream, among them a certain short, sallow-faced man with dark eyes and rat-like features who called four times in one week and whom Holmes was careful to introduce to Watson as plain Mr Lestrade, omitting his professional title of Inspector. Other visitors included a fashionably-dressed young woman, an excitable Jewish pedlar and a railway porter. Holmes explained that these visitors were clients and politely asked for the exclusive use of the shared sitting-room for business purposes.

Clients? Business?

But Holmes offered no further explanation and Watson retired to his bedroom, agog with curiosity but too well mannered to question Holmes point-blank.

And then, on the morning of 4th March, the mystery was finally solved.

For the first time since his arrival in the Baker Street lodgings, Watson was up in time to join Holmes at breakfast. While he waited a little impatiently for Mrs Hudson to lay his place and bring fresh coffee, Watson picked up a magazine from the table and began to read an article in it, entitled, rather ambitiously he thought, 'The Book of Life', which was marked by a pencil. One suspects that Holmes, on hearing Watson coming down the stairs, had hurriedly fetched the magazine from the bookcase and had deliberately marked that particular article in order to draw the doctor's attention to it, intending to use it as an excuse to take Watson into his confidence at last. After all, the game-playing and the mystification, amusing though it had been, could not continue indefinitely.

Watson was unimpressed by the anonymous author's assertion that a careful observer, by following even the most elementary precepts of what he called the 'Science of Deduction and Analysis', could correctly deduce the history as well as the trade or profession of any man on first acquaintance.

'By a man's finger-nails, by his coat-sleeve, by his boot, by his trouser-knees, by the callosities of his forefinger and thumb, by his expression, by his shirt-cuffs – by each of these things a man's calling is plainly revealed.'

While admitting that the reasoning in the article was close and intense, Watson was exasperated by its conclusions, which struck him as far-fetched and exaggerated. Slapping the magazine down on the table, he roundly denounced it as 'ineffable twaddle', adding that he had never read such rubbish in his life. As a betting man, he continued, he was willing to lay a thousand to one that, should the author be 'clapped down', as he expressed it, in a third-class carriage in the underground, he would be unable to name the trades of his fellow-travellers.

Holmes may well have been taken aback by the unexpected vehemence of this criticism, coming from a man whom he had dismissed as a fool and a bore. Certainly, there is a defensive ring to his choice of words when, having acknowledged his authorship of the article, he went on to explain that he was by 'trade' a private consulting detective and that he depended on those theories of observation and deduction for his 'bread and cheese' as if, having created the mystery surrounding himself, he was anxious, in the face of Watson's scorn over the contents of the article, to play down the situation.

Lestrade, he continued, was a well-known detective whom he, Holmes, was helping over a forgery case and his visitors were clients seeking his professional assistance. It was by employing his powers of observation at their first meeting at Bart's, Holmes added, that he had been able to deduce Watson's recent career as an army doctor serving in Afghanistan.

Despite some scepticism, Watson was impressed enough to compare Holmes to two of his favourite fictional detectives, Edgar Allan Poe's Dupin and Emile Gaboriau's Lecoq, and was considerably annoyed when Holmes dismissed them contemptuously. Holmes, Watson concluded, and not without some justification, was bumptious.

He was further exasperated when, in order to change the

subject, he drew Holmes' attention to a man walking along the other side of Baker Street, carrying a large blue envelope in his hand and looking anxiously at the numbers of the houses. Joining Watson at the window, Holmes immediately pronounced him to be a sergeant of Marines, an assertion which Watson silently dismissed as mere 'brag and bounce'.

When, a few minutes later, the man arrived in their sitting-room to deliver the letter to Holmes, Watson, with a touch of excusable malice, seized on the opportunity to take Holmes down a peg or two by asking the man what his trade was. To his discomfiture, he discovered that Holmes was correct and that the man, though now a commissionaire, had indeed once served as a sergeant in the Royal Marine Light Infantry. Although Watson was impressed, a lurking suspicion remained that the episode had been pre-arranged in order to 'dazzle' him, a doubt which was not expelled until Holmes explained step by step the method by which he had arrived at his conclusions regarding the man. Watson was totally won over and from that moment on was to remain a loyal admirer and exponent of Holmes' unique skills as a private consulting detective, an attitude which was to form the bedrock of their friendship.

The events of that morning of 4th March were also significant for Holmes for they showed him that Watson, far from being the gullible fool he had at first imagined, possessed not only a good deal of intelligence and healthy scepticism but was prepared to stand up for himself and express his opinions in a forthright manner. At the same time, he was gratified by the doctor's genuine admiration for his deductive skills. As Watson was later to discover, Holmes was as susceptible to flattery of his professional abilities as any young woman of her beauty.

Watson might be worth cultivating after all, and Holmes was tempted to prove to Watson just how far those skills extended by inviting him to join him as an observer on the Study in Scarlet murder inquiry for which Inspector Gregson had requested Holmes' assistance in the letter delivered by the former sergeant of Marines. It would also be entertaining to have Watson as a witness to the inevitable discomfiture of the official police when Holmes eventually proved them wrong, as he had every confidence of doing.

At the same time, Holmes could not resist squeezing the last few drops of humour out of the situation by pretending indifference to the case, knowing only too well that Watson, with his newly-acquired enthusiasm, would be further astonished and would urge him to accept. It was a subtle game, the artfulness of which Watson did not entirely appreciate, although, once they had arrived at number 3 Lauriston Gardens, Brixton, where Drebber's body had been discovered, he was not completely taken in by the little act which Holmes put on for his benefit. It occurred to Watson that Holmes' show of nonchalance, the lounging manner in which he sauntered up and down the pavement or gazed vacantly about him, bordered on affectation, a conclusion which was not far from the truth. For although Holmes' methods on this occasion were similar to those he often employed on other investigations, he undoubtedly exaggerated the unhurried nature of his preliminary examination of the scene-of-crime in order to impress his companion.

Once the inquiry was under way and the second murder, that of Joseph Stangerson, had been committed, he abandoned these prima-donnaish pretensions and threw himself into solving the case with his usual enthusiastic energy, applying those precepts of scientific analysis and deduction to such dazzling effect that any vestige of Watson's earlier scepticism was finally swept away. Indeed, the doctor was so impressed by Holmes' professional expertise that, once the case was completed and the murderer of Drebber and Stangerson was arrested and had made a full confession, Watson was determined that Holmes' merits as a consulting detective should be made public, especially as an account in the evening newspaper, the *Echo*, gave all the credit for the successful conclusion of the case to the two Scotland Yard inspectors Lestrade and Gregson, just as Holmes had predicted.

It was this sense of justice and fair play as well as his admiration that persuaded Watson to declare that, if Holmes would not publish an account of the case, then he himself would do so on Holmes' behalf. It was a spur-of-the-moment decision which Watson was not to regret over the years he acted as self-appointed chronicler of Holmes' many exploits.

In this role, he has come in for much criticism from commentators. However, it should be remembered that Watson had no formal training either as a secretary or as a recorder of events although his experience both at Bart's and at Netley as a student would have accustomed him to taking lecture notes and he was therefore used to scribbling down the more important facts, relying on his memory when he came to expanding those notes into a more coherent and detailed form.

And despite his notorious carelessness over dates and other facts and figures, he was on the whole blessed with a good memory, particularly for conversations and for the details of his physical surroundings as well as the people he was to encounter, especially women. His accounts are full of vivid descriptions of interiors and landscapes, whether of London streets or of the countryside as, for example, this picture of Dartmoor in autumn, 'the slanting rays of the sun turning the streams to threads of gold and glowing on the red earth new turned by the plough and the broad tangle of woodlands.'

He uses this same talent to describe people as diverse as Miss Violet Hunter with 'her bright, quick face, freckled like a plover's egg', or Charles Augustus Milverton with 'his large, intellectual head' and 'perpetual frozen smile.'*

Holmes, too, is captured again and again in his many moods, sitting cross-legged, for example, on a pile of cushions, 'his old briar pipe between his lips' as, 'in the dim light of the lamp', he ponders the problem of the disappearance of Neville St Clair in *The Man with the Twisted Lip*, or smashing the plaster bust of Napoleon with his hunting crop and, 'with a shout of triumph', retrieving the black Borgia pearl from among its fragments in *The Adventure of the Six Napoleons*.

Watson records conversations with the same lively immediacy and has a keen ear for differentiating between, for example, the Cockney speech of Mr Sherman, the taxidermist from Pinchen Lane, the Scots accent of Inspector MacDonald, and the pompous language of Lord St Simon.

Watson also possesses great skills as a narrator. His accounts never flag but are driven forward with enormous energy and gusto, especially in those passages where the action is all import-

* In *The Adventure of the Retired Colourman*, Watson himself acknowledges that he has 'a quick eye for faces'.

ant, as in this passage from *The Sign of Four*, which with its short, staccato sentences captures the speed and excitement of the night-time pursuit up the Thames by a police boat of the steam launch *Aurora*.

'We flashed past barges, steamers, merchant-vessels, in and out, behind this one and round the other. Voices hailed us out of the darkness, but still the *Aurora* thundered on, and still we thundered close upon her track.'

He is also adept at using other narrative devices to forward the action or to convey information: quotations from newspaper accounts, for example, or direct conversation, either in brief exchanges or in longer passages in which Holmes' clients explain their problems or Holmes himself expounds his theories. On occasions, Watson uses his role as narrator to address the reader personally or, in order to heighten the mystery and tension, expresses his thoughts and feelings in such an open and disarming manner that the reader easily identifies with him.

His methods of recording his material are made clear in *A Study in Scarlet*. Presumably he made use of much the same system in subsequent cases. He kept a journal. He also read newspaper accounts of the case as it progressed, using them as sources of additional information before cutting them out and pasting them into a scrap book, a form of reference which he may have copied from Holmes, who was in the habit of keeping similar records. In addition, he had access to Inspector Lestrade's notes on the murderer's confession, probably not in their original shorthand version but in the extended longhand reports which Lestrade would have had to submit to his superior officers at Scotland Yard.

Apart from these written or printed records, Watson was in daily contact with Holmes, with whom he discussed the cases and from whom he could draw any additional material or information should it be needed.

In the Drebber-Stangerson murder inquiry, he was also given permission to hold a lengthy interview with Jefferson Hope, his notes of which Watson was later to expand and transcribe into five retrospective chapters which form the larger section of Part Two of *A Study in Scarlet*.

His limitations are seen in his negligence over some of the facts of the cases, especially in the matter of dates, over which at times he was infuriatingly imprecise. Watson clearly belonged to that group of people, often but not exclusively male, who are congenitally incapable of remembering dates, even their children's and spouse's birthdays or their own wedding anniversary.

However, it should be pointed out in Watson's defence that it was not the chronological aspect of Holmes' career which particularly interested him. He was not an historian; he was not even a biographer in the accepted sense of the term, even though he claimed to be both in *The Adventure of the Resident Patient*. He was a chronicler of events in which he himself participated and his point of view was therefore subjective. He was, moreover, far more concerned with conveying to his readers an awareness and appreciation of Holmes' skill as a consulting detective and the exciting as well as the baffling aspects of the cases he investigated than in recording the precise dates on which they occurred.

His own reading tastes almost certainly influenced his style. He enjoyed a good yarn, as can be seen in his appreciation of the nautical adventures of the American novelist William Clark Russell, while his admiration for the detective stories of Edgar Allan Poe and Emile Gaboriau, despite Holmes' contempt for their fictional investigators, would have persuaded him to concentrate on the thrill and mystery of Holmes' inquiries. Significantly, out of the four novel-length chronicles and the fifty-six shorter accounts, Watson has chosen to preface the titles of forty-six of them, nearly four-fifths, with the words *The Adventure of. . .*

In further mitigation, it should also be pointed out that Watson was working from brief, handwritten notes, on some occasions months or even years after they were first scribbled down. It was easy enough for him to misread his own handwriting and to mistake a badly formed figure seven, say, for a nine or a scrawled three for an eight.

Other mistakes, particularly over dating, could have occurred when his handwritten manuscripts were copied by a typist, if he employed one, or alternatively by the typesetter. In addition, some could be printer's errors which were uncorrected at the proof stage, either by Watson himself or by the publisher's reader, or by both. It is easily done, as I know from experience.

One of my own books contains the description of a character sitting with his 'things' rather than his 'thighs' wide apart.

During the 1880s, Watson was further handicapped in his task of chronicling Holmes' exploits by the loss of his papers, as he reports in *The Adventure of the Resident Patient* when it was first published in the *Strand* in August 1893. 'I cannot be sure of the exact date,' he writes, 'for some of my memoranda on the matter have been mislaid, but it must have been towards the end of the first year during which Holmes and I shared chambers in Baker Street.' When the account was reprinted in *The Memoirs of Sherlock Holmes* the following year, this sentence was omitted.

On other occasions, Watson deliberately withheld dates and other information in order to protect the identities of those involved in some of the inquiries or for reasons of national security as he was to do in *The Adventure of Charles Augustus Milverton*, a notorious blackmailing case, or in *The Adventure of the Second Stain*, 'the most important case' Holmes ever handled, an account of which he gave Watson permission to publish only if its contents were 'carefully guarded'.

Nevertheless, it would have made the task easier for later commentators on the canon if Watson had shown a little more care over certain of the facts while at the same time depriving them of a great deal of pleasurable diversion in speculating on possible interpretations.

This lack of precision is, however, far outweighed by Watson's other and more important skills as an author as the continuing and world-wide popularity of his accounts has proved.

CHAPTER SIX

BAKER STREET DAYS

1881–1889

'I had no keener pleasure than in following Holmes in his professional investigations, and in admiring the rapid deductions, as swift as intuitions, and yet always founded on a logical basis, with which he unravelled the problems which were submitted to him.'

Watson: *The Adventure of the Speckled Band.*

In *The Hound of the Baskervilles,* Holmes states that he had handled 'five hundred cases of capital importance' up to that time, by which he presumably means from 1877 when he turned professional to 1888, the date of the Baskerville inquiry.* It was a very heavy case load, averaging forty-five investigations a year. Of these, Watson was actively involved with about only a seventh. This is made clear in the opening paragraph of *The Adventure of the Speckled Band,* in which Watson refers to the 'seventy odd cases' of which he had kept notes over the past eight years.

In this instance at least, Watson was correct in his facts. This period of their shared tenancy of the Baker Street lodgings and the initial stage of their association indeed lasted eight years, from the time of their first meeting in the early part of 1881, probably on 1st January, to the spring of 1889 when, as we shall see in a later chapter, an event occurred which was to affect both

* See Appendix One for the dating of this case.

83

their lives, Watson's in particular, and which might have brought an end to their friendship.

He is less accurate in his other comment, already referred to in Chapter Two, in which he states that of the twenty-three years Holmes was in active practice, he co-operated with him 'during seventeen of these'. If Watson is basing this calculation on the Study in Scarlet case, the first investigation on which he accompanied Holmes and which occurred in March 1881, then the number of years of his collaboration was nineteen, not seventeen.

Of the over seventy cases of this 1881–9 period on which Watson says he kept notes, he wrote full accounts of only about a fifth of them, fourteen at most, and referred directly to only another seven.

Because of the problems over dating, it is impossible to establish a definite chronology of these recorded inquiries that Holmes undertook during this period, although in some instances Watson has supplied dates, on occasions with admirable precision, as in *A Study in Scarlet* which is quite positively assigned to 4th March 1881, or the inquiry involving the murder of William Kirwin, which occurred on 26th April 1887, a date which can be established without any doubt from the facts supplied in Watson's account. *'The Adventure of the Reigate Squire.'* Other cases are less precisely dated. The Speckled Band inquiry took place in April 1883 while the Valley of Fear investigation occurred, Watson states, 'in the early days of the late 1880s'.

In other accounts, only the month or the season of the year are given; in some not even these. It is only by internal evidence, such as references to 'our sitting-room', or the date of first publication, that the cases can be assigned to this period, while some commentators have turned to meteorological records or, in the Yellow Face inquiry, to such external evidence as the date of the yellow fever epidemic in Atlanta, in an attempt to establish the date.

However, a tentative chronology can be established, although it is by no means definitive and many Sherlockian commentators will disagree with it. The asterisks refer to those cases where the

---

* This account is published in the States under the title *The Adventure of the Reigate Squires*.

dating is beyond doubt. The cases placed in parentheses are those referred to in the canon but not fully recorded. The question marks are self-explanatory.

A more detailed explanation of the dating of the more problematic cases is given in Appendix One.

Date	Case	First publication
4th March 1881*	A Study in Scarlet	December 1887
October 1881?	The Resident Patient	August 1893
April 1882?	The Yellow Face	February 1893
April 1883*	The Speckled Band	February 1892
Spring 1885?	The Copper Beeches	June 1892
February 1886?	The Beryl Coronet	May 1892
February-April 1887*	(The Maupertuis Scandal)	unrecorded
14th April 1887*	The Reigate Squire	June 1893
January* 1880s	The Valley of Fear	September 1914–
(January 1888?)	in serial form	May 1915
June 1888*	(Vatican Cameos)	unrecorded
Summer 1888?	(The Manor House Affair)	unrecorded
Summer 1888?	The Greek Interpreter	September 1893
August 1888?	The Cardboard Box	January 1893
September 1888*	The Sign of Four	February 1890
late September 1888?	Silver Blaze	December 1892
October 1888?	Hound of the Baskervilles, in serial form	August 1901– April 1902
October 1888?	(King of Scandinavia)	unrecorded
October 1888?	(Grosvenor Square Van)	unrecorded
October 1888*	The Noble Bachelor	April 1892
November 1888?	(Colonel Upwood Scandal)	unrecorded
November 1888?	(Mme Montpensier)	unrecorded

Of these fourteen fully recorded cases which may be assigned to this period, seven involved murder, in some instances more than one; four were crimes of either attempted murder, theft, wrongful imprisonment or attempted fraud; one was a case of accidental death while two, the affairs of the Yellow Face and the Noble Bachelor, involved no crime at all. If the Charles Augustus Milverton case also took place during this time, then blackmail as well as murder may be added to this list.† Out of the criminal

† This case, which is deliberately undated by Watson, is assigned by some

cases, nine were motivated by greed, four by revenge and one by fear.

Of the seven inquiries referred to during this period but of which Watson has left no written account, the nature of the crime can be established for only three, the Maupertuis investigation, which was a case of international fraud; the scandal at the Nonpareil Club, involving the infamous Colonel Upwood and which was presumably concerned with cheating at cards; and the case of Mme Montpensier, a French lady, wrongly accused of the murder of her stepdaughter, Mlle Carère, who was later found married and living in New York.

Little is known about the others except that the Manor House affair concerned a man called Adams and was successfully concluded by Holmes. Holmes gives no details of the case of the Vatican Cameos apart from remarking that it took place at the time of the death of Sir Charles Baskerville in June 1883. As for the inquiry involving the king of Scandinavia*, we know nothing except that it occurred shortly before the case of the Noble Bachelor and that it was of a highly confidential nature. Readers are referred to Appendix One for fuller explanation of the case of the Second Stain and three other inquiries with which Holmes may have been involved between 1881 and 1889: the Bogus Laundry affair, the Darlington Substitution scandal and the Arnsworth Castle case[†]. Other cases which occurred towards the end of this period – the Trepoff murder, the Atkinson tragedy and the mission on behalf of the reigning family of Holland – will be examined in more detail in Chapter Nine.

As Watson explains, out of this list of more than seventy cases,

---

commentators to this 1881–9 period. However, in agreement with other Sherlockian scholars, I have placed it in the later period (1894–1903), after Watson's return to Baker Street.

* Holmes may be referring to King Oscar II (1829–1907), who ruled Sweden and Norway from 1872 until 1905, when Norway gained its independence. The king of Bohemia was engaged to one of the daughters of the king of Scandinavia (see Chapter Nine).

† The case involving Wilson, the manager of a district messenger office, whose good name Holmes saved and possibly also Wilson's life, may belong to this period or to the time when Holmes was practising at Montague Street. One of Wilson's messenger boys, who had helped with that inquiry, also assisted Holmes in the Hound of the Baskerville case.

he found it difficult to choose which to record, selecting only those which best illustrated Holmes' remarkable detective powers while at the same time avoiding either the over-sensational or those in which the facts were too slight or commonplace to satisfy his readers. Watson was not always to keep to this rule. The Cardboard Box inquiry, with its double murder and gruesome evidence in the shape of two severed ears, should surely come into the category of the over-sensational.

Those he has chosen do indeed illustrate Holmes' expertise in scientific detection, perfected during the latter's five and a half years' residence at Montague Street. Examples include the tracing of footprints and animal tracks (*The Adventure of Silver Blaze, The Adventure of the Resident Patient* and *The Hound of the Baskervilles*); the effects of gunshot wounds (*The Valley of Fear*); the analysis of handwriting (*The Adventure of the Cardboard Box* and *The Adventure of the Reigate Squire*): the analysis of cigars and their ash (*The Adventure of the Resident Patient*); the deciphering of codes (*The Valley of Fear*) and the use of disguise (*The Adventure of the Beryl Coronet*).

Holmes was probably 27 and Watson about 28 or 29 when this period began with the Study in Scarlet case and 35 when it ended in the early spring of 1889, Watson then being about 36 or 37. For both men, this eight-year period was to see great changes, not least in the growth of their friendship. After the Study in Scarlet inquiry, Holmes began to treat Watson with increased respect and intimacy, addressing him as 'my dear Watson' or 'my dear fellow' rather than the more formal 'Doctor'. By April 1883, the date of the Speckled Band case, he was referring to Watson as his 'intimate friend and associate', assuring his client, Miss Helen Stoner, that she could speak as freely in front of Watson as she could before himself. Watson reciprocated, using such terms as 'My dear Holmes'.

Both men gained enormous advantages from their growing friendship, in particular from the shared companionship, although Watson undoubtedly appreciated this aspect of their relationship more than Holmes, who was better suited tempermentally to solitude than Watson. As a consequence, Watson began to emerge from his depression and to recover his former good spirits to the extent that Holmes commented on 'his pawky humcur'. However, physically he had not yet fully recovered and the wound in his leg continued to trouble him throughout this period, particularly when the weather was cold or damp.

When in a good humour, Holmes could be a stimulating companion, his conversation covering a wide range of topics: on one occasion miracle plays, medieval pottery, Stradivarius violins, Buddhism in Ceylon and warships of the future. On another, Watson reports how he was kept 'amused and enthralled' by Holmes' 'characteristic talk, with its keen observance of detail and subtle powers of observation'.

Time no longer hung heavy on Watson's hands. Apart from the investigations themselves, which absorbed much of their joint attention and took them to many different locations – not just in London but to various parts of the country including Sussex, Hampshire and, further afield still, to Dartmoor, and even on one occasion to France – he and Holmes went for walks, dined out and went to the opera together.

In addition, Watson was busy keeping up to date with his notes on the cases and writing up full accounts of some of the inquiries with the intention of publishing them and thereby making Holmes' name better known, not with much success until the latter part of this period. This aspect of Watson's life will be examined in the next chapter.

All these activities must have taken up much of his time for, during these eight years, there is no reference to his reading any of his medical books or to preparing himself to return to active practice, and it is safe to assume that at this stage he had abandoned any thought of resuming his former career as a doctor. He appears quite content to continue sharing the bachelor lodgings with Holmes, living on his army pension and acting as Holmes' companion, assistant and chronicler. Any leisure time he had away from Holmes' company was spent either at his club, playing billiards with a man named Thurston, or betting on horses, an activity which he was later to admit cost him half his pension. It was only in September 1888, towards the end of this period, that a meeting was to occur which was radically to change his attitude and to rekindle his old ambitions.

The advantages of the friendship were, however, not all on Watson's side. Holmes gained, too. Watson was a loyal and eager companion, prepared to accompany him even on potentially dangerous inquiries and, if necessary, to go armed, as Watson did on at least three occasions, the Speckled Band, the Baskerville and the Copper Beeches inquiries. In the latter case, Watson used his gun to save the life of Jephro Rucastle when he was attacked by his own guard-dog.

Watson's medical knowledge also had its uses. In the Resident Patient inquiry, he was able to establish the time of Blessington's death from the degree of rigor mortis. He also saved the life of Mr Melas in the Greek Interpreter affair by the prompt adminis- tration of ammonia and brandy when that gentleman had been overcome by charcoal fumes, while in 1887, he was to give Holmes himself direct medical advice and assistance, as we shall see later in the chapter.

On occasions, Watson helped with the inquiries themselves by acting as another pair of eyes and ears, helping Holmes, for example, to trace Silver Blaze's tracks across the moor. In the Baskerville case, he was left virtually in charge of the inquiry, reporting back to Holmes, who had apparently returned to London, on all he saw and heard relating to the investigation.

As well as these more practical contributions, Watson served as a sympathetic listener to whom Holmes could expound the facts of a case, thereby clarifying them in his own mind. Holmes expresses such a need in *The Adventure of Silver Blaze*. 'I shall enumerate them [the facts] to you,' he tells Watson, 'for nothing clears up a case so much as stating it to another person.' In the same inquiry, Holmes appealed directly for Watson's help in solving the mystery of John Straker's death. 'If you can give me any light I shall be infinitely obliged to you,' he says.

By degrees, as Watson's confidence grew, he began to put forward his own ideas as, for example, in the Greek Interpreter inquiry in which he suggests that the young Greek woman found out about her brother's arrival in England only by accident, a theory which Holmes greeted with the exclamation, 'Excellent, Watson! I really feel you are not far from the truth.' It was also Watson who suggested that an almanac might hold the key to the coded letter in the Valley of Fear case.

But Watson's chief role was still that of an appreciative audi- ence. Holmes remained susceptible to flattery, as is seen in *The*

Adventure of the Reigate Squire when Colonel Hayter complimented him by suggesting the inquiry was too petty to interest someone of his reputation. Although Holmes brushed the remark aside, his smile, Watson observes, 'showed that it pleased him'. And it was exceedingly flattering to Holmes' ego to have Watson at his side, constantly exclaiming in surprise and admiration at his, Holmes', brilliant detective skills and superior intellectual powers. However, while he was admittedly not as intelligent as Holmes, Watson was no fool and, one suspects that, kind man that he was – he sometimes deliberately exaggerated his bewilderment in order to give Holmes the pleasure of explaining how he had arrived at his conclusions.

Another indication of their growing intimacy was Holmes' admission of his drug addiction. Watson does not state exactly how or when he learned of Holmes' habit of injecting himself with a 7 per cent solution of cocaine. The first reference to it is in *The Adventure of the Yellow Face,* assigned by some commentators to 1885 or 1886. However, Watson's awareness of Holmes' dependency might suggest that the earlier date of 1882 is correct. It is unlikely that Holmes could have kept his addiction secret from Watson for four or five years. Watson was a doctor and, as we have seen, was already suspicious of Holmes' symptoms within a few weeks of their moving together into the Baker Street lodgings. Over the following years, Watson was to try weaning Holmes from the habit.

Holmes also came to express more openly to Watson that darker, more melancholy side of his nature. In *The Adventure of the Copper Beeches*, Holmes remarks: 'It is my belief, Watson, founded upon my experience, that the lowest and vilest alleys in London do not present a more dreadful record of sin than does the beautiful countryside.' He was in an even more solemn and philosophical mood at the end of the Cardboard Box inquiry.

'What is the meaning of it, Watson?' he inquires. 'What is served by this circle of misery, violence and fear? It must tend to some end, or else our universe is ruled by chance, which is unthinkable. But to what end? There is the great standing perennial problem to which human reason is as far from an answer as ever.'

Holmes must have found considerable relief from having,

possibly for the first time in his life, so close a companion in whom he could confide such thoughts.

However, it was not all gloom. There was a great deal of laughter as well and the image of Holmes as an introspective intellectual, sunk deep in thought, is only partly true. Throughout Watson's accounts, there are numerous references to Holmes either smiling or laughing, from a 'low chuckle' to 'an uncontrollable fit of laughter' in which Watson joined.

Holmes possessed a keen sense of humour, often ironic, as demonstrated by his comment, quoted in *The Valley of Fear* on the style of *Whitaker's Almanac*: 'though terse in its earlier vocabulary, it becomes, if I remember right, quite garrulous towards the end.' However, when that irony turned to sarcasm and was directed against himself, Watson became annoyed at Holmes' 'sardonic' interruptions, as he reports in the same account.

For despite their growing friendship and Watson's unaffected admiration, there were still times when he found Holmes exasperating, particularly when he was in what Watson calls a 'disputatious mood'. It was then that Watson was reminded of the egoism which was 'a strong factor' in Holmes' personality and which he found repellent. Much warmer by nature, Watson also found it difficult to come to terms with Holmes' colder, less emotional character to the extent that on occasions he considered him as a nothing more than a 'brain without a heart', so lacking was he in human sympathy.

This side of Holmes' personality is seen in his attitude to certain individuals, especially those he had reason to dislike, such as Dr Grimesby Roylott (*The Adventure of the Speckled Band*) on whose death, for which he was indirectly responsible, he remarks dismissively, 'I cannot say that it is likely to weigh very heavily on my conscience.'

Once a case was completed, he showed no further concern over his clients, not even for Miss Violet Hunter (*The Adventure of the Copper Beeches*), a young lady of considerable charm and courage. It was Watson, disappointed by Holmes' lack of interest, who went to the trouble of finding out and reporting on her subsequent successful career as the headmistress of a private school.

But, when interviewing clients, Holmes was capable of showing admirable patience, listening to their at times lengthy accounts without interruption. He could even sympathize with their distress, as in the case of Miss Helen Stoner (*The Adventure of the Speckled Band*), whom he pats soothingly on the arm, a rare instance of Holmes' initiating physical contact with another person. Seeing she is cold, he seats her by the fire and orders a cup of coffee for her. However, he is quite adamant in one respect: his clients had to be completely frank with him. When he suspected Mr Blessington was lying to him (*The Adventure of the Resident Patient*), Holmes curtly refused to continue with the case.

Despite this stricture on the part of his clients, Holmes was not able to shake off his own delight in mystifying others and even Watson, intimate friend or not, was kept deliberately in the dark on some occasions, as in the Beryl Coronet inquiry when Holmes adroitly sidestepped Watson's questions by changing the subject. In a later inquiry into the disappearance of the racehorse, Silver Blaze, and the death of its trainer, John Straker, Holmes not only misled Watson but also the horse's owner, Colonel Ross, as well as Inspector Gregson, who was officially engaged on the inquiry. In this instance, there was some justification for Holmes' withholding the truth. A too-early revelation would have ruined the drama of the dénouement. For Holmes could not resist the temptation of introducing an element of the theatrical into his investigations, a tendency he admits in the Valley of Fear inquiry.

'Watson insists that I am the dramatist in real life,' he remarks. 'Some touch of the artist wells up in one and calls insistently for a well-staged performance.'

Once he had established himself in both Mrs Hudson's and Watson's good books, Holmes soon reverted to his old irregular habits of untidiness and late rising, occasionally lapsing, when in one of his manic moods, into acts of irresponsible behaviour, such as his use of the sitting-room wall for target practice, already referred to in Chapter Four.

Nevertheless, over this period, Holmes' character shows definite signs of developing and maturing. One indication of this is his changing attitude to the official police. As the years passed, he grew less contemptuous of both them and their methods, even of Lestrade, whom he refers to as 'the best of the Scotland

Yarders'. In *The Adventure of the Cardboard Box*, Holmes remarks that the inspector can be relied on to supply the missing facts of the case for 'although he is devoid of reason, he is as tenacious as a bulldog once he understands what he has to do.' It is doubtful if Holmes would have paid Lestrade even this back-handed compliment a few years earlier. He is also complimentary about Inspector Gregson, whom he describes as an 'extremely competent officer', though lacking in imagination.

But it is in his dealings with Inspector MacDonald, a young and intelligent Scotland Yard officer, during the Valley of Fear inquiry that Holmes's improved relationship with the police is seen at its best. Watson comments that, although not prone to friendship, Holmes was tolerant of the big Scotsman. Certainly his attitude towards him is relaxed and informal. Holmes refers to him as 'friend MacDonald' and addresses him as 'Mr Mac', a nickname which has a touch of affectionate regard about it. He also had, as Watson remarks, a genuine admiration for the man's professional competence.

Another change is seen in Holmes's willingness to admit he could at times be wrong, a confession he would have also found difficult to make before this period.

'I had come to an entirely erroneous conclusion,' he confesses to Watson at the end of the Speckled Band affair while he is even more frank about his shortcomings over the Yellow Face inquiry which took place at Norbury. He tells Watson, '. . .if it should ever strike you that I am getting a little over-confident in my powers, or giving less pains to a case than it deserves, kindly whisper "Norbury" in my ear, and I shall be infinitely obliged to you.'*

Apart from his heavy case-load, Holmes was also busy during these years with his other interests. If the date of August 1888 is correct for *The Adventure of the Cardboard Box*, then in 1887 he published the two short monographs in the *Anthropological Journal* on the human ear, already referred to in Chapter Two. He also

---

* Although Holmes was not aware of it, he was also incorrect in assuming that the swamp adder in the Speckled Band inquiry was summoned by its owner's whistle. All snakes are deaf, a fact of which Holmes was apparently ignorant. Presumably the snake was tempted back to Roylott's room by the scent of the saucer of milk he put out for it.

continued with his chemical experiments, including an analysis of acetones and a successful attempt at dissolving hydrocarbons.

But it was, of course, the investigations which occupied most of his time. As we have seen, he was dealing with about forty-five cases a year, some of which, such as the Baskerville inquiry, took several weeks to complete. The Maupertuis case took even longer, extending over at least two months of intensive and exhausting inquiries. On occasions, it was not unusual for Holmes to be absent from Baker Street for days and nights at a time.

His clientele came from a wide variety of social backgrounds, from the humble, lowly-paid governess, Miss Violet Hunter (*The Adventure of the Copper Beeches*), to the wealthy banker, Alexander Holder (*The Adventure of the Beryl Coronet*) through to the richest and highest-born in the country such as Sir Henry Baskerville and Lord St Simon (*The Adventure of the Noble Bachelor*). Towards the end of this period, Holmes was to have two even more exalted clients: the Pope, who asked him to investigate the case of the Vatican Cameos, an inquiry which may have necessitated Holmes' presence in Rome, and the King of Scandinavia.

But Holmes was no snob and he treated his clients exactly the same, whatever their backgrounds. 'I can assure you, Watson, without affectation,' he declares in *The Adventure of the Noble Bachelor*, 'that the social status of a client is of less moment to me than the interests of his case.'

It would appear that Holmes never advertised, relying on either his police contacts to introduce him to clients or to ask for his assistance on an inquiry, as happened with the Beryl Coronet and the Cardboard Box investigations, or personal recommendation by former clients. Helen Stoner heard of him through Mrs Farintosh, one of his Montague Street clients, while Lord St Simon was advised by his aristocratic friend, Lord Blackwater, to consult Holmes when the former's bride disappeared under mysterious circumstances.

Holmes' older brother Mycroft, of whom more in the next chapter, was another source of introductions. It was he who called Holmes in to investigate the Greek Interpreter affair and who brought some of the more interesting cases to his brother's attention.

The fees Holmes charged his clients varied according to their financial circumstances. In the case of Miss Helen Stoner, dependent on her stepfather, he asked only for his expenses, but from the wealthy Mr Holder he claimed the full reward of £1,000, at that time a very large sum indeed, offered by the banker for the recovery of the beryl coronet.

His increasing financial success made it possible for Holmes to afford to travel first-class, a luxury he indulged in for his own and presumably also Watson's benefit, when they went by train to Dartmoor to investigate the Silver Blaze affair. As early as 1882, if the dating of *The Adventure of the Yellow Face* to this year is correct, he was already earning enough to pay the wages as well as the board and lodging of a page-boy, referred to in the canon as Billy.

Billy is mentioned several times in Watson's accounts. However, the Billy who features in *The Adventure of the Mazarin Stone*, told in the third person and undated, although it is assigned by some commentators to June 1903, is not the original page-boy. In that account, he refers to the Empty House case of 1894 as being 'before my time'. Billy, like Wiggins, may be a generic name.

Presumably this first Billy, as well as his replacement, slept on the premises, occupying one of the attic bedrooms and eating in the basement kitchen in company with Mrs Hudson and the servant. His duties included answering the door, showing clients upstairs and running errands. He may have performed other tasks as well, such as cleaning boots, relieving Mrs Hudson of some of the burden of caring for her two gentlemen lodgers.

As his practice grew, bringing increased financial reward, Holmes' reputation as a private consulting detective was also spreading. Not only were well-to-do aristocrats such as Lord St Simon and Sir Henry Baskerville calling on his services but he was asked to undertake such *causes célèbres* as the Silver Blaze inquiry which was, as Watson states, 'the one topic of conversation through the length and breadth of England' and which featured in the national newspapers. Some of these cases were also to result in 'sensational trials' which were presumably also reported in the press. As a consequence, his name became well known outside London, not only in England but on the Continent, including Italy and Scandinavia. His international renown culminated in February of the same year as the Reigate Squire case, 1887, with his successful investigation into the Netherland-Sumatra Company. Although the police of three countries had failed to bring Baron Maupertuis, the most accomplished swindler in Europe, to justice, Holmes succeeded in outwitting him, a triumph which brought him European fame.

Unfortunately, for it is one of the most important cases of this period, Watson decided not to publish a full account of the case on the grounds that the events were too recent and the subject-matter too concerned with politics and finance for what he modestly refers to as his 'series of sketches'. One suspects, however, that there were more powerful reasons behind his decision. Pressure may even have been brought on Watson by highly-placed government officials to prevent him from publishing the full facts.

The strain of the Maupertuis inquiry, which lasted for two months and kept Holmes working fifteen hours a day, at times for five days at a stretch, without proper rest, brought about a complete breakdown in his health. On 14th April 1887, despite his iron constitution, he was taken ill in France while staying at the Hotel Dulong in Lyons, where presumably he was still engaged in completing his inquiries into the Maupertuis case. Watson, summoned by telegram, hastened to his side and found Holmes in a state of nervous prostration, suffering from deep depression in a room which was, ironically, ankle-deep in congratulatory telegrams.

Watson immediately took charge, escorting Holmes back to Baker Street. A week later, Watson accompanied him to Reigate in Surrey to stay with his old army friend from his Afghanistan days, Colonel Hayter, for a period of convalescence. However, despite Watson's best efforts to persuade him to rest, Holmes immediately became involved in the Reigate Squire inquiry, a case which he was successfully to solve.

Work was always for him a necessity. It was idleness he could not tolerate. 'My mind rebels at stagnation,' he tells Watson and Watson himself remarks that Holmes' 'razor brain blunted and rusted with inaction'.

The latter years of this period (1881–9) were particularly significant for both of them, marking Watson's first success as an author and bringing Holmes into contact with an arch criminal of such superior intellectual powers that he was to prove not only an adversary worthy of the name but almost a match for Holmes' own remarkable intelligence and investigative skills.

CHAPTER SEVEN

FRIEND AND FOE

1881–1889

'When you have one of the first brains of Europe up
against you and all the powers of darkness at his back,
there are infinite possibilities.'

Holmes on Moriarty: *The Valley of Fear*

In 1887, the same year in which Holmes won European fame
with his investigation of Baron Maupertuis and the Netherland-
Sumatra Company, Watson achieved his own success with the
publication in Beeton's Christmas Annual of *A Study in Scarlet*,
the first case on which he accompanied Holmes in March 1881,
shortly after their meeting.*

With his usual modesty, Watson himself makes no reference to
this minor triumph, although he must have been delighted when,
in the course of the Baskerville inquiry in October 1888, Jack
Stapleton, one of Sir Henry's neighbours, told him that both the
names Holmes and Watson were already familiar to him through
Watson's 'records'. By this, he must mean *A Study in Scarlet*, the
only one of Watson's accounts which had been published at that
date.

It had taken Watson nearly six years for this account to appear
in print and for him to fulfil his promise to Holmes to make his
name better known; rather late for, by the time it was published,

* Although Watson's account was hardly noticed by the critics at the time,
the annual itself was such a success that the publishers issued *A Study in Scarlet*
in a separate edition in 1888.

Holmes' reputation was already established on both sides of the Channel. The fee Watson received must have gone a little way towards helping with his finances although he remained short of money. In August 1888, the possible date of the Cardboard Box case and a particularly hot summer when he was hoping to escape to the New Forest or to the coast at Southsea, he was forced to postpone his holiday and remain in London due to lack of funds.

It would seem that Watson had written up accounts of other cases during this period. In *The Adventure of the Copper Beeches*, which according to the chronology given in Chapter Six is dated 1885, Holmes speaks of 'records of our cases which you have been good enough to draw up'. But as not even *A Study in Scarlet* had appeared in print at that time, Holmes had presumably read these accounts in manuscript form only. Like many other aspiring authors, Watson evidently had problems in finding a publisher willing to take his work, almost certainly a keen disappointment to him although with characteristic self-effacement he never mentions it.

The reference in *The Adventure of the Cardboard Box* to Watson's account of the Sign of Four case is surely another example of Watson's carelessness over facts, a point which has already been examined in Appendix One under the notes on Chapter Six for the dating of this particular account.

Holmes' attitude to Watson as his chronicler is ambivalent. On the one hand, he praises him for choosing those cases which, though trivial in themselves, best illustrate his own skills at 'logical synthesis' rather than concentrating on the *causes célèbres*. However, he criticizes Watson over his style and for putting too much 'life and colour' into his accounts to the detriment of that 'severe reasoning from cause to effect' which Holmes considered the most important feature of his investigations. As he remarks, 'Crime is common. Logic is rare.'

No budding writer likes to have his work disparaged and, quite naturally, Watson was annoyed by Holmes's attitude, seeing it as an example of his egotism, although the reproof was not entirely unjust. As an author, Watson has on occasions a tendency towards exaggeration which is seen, for example, in his description of Alexander Holder (*The Adventure of the Beryl Coro-*

net). It is difficult to believe that the senior partner in the second largest City of London bank would behave quite as hysterically as in Watson's description of him plucking at his hair and banging his head against the wall. Holmes was not the only one with a leaning towards the dramatic.

However, when Holmes himself later turned author and wrote up an account of his own, *The Adventure of the Blanched Soldier*, he was to admit it was not easy to keep rigidly to facts and figures if the material was to interest the reader. When he came to write his second account, *The Adventure of the Lion's Mane*, a case which occurred after his retirement from active practice, his style contains as much 'life and colour' in the way of description as any of Watson's narratives.

Holmes' brother, Mycroft, showed more sensitivity on the subject of Watson's authorship when he was introduced to him at the beginning of the Greek Interpreter case. 'I am glad to meet you, sir,' he says to Watson. 'I hear of Sherlock everywhere since you became his chronicler.' It is an obvious reference to the publication several months earlier of *A Study in Scarlet* and was intended to flatter for, by this time, Holmes' name was already well known. Like his brother, Mycroft could show considerable social charm when the occasion demanded it.

Because of this reference, the Greek Interpreter case is usually assigned to the summer of 1888 although some commentators have preferred to date it much earlier on the grounds that Holmes would not have waited for over six years before even mentioning to Watson that he had a brother, let alone introducing him to Mycroft. However, the time gap is perfectly understandable. As Watson explains in the opening paragraph of *The Adventure of the Greek Interpreter*, Holmes was extremely reticent both about his relations and his early life, an attitude Watson interpreted as an indication of Holmes' lack of emotion. This is certainly part of the explanation. But, as we have seen in Chapter One, Holmes' unhappy childhood could well have caused him deliberately to avoid discussing that period in his life as too painful a subject.

It was an experience which had affected Mycroft as well. Like Holmes, he was a bachelor without friends, and was even more unsociable than his brother, his life being restricted to his

100

Whitehall office, his lodgings in Pall Mall and the Diogenes Club* opposite his rooms, of which he was a founder-member and where he could be found every evening from a quarter to five until twenty to eight. As Holmes says of him, 'Mycroft has his rails and he runs on them.' For him to break his routine and actually visit Baker Street would be as extraordinary as seeing a tram coming down a country lane.

Holmes was evidently in close contact with his brother as he speaks of consulting him 'again and again' over difficult cases. Indeed, Mycroft had expected Holmes to ask for his advice over the Manor House affair shortly before introducing him to Watson. Presumably the two brothers met either at Mycroft's bachelor apartment or at the Diogenes Club in the Strangers' Room, the only part of the premises where conversation was permitted. He never apparently visited Holmes in Baker Street, for when he called there during the Greek Interpreter inquiry his presence was so unexpected that Holmes gave a start of astonishment on seeing him. Under such circumstances, it is hardly surprising that Watson had not met him before 1888.

There was no filial jealousy between the two brothers. In fact, Holmes openly acknowledged Mycroft's superior powers of observation and deduction. But, through lack of ambition and energy as well as an inability to work out the legal practicalities of bringing a case to court, Mycroft preferred to conduct his detection from the comfort of his armchair. If it meant exerting himself, he would rather his deductions were considered wrong than go to the trouble of proving them right.

Much to Watson's amusement, he was treated to a demonstration of Mycroft's superior powers of observation when the latter corrected his brother over the matter of the number of children a passer-by in the street possessed from the toys the man carried under his arm. It was clearly a game the brothers had played before, perhaps even in boyhood, and indicates a close and warm relationship. Holmes' manner of addressing his

* The Diogenes Club has been variously identified as the Athenaeum or the Travellers', which were also situated in Pall Mall. However, both were established too early for Mycroft Holmes to have been a founder-member.

brother as 'my dear Mycroft' suggests affection, while Mycroft's use of the term 'my dear boy' has an almost paternal ring about it, an aspect of their relationship which has already been examined in Chapter One.

Ostensibly Mycroft, who had, as Holmes describes it, 'an extraordinary faculty for figures',* was employed as an auditor in some of the Government departments for a salary of £450. It was only eight years later, in November 1895 during the case of the Bruce-Partington plans, that Holmes confided in Watson Mycroft's true role. With his unique capacity for remembering and correlating facts, Mycroft acted as a confidential adviser to various Government ministers on which policies they should pursue. As such, Mycroft was the most indispensable man in the whole country and at times *was* the British Government, as Holmes rather dramatically expresses it. 'The conclusions of every department are passed to him,' Holmes explains to Watson, 'and he is the central exchange, the clearing-house, which makes out the balance. All other men are specialists, but his specialism is omniscience.'

Some commentators have regarded this long silence on Holmes' part about his brother's true role as curious, given the close friendship between Holmes and Watson. But as it was a highly confidential Governmental matter, Holmes may not have been in the position to divulge it even to Watson until he had received permission to do so from Mycroft.

Physically, the brothers were not alike. While Sherlock was thin, Mycroft, although tall, was stout to the point of corpulence and gave the impression of 'uncouth physical inertia', in contrast to Sherlock's quick and energetic manner. But despite his unwieldy frame, Mycroft's head, with its 'masterful brow, alert deep-set eyes, steel grey in colour, and firm lips', was so strongly suggestive of his dominant mind that one quickly forgot his 'gross body'. It was only in the sharpness of his expression that Watson could see any family resemblance, and Mycroft's eyes had on occasions the same 'far-away, introspective look' of

* Holmes himself was a good mathematician. While travelling down to Devon on the Silver Blaze inquiry, he was able to calculate in his head the speed of the train from the time it took to pass the telegraph posts which were set sixty yards apart.

Sherlock's when he was brooding over some particularly difficult case.

It was during this same period, 1881–9, that one other important encounter was made, two if the Charles Augustus Milverton inquiry is included, although commentators disagree over its date. However, for reasons explained in Appendix One, I am more inclined to assign this case to the later period, 1894–1902, and this investigation will therefore be more fully discussed in Chapter Fourteen.

But there is no doubt at all that at some time between 1881 and 1889, almost certainly towards the latter end of the period, Holmes came into contact with someone who was to play a significant role in his future; Watson's, too, although it was Holmes who was the more deeply affected. This man was Professor James Moriarty, whom Holmes was subsequently to refer to as the 'Napoleon of crime'.

It is not known precisely when Holmes first heard of him nor did he actually meet him face to face until several years later. But by January 1888, the date usually ascribed to the Valley of Fear case, Holmes had already accumulated a comprehensive dossier on Moriarty's background and activities. According to his researches, Moriarty came from a good family and had enjoyed the benefits of an excellent education but had inherited criminal tendencies, thus bearing out Holmes' theory about the importance of heredity and how certain aptitudes and characteristics can be passed on to subsequent generations through the blood line.

Little else is known about Moriarty's background, except for the fact that he was a bachelor and had two brothers. The younger one was a station-master in the West of England and was presumably respectable. Another, an army Colonel, was also called James, a duplication which has led some commentators to assume that James Moriarty was a double-barrelled surname. The family may have been of Irish descent, as other Sherlockian scholars have suggested although this is not known for certain. Neither is his date of birth. While he is clearly older than Holmes, any theories which give the year he was born, and they vary from 1844 to as early as 1830, are speculative.

What is quite evident, however, is Moriarty's remarkable

intelligence. Holmes, even when acknowledging the man's genius for evil, openly admits his admiration for the Professor's 'extraordinary mental powers' and 'phenomenal mathematical faculty'.

'My horror at his crimes,' he was later to confess to Watson, 'was lost in my admiration for his skill.'

At the age of twenty-one, Moriarty had written a treatise on the binomial theorem, as a result of which he was offered the Chair of Mathematics at 'one of our smaller universities', a post he was still holding when Holmes first came to hear of him. Although Holmes does not specify which university this was, Philip A. Shreffler may well be correct in suggesting it was Durham, a theory he put forward in an article, 'Moriarty: A Life Study', published in the *Baker Street Journal* in June 1973. According to this theory, Holmes cannot be referring to either Oxford, Cambridge or London as none of these can be described as 'one of our smaller universities', while the pronoun 'our' suggests an establishment in England rather than Wales, Scotland or Northern Ireland. As the only English provincial university at the time was Durham, it must have been there that Moriarty held the Chair of Mathematics, although there is no record of his having served in this post.

The problem of raising a binomial, that is two terms connected by a plus or minus sign, to the nth power had taxed mathematicians for many years. Although simple cases such as $(a + b)^2 = a^2 + 2ab + b^2$ could be easily worked out, high powers proved difficult and fractional powers impossible. In 1655, Sir Isaac Newton had devised the binomial theorem:

$$(a + b)^n = a^n + {}^n a^{n-1}b + \frac{n(n-1)}{2!} a^{n-2}b^2 \ldots$$

which allowed the binomial, $(a + b)$, to be raised to any power n.

Although the theorem was proved by the Norwegian mathematician, Niels Henrik Abel in the early part of the nineteenth century, Mr Poul Anderson in his article 'A Treatise on the Binomial Theorem', published in the *Baker Street Journal* in January 1955, has suggested that Moriarty was working on the basic idea of number itself and that he had developed a general binomial theorem which could be applied to other forms of algebra.

Moriarty was also the author of *The Dynamics of the Asteroid*, a book which ascended to 'such rarefied heights of mathematics' that it was claimed there was 'no man in the scientific press capable of criticizing it'. An asteroid is a tiny planet revolving round the sun between the orbits of Mars and Jupiter. While it is too small to affect the orbits of the nine major planets, their gravitations simultaneously influence the orbit of the asteroid although no general mathematical solution had been formulated to express even the effect of three of these planets (the three-body problem), let alone the nine.

In the same article, 'A Treatise on the Binomial Theorem', Mr Poul Anderson has suggested that Professor Moriarty had discovered a general solution for the orbit of an asteroid together with a set of equations which could be applied to any similar body, as far as even the n-body problem. Mr William S. Baring-Gould has further suggested that Moriarty may have anticipated Einstein's equation $E = mc^2$, which prepared the way for the development of the atomic and hydrogen bomb, and that he may also have supplied the theoretical groundwork for man-made satellites and space stations.

Whether this is true or not, it is clear Holmes was correct in describing Professor Moriarty's powers as 'phenomenal', although he had deliberately chosen to dedicate his genius to a much more sinister purpose than research into pure mathematics. Instead, he had set up an international criminal organization of over a hundred members, including pickpockets, blackmailers, cardsharpers and murderers which he ruled over with a rod of iron. The punishment for any transgression of the organization's rules was death.

His Chief of Staff was Colonel Sebastian Moran, son of Alexander Moran, the former British minister to Persia. Born in 1840, Colonel Moran had been educated at Eton and Oxford University and later joined the First Bengalore Pioneers,* an Indian Army regiment. He had served with some distinction in several campaigns and had been mentioned in dispatches. He was also the

* Bengalore is spelt Bangalore in some American editions. There is no such regiment as the First Bengalore Pioneers. Because of Colonel Moran's subsequent criminal career, Watson has clearly changed the name in order not to bring shame on Moran's former regiment.

celebrated author of two books, *Heavy Game in the Himalayas* and *Three Months in the Jungle*, and was considered one of the best shots in the world, a skill he was later to put to deadly use.

Although there was no open scandal, he was obliged to retire from the army and, on his return to England, Moriarty recruited him into his organization to carry out those top-class crimes which none of the ordinary gang-members would undertake. Holmes, who considered him the second most dangerous man in London, suspected him of being responsible for the murder in 1887 of Mrs Stewart from Lauder.

Professor Moriarty paid Moran the huge sum of £6,000 a year, more than the Prime Minister's salary. It was money Moriarty could well afford, for his criminal activities brought him considerable wealth. By tracing some of Moriarty's cheques, Holmes had discovered he had six separate bank accounts and suspected he owned twenty in all, the bulk of his fortune being invested abroad in Deutsche Bank or Credit Lyonnais.

The problem was finding evidence which would prove Moriarty's guilt. It was not an easy task. Holmes had visited his rooms on three occasions, twice legitimately, using different pretexts for calling on him but leaving before the Professor returned home. Although Holmes does not give details, he hints that on the third occasion he broke into Moriarty's rooms during his absence and searched his papers but found nothing incriminating. Holmes does not make it clear where these rooms were situated, whether at the university, possibly Durham, or in London where Moriarty may have kept a separate establishment for his use during the vacations. As his criminal organization was London-based, this is perfectly feasible, in which case Holmes would have timed his visits to coincide with Moriarty's presence in the capital.

Nor is it clear how Holmes first heard of Moriarty, although it may have been through a man known by the pseudonym Fred Porlock. The surname is probably a reference to the man from Porlock who called on the poet Samuel Coleridge and interrupted his composition of 'Kubla Khan'. Or Holmes may have already been aware of Moriarty's existence through his own inquiries and established contact with Porlock himself. Whatever the circumstances, Porlock was a useful informer inside Moriarty's organization, what in the language of John le Carré's spy fiction is referred to as a 'mole'.

Porlock, a 'shifty and evasive' character, was a minor member of Moriarty's gang, a pilot fish to his whale, a jackal to his lion. Out of what Holmes refers to as 'a rudimentary aspiration towards right' but principally for financial gain – the 'judicious stimulation of a ten-pound note', as Holmes ironically calls it – Porlock was willing on occasions to supply Holmes with advance information of Moriarty's plans. These sums of ten pounds, a large amount of money in the 1880s, were presumably paid out of Holmes' pocket and were always sent in cash to Camberwell Post Office. Communication between them was in code, using a system which is virtually unbreakable. The message was composed of a set of figures which referred to a page, to lines on that page and to the position within those lines of individual words contained in a certain book, the identity of which was known only to the correspondents. Anyone not knowing which book had been used to compile the cipher had little hope of unscrambling the message.

In the Valley of Fear inquiry, Porlock sent the coded message but lost his nerve at the last moment and failed to supply the name of the volume on which the code was based. It took all of Holmes' ingenuity and knowledge of ciphers, on which he was an expert, in addition to some invaluable assistance from Watson, to deduce that the code was taken from a page in *Whitaker's Almanac*.

Breaking through the web of evil which surrounded Professor Moriarty was to prove a much more difficult task. As Holmes says of him, he had a brain which might have made or marred the destiny of nations. This is an interesting echo of his comment on Mycroft's role. In fact, the two men had much in common. Both possessed great mathematical skills. Both men also concealed their true activities, Mycroft as adviser to Her Majesty's Government, Moriarty as head of an international criminal gang.

But it is between Sherlock Holmes and Professor Moriarty that the closest parallels can be drawn. In *The Hound of the Baskervilles*, Holmes refers to himself as a 'specialist in crime', a epithet which could be applied with equal accuracy to Moriarty; but while

Holmes had dedicated his own phenomenal powers to the fight against crime, Moriarty had concentrated his on building up a Mafia-style underworld organization, the sole purpose of which was the perpetration of crime.

The struggle between the two men was to assume the epic proportions of the primeval contest between the forces of good and evil, Holmes on the side of the forces of light locked in mortal combat with Moriarty who 'had all the powers of darkness at his back'.

None of this was apparent to the casual observer. Outwardly, Moriarty was harmless, a respectable Professor of Mathematics from a provincial university, known only as the learned author of two brilliant but abstruse publications which had caused quite a stir in academic circles. Inspector MacDonald, who called on him after hearing of him from Holmes, found nothing suspicious about him. Indeed, he thought Moriarty would have made 'a grand meenister with his thin face and grey hair and solemn way of talking'. In the opinion of MacDonald and his colleagues in the CID, Holmes had a bit of a bee in his bonnet over the man.

Holmes's description of Moriarty, when he finally came face to face with him, is much less flattering. He was extremely tall and thin, Holmes tells Watson, with a high, white, domed forehead, sunken eyes and rounded shoulders from his years of study. Clean-shaven, pale and ascetic-looking, he had something of the professor in his features although his habit of pushing his head forward and swinging it slowly from side to side gave him a repulsive, reptilian air. Holmes found his style of speech, which was soft and precise, more threatening than an overtly bullying manner.

During his interview with Moriarty, MacDonald was also impressed when, the conversation having turned to the subject of eclipses, the Professor was able, with the aid of a reflector lantern and a globe, to make 'it all clear in a minute', proof of Moriarty's undoubted skill as a teacher.

But what MacDonald failed to take sufficient note of was the painting which hung behind the Professor's desk. It was a portrait of a young girl by the French artist Jean-Baptiste Greuze. A similar painting, entitled *La Jeune Fille à l'Agneau*, had fetched FF1,200,000, more than £4,000, at the Portalis sale in

1865.* How could the Professor afford to buy such a painting on his salary of £700 a year?

The answer was simple. Like Jonathan Wild[†] before him, Moriarty sold his own criminal expertise and that of his organization for a commission, either on a promise of part of the spoils or as a down-payment for organizing the crime before it was committed. In the Birlstone case, he had been paid by the Scowrers, an American secret society intent on destroying the power of the railway and colliery owners in Vermissa Valley in the States, to hunt down and organize the murder of Birdy Edwards, a.k.a. John McMurdo, a Pinkerton detective who had infiltrated the Scowrers and brought about their downfall. Using the alias John Douglas, Edwards had fled to England, where Moriarty's organization had traced his whereabouts. But the attempt on his life failed when Douglas killed his would-be murderer, Ted Baldwin, a former Scowrer member, in self-defence.

This case, a full-length account of which Watson later published under the title *The Valley of Fear*, was the first direct contact Holmes had with both the Pinkerton National Detective Agency, set up in the States by Allan Pinkerton in 1850[‡], and, more importantly, with Moriarty and his gang.

Douglas later disappeared overboard from the *Palmyra* when on his way to South Africa with his wife, after being acquitted of Baldwin's murder. Holmes attributed Douglas's death to Mor-

* Holmes was mistaken over the name Portalis. In fact, it was the Pourtalès Gallery of Art, a private collection owned by the Comte de Pourtalès-Gorgier, which was sold at auction in 1865. The painting referred to by Holmes, entitled *Innocence*, which was bought by an anonymous buyer, was later proved to be a copy of the original by Greuze. It is at present in the Wallace Collection in London.

† Jonathan Wild (c. 1682–1725) was a master criminal who organized a gang of London thieves, setting up their robberies and charging a 15 per cent commission on the sale of the proceeds of their thefts. He betrayed anyone who refused to co-operate with him to the authorities. He was hanged at Tyburn in 1725.

‡ Allan Pinkerton (1819–1884) was born in Glasgow. After emigrating to the States in 1842, he was appointed deputy sheriff of Cook County. Eight years later he set up his own detective agency. One of his detectives, James McParlan, infiltrated the Molly Maguires in Pennsylvania (1873–6) and secured evidence which led to the break-up of this organization of coal-miners, allegedly engaged in terrorism. This closely parallels John Douglas's infiltration of the Scowrers.

iarty, convinced he had stage-managed the apparent accident in order not to appear to have failed in his commission. As Holmes remarks, 'You can tell an old Master by the sweep of his brush. I can tell a Moriarty when I see one.'

Holmes' comparison of Moriarty with Wild was apt. So, too, was his comment that, 'The old wheel turns and the same spoke comes up again.' It had all been done before and would be done again.

Moriarty's methods, such as the use of the paid professional 'hit-man', the investment in overseas banks of illegal money and the iron discipline exerted over gang members, are those still used by contemporary criminals. Even Moriarty's ploy of deliberately seating a person he was interviewing so that either the light from the window or the desk lamp fell directly on his face while his own features remained in shadow, is a stratagem still used by secret police the world over.

Holmes himself was looking into the future when, at the end of the Valley of Fear inquiry, he assures Cecil Barker, Douglas's close friend and associate, that Moriarty can be beaten.

'But you must give me time – you must give me time.'

It was to take Holmes another three years before that promise was fulfilled.

CHAPTER EIGHT

MEETING AND PARTING

September 1888–March 1889

'Love is an emotional thing, and whatever is emotional is opposed to that true, cold reason which I place above all things. I should never marry myself, lest it bias my judgment.'

Holmes: *The Sign of Four*

In September 1888* Watson became involved with Holmes in a case which was to have an important effect on his future happiness for it was during the course of the investigation that he met the young lady who was to become his wife.

She was Mary Morstan, who possibly was born and was certainly partly brought up in India where her father, Major Arthur Morstan, was serving in an Indian regiment. As her mother was dead and there were no relatives living in England, her father had sent her as a child to Edinburgh to be educated at a boarding-school. This may imply that she had at least one relation living in or near Edinburgh, perhaps an aunt with whom she may have spent the school holidays and whom she was later to visit on at least two occasions.

In the meantime, her father had been posted to the Andaman Islands, situated in the Bay of Bengal off the east coast of India, to assist Major John Sholto in guarding a convict settlement on Blair Island, one of the most southerly of the group.

In 1878, Major Morstan, having obtained twelve months' leave,

---

* See Appendix One for the dating of the Sign of Four case.

returned to England and sent a telegram to his daughter, asking her to meet him in London at the Langham Hotel. However, when Mary Morstan arrived there, she found her father had disappeared, leaving his luggage behind. Despite inquiries on her part, nothing more was heard of him and his whereabouts remained a mystery.

Six years later, Mary Morstan, who had taken up the post of governess to Mrs Cecil Forrester's family in Lower Camberwell, saw an advertisement in *The Times*, asking for her address and stating that, if she came forward, it would be to her advantage. On Mrs Forrester's advice, she published her address in the newspaper and received through the post a parcel containing a valuable pearl, the first of six which were to be sent to her anonymously over the next five years.

And then, quite unexpectedly in September 1888, she received a letter telling her she had been wronged and asking her to meet her unknown correspondent that evening at seven o'clock outside the Lyceum Theatre. If she were at all doubtful, she could bring two friends with her but the police were not to be informed. Mrs Forrester who, as we have seen in Chapter Two, had been one of Holmes' clients while he was living in Montague Street, further advised her to consult Holmes which Mary Morstan did, calling on him at Baker Street and laying the facts before him.

It was an intriguing account and Holmes agreed to accompany her on the mysterious assignation, suggesting that Watson came as well, an invitation which he eagerly accepted. For far more fascinating to him than her story was Miss Morstan herself.

He describes her in detail. She was a small, dainty, blue-eyed blonde and, although she was not exactly beautiful, everything about her struck him as charming, from her simple, yet tasteful dress sense to her amiable and sympathetic expression which indicated a sensitive personality. Of a sympathetic nature himself, he was touched by her outward composure which hid an intense inner distress and by the fact that she was alone in the world. She was twenty-seven, a 'sweet age', as Watson describes it, when a woman has lost the self-consciousness of youth and has matured through experience.

He himself was thirty-five or thirty-six and to all outward appearances a confirmed bachelor, content with his single life, spent almost entirely in Holmes' company. During his eight years in Baker Street, the thought of marriage had not crossed his mind. Nor apparently had it occurred to him that he might resume his former medical career. As far as he was concerned, any such ambition had been cut short at the battle of Maiwand.

The meeting with Mary Morstan was to change all that. For him, it was a case of love at first sight, a *coup de foudre*, which altered his whole attitude and set him yearning for a very different future. But these were 'dangerous thoughts' which he dare not allow himself to contemplate. It is, however, highly significant that, as soon as Mary Morstan had left and he was alone, Watson went straight to his desk and 'plunged furiously into the latest treatise on pathology', the only record during those eight years of his reading any medical books.

Yet, despite this sudden interest in his former studies, it all seemed hopeless. Watson had enough common sense as well as honesty to realize that marriage to Mary Morstan was out of the question. Although the future without her seemed black indeed, it was far better to face reality like a man than deceive himself with 'mere will o' the wisps of the imagination'. As he himself realized, he was nothing more than a former army surgeon with, as he says, a weak leg and an even weaker bank balance. As for any hope of making a living as an author, this was so unlikely that Watson does not even mention it.

His chances seemed even more remote when, during the investigation, it was discovered that Mary Morstan's father was dead and that she stood to inherit his half share in the Agra treasure, a fabulous collection of jewels estimated to be worth the huge sum of half a million pounds.

A more mercenary man would have welcomed the news. To Watson, it was yet another barrier between them. For how could he, a man living on a pension and with no immediate prospects of earning any more, propose to a woman who might become the richest heiress in England? His own sense of decency and self-respect prevented him from even considering it, despite the signs that Mary Morstan's feelings for him were as warm as his towards her.

There is a touching scene of them standing in the dark in the desolate garden of Pondicherry Lodge, where Holmes' inquiries had led them, and of Mary Morstan's hand reaching out to grasp Watson's as if she were turning to him instinctively for comfort and protection.

To Watson's enormous relief, and also to hers, the chest said to contain the Agra treasure was later found to be empty, its contents having been thrown into the Thames by Jonathan Small, who had stolen the jewels in the first place and whom Holmes and Watson were pursuing up the river in an attempt to retrieve them. Watson was now free to propose marriage to Mary Morstan who accepted him without any hesitation.

His choice of her as a wife was excellent. Mary Morstan was a quiet, sensible woman with a warm personality which, as Watson says, drew people in trouble to her as naturally as 'birds to a lighthouse'. As a former governess, she was also used to living frugally and making the most of a little money, a necessary quality in the wife of a future GP who was to struggle to build up a neglected practice.

She was to create a happy and stable domestic background for Watson such as he had probably not experienced since his boyhood, so much of his adult life having been spent in student lodgings, army quarters or the bachelor apartment at Baker Street. Although he was content enough sharing digs with Holmes where he was well looked after by Mrs Hudson, it was not quite the same as having his own home and coming back to his own fireside.

Even Holmes remarked that Mary Morstan was one of the most charming young ladies he had ever met and added that, with her intelligence, she could have become a private consulting detective, a rare accolade indeed.

Knowing Holmes' attitude to women and his strong aversion to marriage, Watson must have anticipated his old friend's reaction when he told him of his engagement. Even so, he found Holmes' response a little hurtful.

'I really cannot congratulate you,' Holmes remarked.

It was an honest reply if not exactly tactful although Watson accepted it with good humour. He was wrong, however, in his assumption that the Sholto investigation would be the last in which he assisted Holmes.

The following month, October 1888,* he became involved with Holmes on a complex case which was to take him away from London and Mary Morstan for several weeks.† This was the inquiry into the death of Sir Charles Baskerville the previous June in the grounds of Baskerville Hall on Dartmoor. It was apparently connected with the family legend of a spectral hound which was said to haunt the moor and which, it was feared, might threaten the life of the young Sir Henry Baskerville, Sir Charles's nephew and heir, when he arrived in Devon to take up residence at the ancestral home.

Some commentators, ignoring the references to the dating of this case, have assigned it to the late 1890s, on the grounds that Watson shows no signs of his game leg which had troubled him during the Sholto affair. Nor is there any mention in his account of the Baskerville inquiry of Mary Morstan to whom he had become engaged only the previous month.

As we have seen, Watson states specifically that the wound to his leg only troubled him when there was a change in the weather and even then it did not prevent him from walking. Moreover, it seemed to affect him most when he was idle and he had time to think about the disability. When he was busy and his mind was occupied, he apparently forgot about it in much the same way as Holmes' depression lifted when his energies were fully engaged. For example, during the Sign of Four case, Watson walked to Camberwell and back to visit Mary Morstan, a distance of some twelve or fourteen miles, without showing any apparent discomfort. This suggests that some of the symptoms may well have been psychosomatic.

* See Appendix One for the dating of the Hound of the Baskerville case.
† If the dating of the Silver Blaze inquiry to September 1888 is correct, then the Baskerville case was the second investigation which took Holmes and Watson to Dartmoor that autumn. Presumably the Silver Blaze inquiry occurred between the end of the Sign of Four case in the first weeks of September 1888 and the Baskerville investigation in early October of the same year. With the other cases assigned to this period, including the Noble Bachelor inquiry as well as the unrecorded inquiries relating to Colonel Upwood, Mme Montpensier, the king of Scandinavia and the Grosvenor Square furniture van, the autumn of 1888 was a particularly busy time for Holmes. Readers are referred to the suggested chronology in Chapter Six.

As for his failure to mention Mary Morstan, this is perfectly understandable. It has already been pointed out that, as a narrator, Watson was far more concerned with chronicling Holmes' exploits than in informing his readers of his own personal affairs. In addition, during much of the Baskerville case, Watson was left in charge of the inquiries, a responsibility he took very seriously. In his diary entry for 16th October, he notes that he must devote all his energies to discovering the identity of the stranger seen on the moors who might be behind the mysterious chain of events threatening Sir Henry's life.

He was regularly in touch with Holmes by post. Presumably his correspondence also included letters to Mary Morstan in Camberwell. But the main thrust of his narrative is to convey to his readers the dangerous nature of the investigation, not to indulge in an expression of his own private and more romantic feelings.

With the successful outcome of the Baskerville inquiry, Holmes and Watson returned to London where Holmes became involved in two further cases already referred to in Chapter Six, the scandal concerning Colonel Upwood and the Nonpareil Club and the defence of Mme Montpensier, accused of the apparent murder of her stepdaughter, Mlle Carère, who was found six months later alive in New York. It was also at about this time that Holmes successfully investigated the case of the Grosvenor Square furniture van about which Watson gives no further details.

As he has left no written accounts of any of these, Watson may not have taken part in them. With typical modesty, he never assumed that Holmes would welcome his presence at every investigation and always waited to be invited to assist on a case. As we have seen in Chapter Six, he participated in about only a seventh of Holmes' inquiries during this 1881–9 period. But he was certainly concerned with another scandal which at the time caused a great deal of gossip in high places.

The client was Lord St Simon, who called on Holmes under embarrassing circumstances. His American bride of a few hours had run away during the wedding reception and Lord St Simon wanted Holmes to discover her whereabouts as well as the reason for her sudden disappearance. Inspector Lestrade was also involved with the case and, much to Holmes' amusement, ordered the Serpentine to be dragged after the bride's wedding clothes were discovered floating in the water, wrongly assuming that Lady St Simon had been murdered by Flora Miller, a dancer and former mistress of his lordship.

The inquiry had particular significance for Watson, for it occurred only a few weeks before his own marriage, as he remarks in one of his typically laconic statements dropped almost casually into his account. It is useful for establishing an approximate date for his wedding to Mary Morstan but is infuriatingly imprecise on details. One has to assume that, in the weeks following Watson's return from Devon, he and Mary Morstan were quietly making plans for their marriage, which included a search for a suitable property to serve as their home and as a base for Watson as a general medical practitioner.

Understandably, Watson did not discuss any of these plans with Holmes, not even his decision to return to medical practice. It was only when the two men met again after the marriage that Holmes was aware of this fact, which he deduced from Watson's appearance.* Watson's failure to confide in Holmes was not out of any desire for secrecy. He was by nature frank and, if Holmes had asked what his plans were, Watson would have told him. But Holmes did not ask, an omission which Watson accepted without any resentment.

Theirs was an essentially male friendship in which the exchange of personal confidences was not expected and much was therefore left unsaid. Apparently, not even Watson's departure from the Baker Street lodgings on the occasion of his marriage was discussed. At least, there is no record of any such conversation in the published canon. Both men must have

---

* Holmes says: 'If a gentleman walks into my rooms smelling of iodoform, with a black mark of nitrate of silver upon his right forefinger, and a bulge on the side of his top hat to show where he secreted his stethoscope, I must be dull indeed if I do not pronounce him to be an active member of the medical profession' (A Scandal in Bohemia). Some commentators have remarked a little derisively on Watson's method of carrying his stethoscope but there is no indication it was a habit of his. He may have placed it there temporarily in order to leave his hands free to greet Holmes. All the same, it is a strange place to put it and is an example of Watson's endearing eccentricities of character, less marked than Holmes' but nonetheless a part of his character.

117

realized it was inevitable but preferred not to speak of it, let alone openly express their feelings about such a parting or the immense changes it would bring to both their lives.

In the weeks leading up to Watson's marriage there was not much opportunity anyway to discuss these personal matters even if they had wished to. Holmes was out of England for most of the latter part of 1888 and the beginning of 1889. Once again, Watson fails to give precise dates and the exact period can only be guessed at by implication.

Holmes was certainly still in England at the end of November 1888. Sir Henry Baskerville, accompanied by Dr Mortimer, his personal physician, called on him and Watson then at Baker Street before embarking on a recuperative voyage which was intended to restore Sir Henry's shattered nerves after his terrifying experiences during the Hound of the Baskerville case.

That same evening, as they sat beside a blazing fire, Holmes at last found time to give Watson a full explanation of the Baskerville affair and to tie up some of the loose ends which still remained unresolved. Later, as a belated celebration, they went out to dine at Marcini's before going to the opera to hear the De Reszke brothers sing in a performance of Meyerbeer's *Les Huguenots*. Holmes hired a box for the occasion, further proof of his improved financial situation, a fact which would have set Watson's mind at rest over the matter of the shared rent of the Baker Street lodgings. Holmes was now in a position to afford to pay the whole of it himself.

It must have been shortly after this that Holmes was summoned to Odessa to inquire into the Trepoff murder and then, after its conclusion, travelled to Ceylon (now Sri Lanka) for the case involving the Atkinson brothers at Trincomalee. That, at least, is the inference for, although Watson is far from clear on the details of this latter investigation, by using the phrase 'at Trincomalee', he seems to suggest that the case required Holmes' presence at the scene of the tragedy.

During this same period, Holmes was also engaged on a delicate mission on behalf of the Dutch royal family,* the word

* The King of the Netherlands at this time was William III (1817–90) who reigned from 1849 until his death.

'mission' again implying that he was required to travel to Holland in order to undertake the inquiry, which he successfully concluded. This was the second occasion during this period that royalty had asked for Holmes' assistance, the first request having come from the King of Scandinavia, and suggests that his reputation for handling highly confidential matters of state was spreading among the reigning European monarchs, many of whom were inter-related.

Of the two other cases, the Trepoff murder and the Atkinson tragedy, Watson supplies no details of their outcome. He himself only learned about them from newspaper accounts, suggesting he and Holmes were not in direct contact during this period.

Although Watson gives no dates, it is possible to establish a rough timetable of Holmes' activities over these months. We know the discussion with Watson over the Baskerville case took place at the end of November 1888 and that Holmes was back in Baker Street at some time before 20th March 1889 when, as will be seen in the next chapter, Watson called on him there.

If one assumes that Holmes left England for Russia on or about the 21st November and spent three weeks travelling to Odessa and investigating the Trepoff case, then he could have been back in England by mid-December. Assuming also that he departed for Ceylon almost immediately, a journey which would have taken about a month by sea, and that the Atkinson case was completed within a fortnight, it is quite possible that Holmes, even allowing another month for the return voyage, was home before the end of February. This would have given him enough time to undertake the mission on behalf of the Dutch royal family before returning to Baker Street before 20th March. It would have been a packed itinerary but one that was perfectly feasible within the available time.

Meanwhile, in Holmes' absence, Watson's marriage plans were taking shape. He and Mary found a suitable property in the Paddington district, not far from the mainline station, the staff of which was to prove a useful source of patients. Although Watson gives no clue to the exact whereabouts of his practice, it was probably only a few minutes' walk from the station, for one of the guards took Mr Hatherley, an injured passenger, to Watson's consulting room for treatment rather than to St Mary's Hospital, which was almost next door to the terminus.

It is most unlikely that Watson and Mary Morstan went house-hunting in the Norfolk Square or Westbourne Terrace areas. These fashionable terraces of tall, stuccoed residences with their balconies and imposing porticoes would have been too expensive. But Watson could well have found an affordable property in such turnings as London Street or Spring Street, almost opposite Paddington station. Some of these houses are still standing, their exteriors largely unaltered since Watson's time. Brick-built and of three or four storeys, they are more modest but still respectable and any one of them would have been suitable as a doctor's premises. They are large enough to accommodate a consulting-room on the ground floor with plenty more space on the upper floors for private living quarters.

Apart from a few scattered references, there is no detailed description of either the interior or the exterior of the house. It was next door to another doctor's practice, a fact which, like its proximity to Paddington station, was to prove useful to Watson in the coming months. There were well-worn steps up to the front door – Holmes comments on them – and the hall floor was covered in linoleum, a practical touch this. With the coming and going of patients, sometimes in muddy boots, a carpet would soon have become worn out. In addition to Watson's consulting-room, there was also a sitting-room on the ground floor. It is possible there was a more formal first-floor drawing-room. In *The Adventure of the Stockbroker's Clerk*, Watson writes of going upstairs to speak to his wife.

The practice had belonged to Mr Farquhar, an elderly gentle-man who suffered from St Vitus' Dance. Because of his age and infirmity, the number of patients had decreased and the income had dropped from £1200 a year to a mere £300. But Watson could still draw his army pension which, added to the money he could expect from the practice, gave him an annual income of £500, enough for the Watsons to live on in reasonable comfort and to afford a servant. Besides, Watson had every confidence that, with his youth and energy, he could gradually build up the practice over the coming months.

He does not say how much he paid for the practice but the

usual price at that time was one to one and a half times the annual income. Watson therefore probably paid between £300 and £450. Neither he nor Mary Morstan could have had much capital. Both had modest incomes, Watson relying entirely on his army pension and Mary Morstan on her salary as a governess which in the late 1880s was about £50 a year, including board and lodging.* They had probably managed to save a little but not enough to buy a suitable house and furnish it adequately.

However, Mary Morstan was in possession of the six pearls, part of the Agra treasure, which had been sent to her by Major Sholto, her late father's army colleague. Presumably some, if not all, were sold to raise the necessary capital.

Watson says nothing at all about the wedding itself, whether it was a church or registry office ceremony. But wherever it was held, it was almost certainly a quiet affair. Neither he nor Mary had the money or the inclination for a lavish celebration and, as neither of them had any relatives living in England or few close friends, the number of guests was probably small.

Mrs Cecil Forrester and her family were probably present. So, too, was Mrs Hudson. It is unlikely Watson would have left her off the guest list. Colonel Hayter, Watson's former army acquaintance from Reigate, may also have been invited as well as Mr and Mrs Whitney. The Whitneys were to play a small part in a subsequent case. Kate Whitney was an old school friend of Mary, and her husband, Isa, was to become one of Watson's patients. Stamford, Watson's former dresser at Bart's who introduced Watson to Holmes, is another possible guest.

But one old friend was certainly not at the wedding. This was Holmes himself, who was most probably out of England on one of his foreign investigations at the time. His absence is made quite clear. When several months later he called on Watson in June 1889, he asked after Mrs Watson, expressing the hope that she had recovered from the excitements of the Sholto affair. He had therefore not seen her since September 1888, the date of that case.

* In *The Adventure of the Copper Beeches*, a case which occurred not long after Watson's marriage, Miss Violet Hunter says that in her last post as a governess her salary was £4 a month.

The date of the wedding cannot, however, be fixed. But it must have occurred between late November 1888, when Watson was still living in Baker Street, and well before 20th March, by which time Watson was already married and settled into the Paddington practice. Commentators have suggested various possibilities from December 1888 to January or February 1889. One of the two later months is the more likely. A December wedding would have hardly given Watson time to make all the necessary arrangements.

As it was, there was evidently some problem over the purchase of the Paddington practice. Watson states that they moved into the property shortly after the marriage. The delay may have been caused by a legal complication or the difficulty of finding suitable premises. Or they may have had to wait while builders or decorators finished refurbishing the house.

But, once installed, Watson was delighted with the arrangements. It was the first time he had owned his own home and he refers proudly to being master of his own establishment. A servant, Mary Jane, was engaged but soon proved unsatisfactory. She was a clumsy, careless girl and Mrs Watson was forced to give her notice.

Apart from this minor domestic inconvenience, Watson was a deeply contented man. During these first few weeks of marriage he put on seven and a half pounds in weight, a sure sign of a man at peace with himself and his world. However, when he picked up his newspaper and read the reports of Holmes' latest exploits, he may have felt a small twinge of nostalgic regret for the old Baker Street days.

The events of the evening of 20th March 1889 certainly suggest that, for all his domestic happiness, he missed that element of adventure and excitement which his long association with Holmes had given him.

CHAPTER NINE

SCANDAL AND REUNION

20th March 1889

'He (Holmes) never spoke of the softer passions, save
with a gibe and a sneer . . . And yet there was but one
woman to him, and that woman was the late Irene Adler,
of dubious and questionable memory.'

Watson: *A Scandal in Bohemia*

In the months following his marriage, Watson saw nothing of
Holmes. As we have seen, Holmes was out of England for most
of this period and when he finally returned to Baker Street, he
preferred his own solitary life, shunning society and 'alternating
from week to week between cocaine and ambition', as Watson
expresses it. This regular use of the drug could suggest more
than his usual dependency. In his loneliness after Watson's
departure, he may well have found solace in cocaine, although
he would never have admitted this. When not drowsy with
drugs, he threw himself into solving those cases which had
baffled the police. Watson does not specify what these cases
were.

Watson himself was also busy with what he calls his 'home-
centred interests' and with building up his practice. He admits
that his marriage had caused Holmes and himself to drift apart.
It was a state of affairs which might have continued and grown
worse as the weeks passed until the gap between them grew too
wide to be bridged, unless one or other of them made an effort
to close it.

123

Characteristically, it was Watson who took the initiative. It is doubtful if Holmes would have gone out of his way to seek out Watson first. His pride would have prevented it. It was also typical of Watson that he acted on impulse.

On the evening of 20th March 1889,* he happened to be passing his former lodgings in Baker Street on his way home from visiting a patient. On reaching the familiar front door, he was seized by a sudden desire to see Holmes again and he gives a vivid description of standing outside on the pavement, watching his old friend's tall, spare figure passing in silhouette across the blind as he paced up and down in the lighted sitting-room beyond.

To give Holmes his due, he welcomed Watson with his usual unaffected bonhomie. After waving him towards an armchair and tossing over his cigar-case, Holmes invited him to help himself to a whisky and soda before remarking on how well he was looking.

'Wedlock suits you,' he commented.

It was a wise approach. A more effusive welcome would have been out of character and embarrassing to both of them. A cooler response might have driven a final wedge between them. But with that one remark, Holmes signalled his acceptance of Watson's marriage and his willingness to continue their friendship on its old footing. The ice, if any existed, was broken, and when Holmes followed it up with one of his brilliantly clever deductions from a few simple observations, a skill which had never failed to impress Watson, the gap was finally closed. In this instance, it concerned the state of Watson's left shoe from which Holmes correctly deduced the existence of Mary Jane, the Watsons' incorrigible servant-girl, to whom Mrs Watson had given notice.

From there, the conversation passed quite naturally to the latest case which Holmes had been asked to investigate on behalf of an anonymous client who by a lucky chance arrived shortly afterwards. With characteristic diffidence, Watson offered to leave but was urged by Holmes to stay.

'I am lost without my Boswell,' he admitted, the nearest

* Watson gives the year as 1888, clearly a mistake as he was not married at this date.

124

Holmes came to confessing he had missed Watson and how much he had relied on his help and companionship. And so Watson stayed and became involved not only in the case concerning the former opera singer, Irene Adler, and the king of Bohemia but also in many other subsequent inquiries, some of which he was later to chronicle. It was almost like old times.

In fact, Watson became so caught up with the case that he returned to Baker Street the following afternoon and stayed that night, the eagerness with which he seized on the chance to renew their former partnership suggesting that he had indeed missed Holmes' company and the opportunity for adventure which it had afforded him.

The facts of Irene Adler's background and career were already indexed in one of Holmes' encyclopaedias of reference and he was able to report that she was American, born in New Jersey in 1856, which made her 31 at the time of the events of March 1889. A contralto, she had sung at La Scala, Milan, and also at the Imperial Opera house in Warsaw but had since retired from the stage and was living in London. During her career in Warsaw, she had met and formed a relationship with the king of Bohemia, of whom more later.

Watson is too discreet to define the exact nature of the connection between the two of them but it involved some compromising letters sent to her by the king and a photograph of them both taken together. It was the photograph in particular which the king wanted Holmes to retrieve, for Irene Adler had threatened to send it to the king of Scandinavia whose daughter Holmes's royal client was planning to marry. Such a scandal would have brought an end to the engagement. As we have already seen, the king of Scandinavia was one of Holmes' clients during the latter end of the 1881–9 period.

The king of Bohemia refers to Irene Adler as a well-known adventuress, which may be an exaggeration. Given the circumstances, his attitude towards her was probably biased. She was certainly a beautiful and fascinating woman. Watson, always susceptible to feminine charms, was much taken with her. Even Holmes was attracted, although Watson is at pains to point out that his old friend was not in love with her. It was not in Holmes' nature to feel any romantic passions, but by opening his account of the case with the striking sentence: 'To Sherlock Holmes she is always *the* woman', Watson may have been indulging in a little wishful thinking. If only Holmes were capable of love, then Irene Adler could well have been the type of woman he might have married: beautiful, talented, high-spirited with a mind and a will of her own.

Holmes is undoubtedly on the defensive about her. When he describes her as 'the daintiest thing under a bonnet on this planet', he is careful to make it clear that he is expressing the opinion of the ostlers in the mews behind her house, whom he had questioned in the course of his inquiries.

She was also intelligent, a necessary quality, for Holmes would not have been attracted to her if she had not possessed as fine a mind as his own. Despite his carefully organized plan to secure the photograph and the letters, Irene Adler managed to elude him and escape with her newly-married husband, taking the compromising photograph, and presumably the letters as well, with her. In their place she left a photograph of herself alone. It was this photograph which Holmes claimed as his fee from the king of Bohemia, although he was later to receive a magnificent gold and amethyst snuff box from his client.

Holmes also kept the sovereign which Irene Adler had given him as payment for acting as a witness to her marriage to Godfrey Norton and which, Holmes informs Watson, he intended wearing on his watch-chain as a memento, the only recorded instance of Holmes showing any sign of sentimentality, although he may have intended it as an ironic reminder of the fact that Irene Adler had outwitted him. It was the first time Holmes had ever been beaten by a woman, a fact which he was still referring to ruefully seven months later, in September 1889 during the case of the Five Orange Pips.

But if Irene Adler's identity can be established, what about Holmes' supposedly royal client?

Whoever he was, he certainly was not the king of Bohemia.*

* Sherry Rose-Bond has pointed out that a list of the present Archduke von Hapsburg's inherited titles, numbering over 40, which was printed in an article in *Vanity Fair* for July 1993, included among them that of king of Bohemia. However, although Watson hints that his king of Bohemia had Hapsburg connections, this may well be part of his ploy to hide his client's real identity.

That country had ceased to be a separate kingdom in 1526 when, after the death of its own monarch, King Ferdinand of Austria contrived to have himself elected to the throne. In 1889 it was ruled over by the Hapsburg emperor, Franz Joseph, as part of the Austro-Hungarian empire. Therefore Watson's account of how Holmes deduced his client's Bohemian background by examining the watermarks in his writing paper must be discounted. Holmes may indeed have made a similar examination but with entirely different results.

Nor should too much reliance be placed on Watson's description of the king as a flamboyantly dressed giant of a man, six feet six inches in height, with the chest and limbs of a Hercules. Watson has obviously disguised the man's appearance in order that he should not be easily identified. The so-called king of Bohemia would not have given his permission for the account to be published had his real name and status been too obvious. All of these details should therefore be regarded as red herrings, designed to throw the reader off the scent. So, too, is the implication that the king of Bohemia had links with the Austrian Hapsburg family. Nevertheless, Watson has managed to include in his description of the king several clues which could point to his identity.

He was German; he was a thirty-year-old bachelor; he was hoping to marry a princess; he was of royal blood and possessed the hereditary title to a kingdom; at the time he consulted Holmes he had some connection with a Scandinavian monarch which a scandal might destroy and which was causing him great anxiety. Moreover, although the king was masked when he first arrived, Holmes recognized his voice and was familiar with his features once the mask was removed. In addition, Holmes openly shows his disapproval of him during the interview. Finally, he was in London in March 1889.

Despite the obvious difficulties of identifying him, various candidates have been suggested, including Emperor Franz Joseph's son, Crown Prince Rudolph, and even Edward, Prince of Wales, later Edward VII, both well-known womanizers.

Neither is convincing. In March 1889 Prince Rudolph was already dead. Two months earlier, on 30th January, his body was found at the hunting-lodge at Mayerling, together with that of his seventeen-year-old mistress, Baroness Mary Vetsera. Both had been shot in circumstances which suggested that Prince Rudolph had first killed the Baroness before committing suicide.

As for Bertie, Prince of Wales, he is just as unlikely. Although he had married a Danish princess, Alexandra, which might accord with the king of Bohemia's engagement to the daughter of the Scandinavian king, the wedding had taken place twenty-six years earlier in 1863. At the time of the events Watson is describing, the prince was forty-nine and so corpulent that he was known behind his back as 'Tum-Tum'. Besides, however much Holmes might have disapproved of Bertie's hedonistic life-style, he would not have treated the heir to the throne in quite so openly a cold and contemptuous manner.

Nor is there any obvious candidate among the numerous minor royal princes, grand dukes, dukes and counts scattered about Europe in the late 1880s.

There is, however, one man whose identity matches the majority of Watson's clues. He was a German count who, although not of royal descent, was the son of a prince and who could be regarded as heir, if not to a royal throne, then to a position of such power and prestige that it far outweighed any regal claim to some minor princedom. He was also a bachelor who, it was rumoured, was in love with a princess whom he was hoping to marry. She was not Scandinavian but German and a member of that other great European royal dynasty, the Hohenzollern family, to which the count in question had very close ties. There were, however, Scandinavian connections but of a political rather than a matrimonial nature. In addition, his identity, if correct, would go a long way to explain Holmes' cold and dismissive attitude towards him.

For good measure, there was also an opera singer – not Irene Adler it should be stressed – whose secret love affair with a semi-royal prince and a former suitor for the hand of the same Hohenzollern princess whom the count hoped to marry, led to his fall from grace and his retirement from public life shortly before the events of March 1889. His humiliation may well have served as an awful warning to the count of what might happen to him if his own liaison with an opera singer was made public.

128

As a final and deciding factor, the count in question was in London in March 1889 on a delicate diplomatic mission which the least breath of scandal could well have ruined. It is quite possible that Mycroft Holmes, who had important Government contacts, had invited his brother to a reception in the count's honour, which was how Holmes was able to recognize his client by his voice even before he removed the mask.

He was Count Herbert von Bismarck, German Secretary of State for Foreign Affairs and the son of Otto von Bismarck, the all-powerful chancellor to William II, the young German emperor, who had been awarded the title of Prince for services to the Hohenzollern imperial family. As Bismarck's son, Count Herbert may well have set his sights on succeeding his father as chancellor to the Second Reich. In March 1889 he was forty years old and still a bachelor. Although this makes him ten years older than the age Watson ascribes to the king of Bohemia, this may be another red herring to confuse the scent.

The princess he was said to have fallen in love with and hoped to marry was Victoria, known in the family as Moretta. She was the second daughter of the late emperor, Kaiser Frederick III, and the former Empress Victoria (Vicky) who was herself the eldest daughter of yet another empress, Victoria, the English queen and matriarch. Moretta was therefore Queen Victoria's granddaughter and niece to the Prince of Wales as well as being sister to the new young Kaiser, Wilhelm II, who had succeeded to the imperial throne less than a year earlier in June 1888, on the death of his father, Frederick III.

Count Herbert's mission to London in March 1889 was to make friendly overtures to Great Britain in order to promote an Anglo-German alliance, a difficult task as the relationship between the two countries was far from cordial. There were deep-seated personal as well as political problems.

Bertie, Prince of Wales, made no secret of his dislike and distrust of the autocratic chancellor and his son, whom he referred to as 'those wicked Bismarcks'. To make matters worse, Vicky, the former empress, was disliked by the Germans for her too-liberal English views and for the influence Queen Victoria continued to exert over her eldest daughter, an unpopularity

129

which the English royal family blamed largely on the Bismarcks for conducting a personal vendetta against the former princess royal.

The bad feeling was not only on the part of the English royal family either. The young Kaiser, Wilhelm II, deeply resented his uncle Bertie's treatment of him as a mere nephew which he felt was not in accordance with the dignity of his imperial status.

There were other long-standing political disagreements between Great Britain and Germany, one of which was the Schleswig–Holstein question, which was so complicated that Lord Palmerston said only three people had ever understood it: the Prince Consort, who was dead; a German professor, who had gone mad; and himself, and he had since forgotten what it was all about. The Schleswig–Holstein situation was one of the reasons for the coolness in the relationship between the two countries, which Count Herbert von Bismarck was hoping to improve during his visit to London. It is in this diplomatic area that the Scandinavian connection can be seen. Although not part of Danish territory, the duchies of Schleswig and Holstein were ruled over by the king of Denmark until 1863 when Austria and Prussia combined to force the Danish king to relinquish them.

Britain largely supported the Danes and the dispute took on a more personal nature when the Prince of Wales married the Danish princess, Alexandra, in March of that same year. In fact, Princess Alexandra so hated the Germans that for eleven years she refused to visit Berlin and was reluctant even to travel to Germany for the funeral of her late brother-in-law, Kaiser Frederick III. It was only on Queen Victoria's special pleading that she finally agreed to attend.

To make matters worse, in January 1889, two months before Count Herbert's arrival in London, an old scandal involving Sir Robert Morier, the British Ambassador to St Petersburg, had been stirred up again in the *Cologne Gazette*, largely, it was suspected, at the instigation of the Bismarcks, father and son. This concerned the allegation that in 1870, during the Franco-Prussian war,* Sir Robert had passed on military information to

* The Franco-Prussian War (1870–71) led to the defeat of France and the subsequent domination of Europe by a Prussian-controlled German empire. It

the French marshal, Bazaire, about troop movements of the German army, a charge vigorously denied by Sir Robert. In an attempt to clear his name, Sir Robert had appealed personally to Count Herbert to publish an official denial of the allegation, a request which the Count had refused in a 'curt and crude reply'.

Diplomatically, the timing of this renewed attack on Sir Robert could not have been more ill-judged for it helped neither Anglo-German relations nor Count Herbert's reputation in England. In a leading article for 4th January 1889 *The Times* took a strong line, accusing the Bismarcks of inflaming anti-British feeling in Germany and warning them that 'their barrack-room manners' were not conducive to a good understanding between the two countries.

'We must beg the German Chancellor,' the article continued, 'and those who take their tone from him to treat English public men as English gentlemen.'

As a further complication, the British Government, anxious to preserve its isolationist policy, regarded with some suspicion Germany's attempts to form alliances with other European nations, particularly with Great Britain's traditional enemies, France and Russia, a situation which added to Count Herbert's problems. In the event, Lord Salisbury, the prime minister, refused to sign the Anglo-German alliance and the count returned home empty-handed.

In treating his client with such brusqueness, Holmes may have been expressing this official mistrust, or his coldness might have arisen from a more personal antipathy. Count Herbert was a conceited, overbearing man, a heavy drinker with a tendency towards violence when drunk, and with an unfortunate habit for someone in his position as German Secretary of State for Foreign Affairs, of issuing orders to his opposite numbers rather than sitting down round the international table to discuss matters diplomatically. Holmes' attitude towards him may reflect the private opinion of Mycroft and his colleagues in the British Foreign Office, who could well have experienced the count's

marked the beginning of a period of instability in European politics which led eventually to the outbreak of the First World War.

highhanded manner during the negotiations over the Anglo-German alliance.

With so much depending on a successful mission to London, it is understandable that Count Herbert was anxious that no scandal concerning himself and the former opera singer, Irene Adler, should be made public, especially as a similar liaison between a prince and another professional singer had caused so much gossip only a short time before.

But who were this prince and his opera singer whose relationship so closely matched that of Count Herbert's and Irene Adler's?

He was the handsome Prince Alexander (Sandro) of Battenburg, second son of Prince Alexander of Hesse. Because of the latter's morganatic marriage to a commoner, a former lady-in-waiting to his sister, the Empress of Russia, Sandro's father had been obliged to give up the right to the Hessian title for his three sons.

Capable and intelligent, as well as exceedingly good-looking, Sandro had been elected in 1879 to rule Bulgaria, a newly-created state formed from the eastern part of Armenia after the Russians had defeated the Turks and driven them out of the territory. By supporting Sandro's nomination to the Bulgarian throne, the Russians assumed he would rule as a puppet prince, willing to carry out the tsar's policies.

Sandro's charm and dark, good looks so enchanted Queen Victoria that she compared him to her beloved Albert, the late Prince Consort. He also captivated the heart of the nineteen-year-old Princess Victoria (Moretta) daughter of Vicky, the former German empress, and the same princess whom Count Herbert later hoped to marry. But some of the stuffier and more conservative members of the Hohenzollern family, supported by Bismarck, considered the match between Sandro and Moretta unsuitable because of the morganatic marriage of Sandro's parents. Consequently, the young Prince of Bulgaria was ordered to give up all claim to Moretta's hand.

Matters came to a head in 1886 when Sandro, who had angered the tsar by his independent attitude, was kidnapped by Russian agents and forced to abdicate at gunpoint, much to Bismarck's delight and to the distress of Queen Victoria, who had set her heart on a wedding between the charming prince and her grand-daughter, Moretta.

In spite of these setbacks and the disapproval of some members of her family, Moretta still clung to the hope that one day she would be permitted to marry her handsome Sandro. It was at this time that the rumours began to circulate of Count Herbert von Bismarck's interest in Moretta. The match was approved of by his father, the German chancellor, who could see the advantages of a marriage between his son and the Hohenzollern princess which would have made Count Herbert a member of the imperial family and strengthened his own ties with the young kaiser.

But Sandro proved less constant in love than the faithful Moretta. In the interval, he transferred his affections to Joanna Loisinger, an opera singer, whom he secretly married in February 1889, a mere month before Count Herbert's arrival in London. Because of this liaison, Sandro forfeited his title of Prince and, taking the name of Count Hartenau, retired from public life. His fate must have served as a warning light to Count Herbert of the likely consequences should his own entanglement with an opera singer become common knowledge.

What happened to them all afterwards?

Sandro died of peritonitis at the tragically early age of thirty-six and was buried in Sofia, the capital of what had once been his Bulgarian princedom. The year following his death, all hope finally abandoned, Moretta became engaged to Prince Adolf zu Schaumburg-Lippe whom she later married. Ten years after his death, at the age of sixty-one, she married Alexander Zubkov, a Russian half her age who, after squandering her fortune, deserted her, leaving her penniless. She died two years later in 1929, disowned by her family.

Irene Adler also died tragically young although the date and cause of death are not known. Writing an account of the events of March 1889, published just over two years later in July 1891 under the title *A Scandal in Bohemia*, Watson refers to her as 'the late Irene Adler' but gives no further details. Perhaps the full facts were unknown to him.

Like Prince Alexander, Count Herbert von Bismarck also retired from public life but not through any scandal involving an opera singer. On 10th March 1890, a mere year after his meeting with Sherlock Holmes, his father, Prince Otto von Bismarck, was forced to resign by the arrogant young German emperor, Wilhelm II, who had grown tired, as he himself expressed it, of being treated like a schoolboy by his elderly chancellor. Both he and his son went into retirement, Prince Otto dying in 1898, Count Herbert in 1904.

As for Wilhelm II, perhaps better known as Kaiser Bill, his fate closely mirrored that of his chancellor. After the defeat of the German armies by the Allies in 1918 at the end of the First World War, he was obliged to abdicate and went into exile in Holland, where he spent the next twenty-two years of his life, dying in 1941 at the age of eighty-two, in time to witness the rise of Hitler and the outbreak of the Second World War but not the fall of the Third Reich and the second defeat of Germany in twenty-seven years.

CHAPTER TEN

MARRIAGE AND FRIENDSHIP

20th March 1889–24th April 1891

'I am glad to have a friend with whom I can discuss my results.'

Holmes to Watson: *The Adventure of the Blue Carbuncle*

Once Watson had re-established contact with Holmes through the Scandal in Bohemia case, their relationship resumed on almost the same footing as before; almost, for there were, of course, significant changes. Watson was now a married man and a busy GP, living in Paddington, about a mile from his former lodgings in Baker Street. This renewal of their old association was a gradual process which took time to build up a momentum, reaching its climax in the summer of 1889 before tapering off during the years 1890 and 1891, as may be seen from the suggested chronology for the period.

Readers are again referred to Appendix One for a detailed explanation of the dating of some of these cases and for an analysis of the crimes involved.

Date	Case	First Publication
20th March 1889*	Scandal in Bohemia	July 1891
April 1889?	Case of Identity	September 1891
June 1889*	Stockbroker's Clerk	March 1893
June 1889*	Man with the Twisted Lip	December 1891
July 1889*	Naval Treaty	Oct/Nov 1893
Summer 1889*	Crooked Man	July 1893

Summer 1889*	Engineer's Thumb	March 1892
September 1889?	Five Orange Pips	November 1891
27th December 1889*	Blue Carbuncle	January 1892

(Unrecorded cases for the year 1889: the Paradol Chamber; the Amateur Mendicant Society; the loss of the British barque, *Sophy Anderson*; the case of the Grice Pattersons on the island of Uffa†; the Camberwell poisoning. As Watson 'kept notes' on these inquiries, he clearly took part in them.)

June 1890?	Boscombe Valley Mystery	October 1891
October 1890?	Red-Headed League	August 1891
November 1890*	Dying Detective	December 1913
24th April 1891*	Final Problem	December 1893

As the chronology shows, there was a gap of about a month between the Scandal in Bohemia case and the Mary Sutherland inquiry (*A Case of Identity*). Holmes himself remarks that he had not seen Watson for several weeks which would accord with this suggested dating scheme. In the meantime, Holmes had received two magnificent gifts from his former royal clients in token of his services: a gold snuff box with a huge amethyst on its lid from the flamboyant king of Bohemia, and a splendid ring containing a stone of remarkable brilliance, possibly a diamond, from the Dutch royal family.

At the time of the Case of Identity inquiry, Holmes had twelve other cases on hand, including an 'intricate matter' which had been referred to him from Marseilles as well as the Dundas separation case, the latter the only recorded instance of Holmes' association in a matrimonial dispute. It was a squalid affair in which the wife complained of her husband's habit of taking out his false teeth and hurling them at her at the end of every evening meal, perhaps in protest at her lack of culinary skills. As Holmes was engaged in clearing up only some small points in connection with it, he was presumably not deeply involved in the case. One hopes not.

† Dr Jay Finley Christ has suggested that Uffa is a combination of the names Ulva and Staffa, two islands three-quarters of a mile apart off the west coast of Scotland.

As in the Scandal in Bohemia investigation, it was Watson who initiated the contact with Holmes in the Case of Identity inquiry, having called on him one evening at Baker Street. It was during this visit that Mary Sutherland arrived with her extraordinary story of the disappearance of her husband-to-be on their wedding day and once again Watson was drawn ineluctably but also very willingly into the affair. In fact, out of the nine recorded cases for 1889, it was Watson who made the initial approach to Holmes in five of them. In the case of the Engineer's Thumb, Watson actually involved Holmes directly in the inquiry by rushing Mr Hatherley, one of his patients, round to Baker Street to tell his story. It was one of the two investigations which, Watson states, he was able to introduce to Holmes, the other being the inquiry into Colonel Warburton's madness, an account of which Watson failed to publish. However, the Naval Treaty inquiry* should also be included in this list for it was through a letter sent to Watson by his old school chum Percy 'Tadpole' Phelps, appealing for help in finding the missing document, that Holmes became associated with the inquiry. In this case, too, Watson immediately hurried off to Baker Street to lay the facts before Holmes, a measure of his eagerness to maintain contact with his old friend.

In fact, at the time of the Five Orange Pips inquiry, Watson had actually moved back temporarily into Baker Street while his wife was visiting her aunt, possibly the same relative who, as suggested in Chapter Eight, may have lived in Edinburgh and with whom Mary Morstan, as she then was, spent her school holidays. It should, however, be pointed out that, although based at Baker Street, Watson continued to run his practice, attending patients and presumably returning to his Paddington practice during the day. Watson's association with the Blue Carbuncle case rose out of another call he made on Holmes on

* This is the first recorded case of Holmes' involvement in an inquiry which could have had serious international repercussions, although the theft of the treaty was not the work of a professional spy. The treaty involved two secret Mediterranean agreements signed by Great Britain with Italy and Austria in 1887. Readers are referred to Appendix One, for the dating of the Naval Treaty case and its political significance, and also to Chapter Seventeen for a more detailed examination of the part Holmes was to play in international affairs leading up to the First World War.

27th December in order to wish him the compliments of the season.

It was not until June 1889 that Holmes paid his first visit to the Watsons, as is evident in *The Adventure of the Stockbroker's Clerk* in which Holmes, in asking after Mrs Watson's health, makes it clear he has not seen her since the Sign of Four case in September 1888, over nine months earlier.

This bears out Watson's own comment that, while he 'continually visited' Holmes, he only occasionally persuaded him to call on himself and his wife. Admittedly, Holmes was not in the habit of paying social visits on anyone, but one has the impression that Holmes hung back from such direct contact with Mrs Watson, preferring to confine his relationship exclusively to Watson, as it had been in the old Baker Street days. It is almost as if he wished to ignore the fact of Watson's marriage and the very existence of his wife, an attitude which was to take an even more extreme form when, as will be seen later in the book, Watson married for a second time. Nevertheless, after that first visit to the Watsons, Holmes relented to the extent of staying the night with them at the beginning of the Crooked Man inquiry.

Some commentators have criticized Watson for neglecting his practice and leaving his patients in the care of two colleagues, Jackson, who owned the practice next door to his in Paddington, and Anstruther, a Kensington neighbour*, while he went gallivanting off with Holmes. Some have even questioned his medical competence, assuming that, as a doctor, he was lacking in responsibility and that therefore his patients suffered. The evidence, however, does not support such strictures. Watson states quite clearly that the arrangement with Jackson, and presumably also with Anstruther, was mutual and that he, in turn, reciprocated by looking after their patients when the need arose. After all, like anybody else, doctors are entitled to some leisure time.

And when the cases are analysed and the actual number of working days lost by Watson is calculated, the total is, in fact, quite small. Leaving aside, temporarily, the case of the Final Problem and taking only those recorded inquiries which took place between 20th March 1889 (*A Scandal in Bohemia*) and

* On Anstruther see the footnote on page 147.

138

November 1890 (*The Adventure of the Dying Detective*), a period of one year and eight months, Watson spent only eleven days away from his practice. Three of these investigations, the Case of Identity, the Five Orange Pips and the Blue Carbuncle inquiries, took place in the evenings and therefore out of normal working hours, except in emergencies, when presumably Jackson would have acted as locum. Three more inquiries, the Stockbroker's Clerk, the Man with the Twisted Lip and the Red-Headed League, occurred at weekends, when again one assumes that, although Watson's consulting room was probably open on Saturdays, it was almost certainly closed on Sundays and he therefore lost only three working days. Moreover, in the Red-Headed League case, Watson states that, although the main events took place on Saturday, he had no patients to visit that day.

The Crooked Man, the Engineer's Thumb and the Dying Detective cases each took up one whole day, Jackson taking care of Watson's practice in the Crooked Man inquiry as he may have done with the other two investigations. Although Watson spent the night with Holmes in Kent during the Man with the Twisted Lip case, he was back in Baker Street by breakfast time and had presumably returned to Paddington before his first patient arrived.

Apart from the Final Problem, only two cases involved longer periods of absence, the Naval Treaty and the Boscombe Valley inquiries, both of which occupied two whole days. The Naval Treaty inquiry, however, occurred, as Watson states, at 'the slackest time of the year' while, although the Boscombe Valley mystery took place when he had a long list of patients, Watson made arrangements for Anstruther to take over his practice.

Watson has left no details of the five unrecorded cases of 1889 and it is therefore not known how many working days he lost over these. But, if Watson followed the same pattern set out above, he may well have so arranged matters that he forfeited the minimum time over these as well or asked either Jackson or Anstruther to look after his patients in his absence. There is no evidence in the canon of Watson taking any protracted time off, even for a holiday, during this period. Indeed, the fact that on two occasions Mary Watson went away alone on visits suggests that Watson was too occupied with his professional duties to accompany her. The case of the Final Problem, during which Watson was absent on the Continent with Holmes for about a fortnight, was exceptional and will be examined in more detail in the next chapter.

In addition to the inquiries in which he assisted Holmes, Watson was also spending at least some of his leisure time in the evenings writing up his notes on previous investigations. When Holmes calls on him at the beginning of the Stockbroker's Clerk case, Watson remarks that, on the previous night 'I was looking over my old notes and classifying our past investigations.' However, he did not publish any accounts of these cases during this period, either because he was too busy or he may have felt that, with Holmes' reputation now firmly established on both sides of the Channel, there was no need for him to promote his old friend's professional expertise.

Rather than Watson's practice suffering from these excursions with Holmes, the facts tend to show the opposite is true. By the summer of 1889, the time of the Crooked Man inquiry and only a few months after his marriage and the purchase of the Paddington practice, Watson was evidently successful enough to afford extra live-in domestic help for, in his account of the case, he refers to the 'servants' as having gone to bed. One was certainly a maid who had presumably replaced the unsatisfactory Mary Jane who, as we have seen, was under notice in March of that year. The other may have been a cook-general. Moreover, before the time of the Red-Headed League inquiry, Watson's finances had sufficiently improved for him to move to Kensington, a more fashionable and expensive area than Paddington, and a sure indication of his increasing success as a medical practitioner.

It is not surprising. While Watson might not have been a highly-qualified consulting surgeon, he was an able and caring GP. This is confirmed by the fact that he had cured a guard at Paddington station of a 'painful and lingering disease', presumably when other medical treatment had failed. In gratitude, the man extolled Watson's virtues as a doctor and consequently more members of the railway staff joined his list of patients. This man may have been one of those whom Watson treated without charging a fee because he found their cases medically instructive, an aspect of Watson's professional attitude which Holmes comments on in *The Adventure of the Red Circle*.

Watson was also prepared to turn out late at night to tend his patients. When Holmes calls unexpectedly at a quarter to twelve one evening, Watson, who was on the point of going to bed, assumes the visitor has come on behalf of a patient and, although he makes a wry face, he is perfectly willing to comply, even though it might be an all-night sitting. Another late call occurred in the same summer of 1889 when Mrs Whitney arrived to ask for Watson's help in tracing the whereabouts of her husband, one of Watson's patients, who had been missing for two days and who she suspected was at an East End opium den. Despite the lateness of the hour, Watson set off immediately in a hansom. Although Mrs Whitney was a friend of Mrs Watson, one feels that he would have reacted similarly, whichever of his patients had asked for his help.

In fact, far from being neglectful of his patients, Watson was careful to put their needs first. In the Mary Sutherland inquiry (*A Case of Identity*), Watson limits his involvement in the case to the evenings, spending the day at the bedside of a gravely ill patient, despite his eagerness to know the outcome of the case.

Part of Watson's success as a GP was undoubtedly his sympathetic nature, which would have given him a good bedside manner. He cared about people, an attitude already seen in his concern over some of Holmes' clients, particularly women. Holmes later remarks on this quality of Watson's in *The Adventure of the Second Stain*. 'The fair sex is your department', he tells him, while in *The Adventure of the Retired Colourman*, he speaks of Watson's 'natural advantages' with the ladies. Quite clearly, women found him attractive. This, too, would have contributed towards his success as a GP. It was often the lady of the house who selected the family doctor and Watson, steady, reliable, caring, would have been an excellent choice.

Nevertheless, despite the calls on his time by his professional duties, Watson could not resist the opportunity to become involved in some of Holmes' cases. It was as thrilling and as irresistible as the sirens' song, appealing to that urge for adventure which ran deep in his veins and to that need to maintain the unique male friendship with Holmes which had been built up over the past eight years when they had shared not only their lives together at the Baker Street lodgings but also so many exciting and dangerous exploits. And once back in Baker Street, it was so very easy to pick up the threads of the old, familiar companionship, as Watson found in the Red-Headed League inquiry in which he accompanies Holmes to St James's Hall to hear Sarasate, the celebrated Spanish violinist, give a concert, or to sit up with Holmes until the early hours of the morning over a whisky and soda, discussing the case.

Mary Watson understood this need in her husband. An intelligent, warm-hearted and generous woman, she perceived, perhaps more clearly than Watson himself, the strength of the bond between the two men and went out of her way to encourage it. A meaner-spirited woman might have tried to break it, with possible damaging effects on her own relationship with her husband. In the Boscombe Valley case, it is she who urges her husband to accompany Holmes when Watson hesitates to accept the invitation.

Even Watson himself seems more aware of the nature of the relationship between himself and Holmes as if, having moved away from Baker Street and distanced himself physically as well as psychologically from his day-to-day contact with Holmes, he was able to assess his own attitude more objectively.

'It was difficult to refuse any of Holmes' requests, for they were always so exceedingly definite, and put forward with such an air of mastery,' Watson confesses in *The Man with the Twisted Lip*, acknowledging for the first time in quite so frank a manner the force of Holmes' dominant personality. His response to it was based partly on his genuine admiration for Holmes' superior intellectual powers.

'I have so deep a respect for the extraordinary qualities of Holmes that I have always deferred to his wishes, even when I least understood them,' he was later to admit in *The Adventure of the Dying Detective*.

Nowhere in his accounts of the adventures he shared with Holmes during this 1889–91 period is there any reference to the exasperation he had felt at Holmes's egotism or cold-bloodedness which is found in his earlier accounts. Once he had left 221B Baker Street and was no longer subjected to the inevitable tensions of living in such close proximity with him, he was less affected by the more infuriating aspects of Holmes' personality.

Holmes himself was perfectly well aware of the influence he had over Watson and there are signs that he used it deliberately on occasions to manipulate his old friend to his own advantage.

'I know, my dear Watson, that you share my love of all that is bizarre and outside the conventions and humdrum routine of everyday life,' he remarks in *The Red-Headed League*, making it clear he understands the deep need in Watson for adventure, a need which Watson himself openly acknowledges in *The Adventure of the Crooked Man*, in which he describes himself as 'tingling with that half-sporting, half-intellectual pleasure which I invariably experienced when I was associated with him [Holmes] in his investigations.'

Indeed, Holmes' reference to the 'humdrum routine of everyday life' could be taken as much as a comment on Watson's daily round as a married man and a GP, which to Holmes must have seemed rather dull and conventional, as on his own circumstances when no investigation was on hand to relieve his boredom. At times, his attitude to Watson's responsibilities as a doctor could be cavalier, even selfish, as seen in this exchange quoted by Watson in *The Adventure of the Naval Treaty*.

'My practice—' I began.

'Oh, if you find your own cases more interesting than mine—' said Holmes, with some asperity.

Watson's reply – 'I was going to say that my practice could get along very well without me for a day or two, since it is the slackest time of the year' – has a defensive, almost apologetic ring to it. Holmes is quite clearly putting pressure on Watson to give priority to his, Holmes', needs rather than to those of his patients.

Watson wasn't the only person to feel the force of Holmes' personality. Mrs Hudson was also subjected to it. In *The Adventure of the Dying Detective*, she excuses her failure to call in a doctor when Holmes, who was apparently gravely ill, had forbidden her to do so by confessing to Watson, 'You know how masterful he is. I didn't dare disobey him.'

The case of the Dying Detective also illustrates that callous, cold-blooded side to Holmes' character which has already been mentioned in an earlier chapter and which will be demonstrated in an even more extreme form in the series of events which were to occur later in 1891.

In the Dying Detective case, Holmes deceives both Mrs Hudson and Watson into believing he is mortally ill with a rare coolie disease, contracted during an investigation in the dockland area of Rotherhithe. Holmes even goes to the extent of using rouge and vaseline as well as encrusting his lips with beeswax to give the impression he is suffering from a high fever, another example of his use of disguise and his love of the dramatic.* He appears, however, to have given no thought to the effect all of this would have on Mrs Hudson and Watson, two people who genuinely cared about his welfare. Mrs Hudson is reduced to tears while Watson, horrified at his old friend's pitiable condition, is plunged into a state bordering on despair. He is also 'bitterly hurt' by Holmes' refusal to accept medical treatment from him.

'After all,' Holmes tells Watson, 'you are only a general practitioner with very limited experience and mediocre qualifications.'

It should be pointed out in Holmes' defence that the purpose of this elaborate deception is to lure Culverton Smith, who has murdered his nephew, Victor Savage, and made an attempt on Holmes' life, to Baker Street where Inspector Morton will arrest him. Nevertheless, Holmes' explanation for his behaviour rings a little hollow.

'You will realize,' he tells Watson, 'that among your many talents dissimulation finds no place, and if you had shared my secret you would never have been able to impress Smith with the urgent necessity of his presence, which was the vital point of the whole scheme.'

This may well be true. Watson was too honest by nature to lie convincingly. But this is hardly an acceptable excuse, even if Holmes followed it up, after apologizing profusely, by assuring

---

* A further example of Holmes' love of the dramatic is seen at the conclusion of the Naval Treaty case in which he arranges for Percy Phelps to find the missing document served up on the breakfast table under a covered dish.

Watson of his respect for his medical competence and by taking him out to dinner that night at Simpson's, especially as the treat was as much for his own benefit as Watson's. Holmes had been starving himself for three days in order to give himself a suitably gaunt appearance. Nor was the apology adequate compensation for the emotional trauma to which Watson, and Mrs Hudson, had been subjected, quite apart from the inconvenience to Watson, who had abandoned his practice to hurry to Holmes' bedside.

In fact, Holmes is far more concerned with the success of his deception than with its effects on his old friend and his landlady. He has carried out the pretence, he declares in a little burst of self-congratulation, 'with the thoroughness of the true artist'. As a further insult, Holmes, in his excitement over the arrest of Smith, forgets that Watson, who is acting as unwitting witness to Smith's confession, has hidden himself behind the headboard of the bed.

'To think that I should have overlooked you!' he exclaims as Watson emerges from his hiding-place.

To think, indeed!

Watson makes no comment on either Holmes' attitude or actions, merely expressing relief that his old friend is not, after all, at death's door, a reaction which is another indication of the strength of his regard for Holmes as well as his own good nature. A less tolerant or forgiving man might have left the house in a huff.

But Holmes needed Watson's friendship as much as Watson needed his, a fact Watson was aware of even if Holmes only rarely gave expression to such feelings. Apart from Watson, he had no friends who called on him socially, as he admits in *The Five Orange Pips*. 'I do not encourage visitors,' he adds, although he must have been in close contact with his brother Mycroft, at least towards the end of this period, as later events were to prove.

He quite clearly missed Watson's companionship, in particular his ability to listen to him without interruption. He was also the only person to whom he could freely express his thoughts. 'You have a grand gift of silence,' he tells Watson in *The Man with the Twisted Lip*. 'It makes you invaluable as a companion. 'Pon my word, it is a great thing to have someone to talk to, for my own thoughts are not over-pleasant.'

And he still valued Watson's advice on occasions as well as the more practical help he was able to bring to an investigation. In both the Crooked Man and the Dying Detective inquiries, Holmes wanted Watson to act as a witness to the events, while in the Naval Treaty case Watson is pressed into service as a companion as well as a medical supervisor to Percy Phelps when Holmes sent him back to London with Watson to stay overnight at Baker Street. Watson's medical knowledge also came in useful in the case of the Stockbroker's Clerk in which he was able to save the life of Beddington, the notorious forger and safe-breaker, after his suicide attempt.

Nevertheless, there are indications during 1889 that Holmes was making too many demands on his relationship with Watson, a situation which could have become overexacting or even psychologically damaging to Watson whose self-esteem shows signs of suffering during this period when he compares his own intelligence with Holmes'.

'I trust I am not more dense than my neighbours, but I was always oppressed by my own stupidity in my dealings with Sherlock Holmes,' he confesses in *The Red-Headed League*.

It was saved from becoming so by two factors: Watson's removal to Kensington and Holmes' involvement in a case of such immense importance and confidentiality that not even Watson could be informed of it.

At some time between 27th December 1889, the suggested date of the Blue Carbuncle case, and October 1890, the date generally accepted for the Red-Headed League inquiry, Watson sold his Paddington practice and moved to Kensington, although it is not known exactly when this took place. Watson himself only mentions this change of address in a passing remark in *The Red-Headed League*, when he refers in a typically laconic manner to driving home to his house in Kensington. It was near Church Street for, in *The Adventure of the Empty House*, Holmes, disguised as an elderly bookseller, refers to himself as Watson's neighbour as his shop is on the corner of Church Street. Apart from this and the fact that Watson had an 'accommodating neighbour' called Anstruther, very little else is known about it. Even its exact

146

address is disguised. In *The Adventure of the Final Problem*, a case which will be examined in more detail in the next chapter, Watson describes Holmes scrambling over the garden wall into Mortimer Street where he hailed a hansom. However, as there is and never has been a Mortimer Street in the Kensington area, one must assume that Watson deliberately falsified the address so that it could not be identified, in much the same way as he disguised other facts, such as personal names and the exact location of 221B Baker Street.

During the year 1890 only three cases occurred of which, as Watson states, he kept any records. Although critics disagree which these three inquiries were, according to the suggested chronology given earlier in the chapter they were most probably the Boscombe Valley mystery, the Red-Headed League inquiry and the case of the Dying Detective, the last two taking place after Watson's move to Kensington.*

This decrease in the number of cases with which Watson was associated with Holmes may have been partly caused by this change of address. Kensington was about two miles from Baker Street, twice the distance Paddington was, and it was not so easy for Watson to call in casually at his former lodgings as he had done in the previous year, 1889. Although his new practice was smaller than his old one in Paddington, he was still kept busy. In *The Boscombe Valley Mystery*, Watson speaks of a 'fairly long list of patients'.

Holmes, too, as we shall see in the next chapter, was fully occupied with one particular investigation, which was to absorb much of his time and attention during the latter part of this period.

---

* In *The Boscombe Valley Mystery*, Mrs Watson suggests that Anstruther would be prepared to take over Watson's practice while he is away in Herefordshire with Holmes. Although Watson does not state as much, he had almost certainly moved to Kensington by this date, a suggestion borne out by the fact that, in going to meet Holmes at Paddington station, Watson takes a cab. Had he been still living in Paddington where, he states, his practice was 'no very great distance' from the terminus, he would surely have walked. This theory would tend to support the suggested date of June 1890 for the Boscombe Valley case as in June 1889 Watson was quite definitely still living in Paddington. It would also suggest that Watson had moved to Kensington before June 1890. Presumably, Anstruther was also the 'accommodating neighbour' who acted as Watson's locum during the Final Problem.

Evidently, Holmes paid no call on the Watsons during 1890 and of the three cases in which Watson became involved, he was summoned to two of them by Holmes, once by telegram (*The Boscombe Valley Mystery*) and on the other occasion by Mrs Hudson, who took it upon herself to call on Watson when Holmes was apparently ill (*The Adventure of the Dying Detective*). However, it is clear from her remarks that the request for Watson's presence had come from Holmes himself. Although at first refusing any medical attention, Holmes had at last reluctantly agreed to see a doctor, adding, 'Let it be Watson, then.'

The only case with which Watson became associated through his own initiative was the Red-Headed League inquiry, when he called at Baker Street, the only recorded instance of his doing so during 1890. Business was apparently slack at the time for Watson tells Holmes, 'I have nothing to do today.' His added comment, 'My practice is never very absorbing,' should not, I believe, be taken too literally. Watson was probably salving his professional conscience by making the remark, although he may have been expressing a temporary boredom with his daily routine. He was, after all, thirty-seven or thirty-eight and the first flush of enthusiasm at returning to the medical profession was probably waning a little. And so, feeling in need of some excitement and finding himself with time on his hands, he called on Holmes.

Before the Boscombe Valley mystery, he was evidently so busy that he was in two minds whether or not to accept Holmes' invitation to travel to Herefordshire with him to investigate the case. It was only on his wife's urging that Watson agreed to go.

'Oh, Anstruther would do your work for you. You have been looking a little pale lately. I think the change would do you good,' she assures him, expressing both her understanding of the relationship between Watson and Holmes and a wifely concern for her husband's well-being.

In fact, towards the end of this period, there is evidence that the two friends were slowly drifting apart as they grew more and more absorbed in their own separate lives. Watson was aware of it for he expresses this sense of growing separation in *The Adventure of the Dying Detective*.

The 'very intimate' relations which had existed between himself and Holmes became, he states, 'to some extent modified,' and between November 1890, the date of the Dying Detective case, and the early spring of 1891, Watson had seen nothing of Holmes, his only knowledge of his old friend's activities being gleaned from the newspapers, from which he learned that Holmes was engaged by the French government on some matter of supreme importance, and from two short letters Holmes sent him from Narbonne and Nimes which suggested Holmes expected to remain in France for some considerable time.

Watson was therefore quite unaware of the fact that Holmes was also engaged on an even more important investigation which, if it succeeded, would be his greatest triumph yet.

CHAPTER ELEVEN

THE FINAL PROBLEM

24th April 1891–4th May 1891

> 'Your memoirs will draw to an end, Watson, upon the
> day that I crown my career by the capture or extinction of
> the most dangerous and capable criminal in Europe.'
>
> Holmes: *The Final Problem*

Watson's ignorance of the fact that during these intervening years between 1888, the suggested date of the Valley of Fear case, and April 1891 Holmes had continued his investigation into the criminal career of Professor Moriarty is not altogether surprising. Holmes had deliberately kept Watson in the dark before over much less important cases. And for this inquiry, which must have involved a great deal of undercover work and secret information gathering, it was imperative that no whisper of his activities became known. It was not that Holmes mistrusted Watson's discretion. Time and again Watson had proved his trustworthiness.

Holmes' silence may be partly due to that innate secretiveness which, as we have seen, was an important element of his personality. But it was largely because of the dangerous nature of the enterprise. Moriarty, whose gang had already been responsible for over forty murders, was quite capable of ordering Watson's death, should he suspect Watson was actively involved in Holmes' investigations. As for the danger to his own life, this was a risk Holmes was prepared to take. This need to protect Watson may also partly explain why after November 1890, the

150

date of the Dying Detective case, Holmes made no attempt to contact Watson although, as we have seen, Holmes was in France for much of this time, working for the French government.

That mission to France may, in fact, have been connected with the Moriarty inquiries, as Edward F. Clark Jr has suggested in his essay 'Study of an Untold Tale', in which he puts forward the theory that Holmes was engaged in recovering a painting stolen from the Louvre by Moriarty's organization. However, there is no evidence for this in the canon.

Because of Watson's ignorance of Holmes' continuing interest in Moriarty, it is impossible to give a detailed chronology of Holmes's activities during the early months of 1891, only a broad outline based on the condensed account he later gave to Watson when his investigation was drawing to its conclusion. From this, one can piece together a fairly coherent record of at least the latter part of these inquiries.

Since Holmes' first brush with Moriarty during the Valley of Fear case, the Professor's teaching career had suffered a setback. Although nothing could be proved against him, 'dark rumours' had forced him to resign his chair of Mathematics at the provincial university and he had come to London, where he was ostensibly earning a living as an army coach, that is as a private tutor preparing potential officers for their qualifying examinations. It was a professional come-down for Moriarty which also had the effect of bringing him within Holmes' orbit. Once Moriarty was established in London, it was much easier for Holmes to monitor his activities. It would appear that Moriarty's arrival in London had taken place only three months before the events of 24th April, suggesting that the Professor had left his university post in December at the end of the Michaelmas term.

Despite this closer proximity, Holmes was finding it no easier to obtain the evidence he needed to prove Moriarty's guilt in a court of law. As Holmes explains to Watson, Moriarty himself was never involved directly in any of the crimes. These were carried out at his orders by members of his organization and, if any of them were arrested, the money needed for their defence or bail was supplied by the syndicate. Nevertheless, throughout the early months of 1891 Holmes' inquiries were progressing to the point at which they were not only causing Moriarty considerable inconvenience but were severely hampering his plans. In fact, by 24th April Holmes needed only three more days to complete his inquiries, after which Moriarty and his gang could be rounded up by Inspector Patterson, the Scotland Yard detective in charge of the official side of the investigation.

The Moriarty inquiry came at a crucial point in Holmes' professional career. He had, as he tells Watson, dealt with over a thousand cases during his years in practice and he was growing tired and disenchanted. Although only thirty-seven, he was seriously considering retirement but felt he could not do so until Moriarty was arrested.

'I tell you, Watson, in all seriousness, that if I could beat that man, if I could free society of him, I should feel my own career had reached its summit, and I should be prepared to turn to some more placid line in life,' he confided to his old friend, and in his last letter to Watson he also writes of his career reaching a 'crisis' and of a desire to bring it to a conclusion.

He could afford to retire. The fees he had received from the Scandinavian royal family in 1888 and more recently from the French government had been generous enough to make this possible. Once Moriarty and his gang were arrested, he intended to live quietly and devote his time and energy to chemical research. There is, however, no suggestion at this point that he intended to retire to the country or to go abroad.

It is important to examine his psychological state at this period of his life, for it was to have a significant effect, I believe, on his subsequent actions. There are signs within the canon that, over these three years, Holmes may have been going through a period of manic depression, triggered perhaps by the loss of Watson's companionship, combined with a heavy case-load, and exacerbated by a more frequent use of cocaine. As we have seen, in *A Scandal in Bohemia*, Watson writes of Holmes 'alternating from week to week between cocaine and ambition', the drug intensifying those 'high' and 'low' states of mind from which he naturally suffered. In his accounts of this period Watson also refers several times to extreme forms of behaviour on the part of his old friend. On one occasion, in a state of 'uncontrollable excitement', Holmes raised his clenched fists and 'raved in the air'. On another, he suffered a fit of 'uncontrollable agitation', following a mood in which he was 'more depressed and shaken' than Watson had ever seen him. The repetition of the word 'uncontrollable' is, I believe, significant.

Although Holmes was still too young to be experiencing a mid-life crisis, he may well have reached a point when he began to question the validity of his whole life and career. What was the point of it all? Where was it leading him? In such a frame of mind, even life itself had lost its zest. 'My life is spent in one long effort to escape from the commonplace of existence,' he confesses to Watson in *The Red-Headed League*.

He was also turning to other forms of mental and spiritual consolation, as if logic and reason no longer satisfied him. In *The Adventure of the Naval Treaty*, Watson describes him examining a rose, and this the action of a man whose knowledge of botany Watson had once marked as Nil*. 'It was a new phase in his character to me,' Watson remarks, 'for I had never before seen him show any interest in natural objects.' In his last letter to Watson, Holmes was to express this urge in even more specific terms. 'Of late,' he writes, 'I have been tempted to look into the problems furnished by Nature rather than those more superficial ones for which our artificial state of society is responsible.' This last remark is surely a reference to crime and its detection.

Such a shift in mood is also seen in his changing attitude to the concepts of law and justice and to his own role in upholding them. In two investigations of this period, the Blue Carbuncle inquiry and the Boscombe Valley mystery, the first a case of theft, the second the much more serious charge of murder, Holmes was prepared to let the criminal escape prosecution, justice being better served, he felt, by leniency than by a strict enforcement of the law.

This change in emphasis reaches its apotheosis in his attitude to Moriarty. The man is not simply a criminal; he is the embodiment of evil. Society must be cleansed of his presence and, in undertaking the task, Holmes is assuming an obligation which has all the qualities of a moral, not to say religious, crusade.

By 24th April that crusade was almost completed. Through a

* Readers are referred to Watson's list of Holmes' limitations in Chapter Five.

'little slip' on Moriarty's part, of what nature Holmes does not specify, the net was rapidly closing round the Professor and his organization. The 'final steps' were taken and their arrest was timed for the following Monday, in three days' time. Again, Holmes does not state what these final steps involved but they may have been connected with the papers Holmes was keeping in his desk in a blue envelope labelled Moriarty, which he had filed in the 'M' pigeon-hole and which he was later to ask Watson to pass on to Inspector Patterson. These documents were vital for the conviction of Moriarty's gang when they were brought to trial.

As they contained such crucial evidence, it was surprisingly irresponsible of Holmes to leave them in his desk at his lodgings. He knew Moriarty's associates were quite capable of breaking into premises and stealing documents at the Professor's orders. In fact, an attempt was made that very night to burn down 221B Baker Street, although fortunately only minor damage was done. There seems to be no excuse for Holmes's negligence unless he had good reason to believe the documents were safer in his possession than Inspector Patterson's. Although Holmes makes no outright accusation, there are hints in the canon that Moriarty had inside knowledge of Holmes' tactics in collecting evidence against him.

'He saw every step I took to draw my toils round him,' Holmes was later to tell Watson, while Moriarty himself informed Holmes that he knew 'every move' of his game, an admission which might hint he had an informer inside Scotland Yard.

Nothing is known about Inspector Patterson. There is no other reference to him in the canon and this suggests that, unlike Lestrade and other Scotland Yard detectives, he was never associated with Holmes on any investigations either before or after the Moriarty inquiry. As a police officer, Patterson was incompetent. He not only allowed Moriarty to escape but also Colonel Moran, the Professor's Chief of Staff, as well as two other members of the gang. He also sent incorrect information to Holmes.

All of this could suggest that Patterson or one of his colleagues was in Moriarty's pay and Holmes suspected as much. Corrupt policemen are unfortunately not unknown and such a theory would explain why Moriarty knew Holmes' every move and how he, along with other gang members, managed to elude arrest. It might also account for Holmes' otherwise inexplicable behaviour in keeping such important documents in his desk. In instructing Watson to hand over the envelope to Patterson, Holmes had, of course, no choice. Whatever private suspicions he may have had against Patterson or one of his colleagues, the inspector was nevertheless officially in charge of the case and, with no proof against him or any other officer, Holmes was obliged to make any evidence available to Scotland Yard.

Whether or not Moriarty was kept informed by a contact inside the Metropolitan police force, he was sufficiently alarmed by the turn events were taking to drop all pretence of respectability and to approach Holmes in person on the morning of 24th April. His arrival at Baker Street came without warning and took Holmes completely by surprise, although he had the presence of mind to slip the gun that he kept as a precaution in his desk drawer into his dressing-gown pocket as Moriarty entered the room. In fact, this meeting was probably the first face to face encounter between the two protagonists and shows the desperate measures which the Professor was prepared to take in order to protect himself and his organization.

His motive in coming was simple. It was to warn Holmes that, unless he dropped his inquiries, he would personally order Holmes' death. It was no idle threat, as Holmes was soon to discover. He also knew that it was useless to ask for police protection. Moriarty's agents were too numerous. The fatal blow could fall anywhere and at any time.

As Moriarty must have anticipated, Holmes refused to drop his inquiries. The Professor was a highly intelligent man and, in the same way that Holmes had been compiling a dossier on him, Moriarty must have been gathering information about his adversary.

Holmes' movements after Moriarty had left can be established in some detail. At midday, he set off for Oxford Street to transact some business, of what nature he does not specify. While in the area, two attempts were made on his life, the first occurring at the corner of Bentinck Street and Welbeck Street when he was nearly run down by a two-horse van driven at speed. A second attempt was made shortly afterwards in Vere Street where a brick came hurtling down from the roof of a house, missing him by inches. Moriarty had wasted no time in putting his death threat into operation.

On this second occasion, Holmes called the police but could not prove the attack was intentional. Bricks and slates were found piled up on the roof in preparation for repairs to be carried out and one might have been blown off accidentally by the wind.

After this last incident, Holmes visited his brother Mycroft in his Pall Mall lodgings, prudently going there by cab. Although he does not state the purpose of this visit, it was probably to make arrangements with his brother for the disposal of his property in the event of his death, a possibility which, in the light of the day's happenings, seemed more and more likely.

Having spent the afternoon with Mycroft, Holmes then decided to call on Watson in Kensington. Although Holmes may have already made up his mind to go abroad while the police rounded up Moriarty and his gang, his decision to invite Watson to accompany him was probably only made during that visit to his brother. In fact, Mycroft may have suggested it. He must have been deeply concerned about Sherlock's safety and the thought of his travelling with a companion, who was, moreover, a doctor and used to acting calmly in a crisis, would have seemed eminently sensible.

Holmes himself was clearly not averse to the idea even though he was aware of the danger to Watson should he agree with the proposal. But both Mycroft and Sherlock must have been convinced that, provided a plan of action was carefully devised and carried out, the risk was minimized. As well as the arrangements regarding Holmes' property, this plan must also have been discussed in some detail by the two brothers that afternoon. Their strategy was this: if Watson agreed to accompany Holmes to the Continent for a week, he would send his luggage unaddressed to Victoria station that same evening by a messenger. Early the following morning, the same man would call a hansom, taking care not to choose the first or second one in the rank, in case Moriarty had deliberately placed them there. Watson would then drive to the Strand end of the Lowther Arcade, hurrying through it on foot and arriving at the far end at exactly quarter to nine. Here he would find a brougham waiting for him. Unknown to Watson, its driver would be Mycroft. This is another example of Holmes' innate secretiveness. There is no reason why Watson should not have known this at the start.

The carriage would then take him to Victoria in time to catch the Continental express, where Holmes would be waiting for him in a reserved first-class carriage, the second from the front.

The plan seemed foolproof. There was small chance that Moriarty would learn of it and send one of his agents to track them down. It cannot have occurred to either of them that Moriarty would take it upon himself to pursue them and personally attempt to carry out his threatened revenge.

Holmes was soon reminded, however, of the continuing danger to his life while he remained in London. Even on his way to Kensington to lay the plan before Watson, he was attacked by one of Moriarty's gang, who must have been tailing him that afternoon. With his skill at boxing, Holmes was soon able to knock him down before handing him over to the police. However, there still remained the threat posed by Colonel Moran, Moriarty's Chief of Staff, an excellent shot, whom Holmes already knew was in possession of an air rifle, specially made by Von Herder, the blind German mechanic, on Moriarty's orders. Holmes' first action on arriving at Watson's house was to close the shutters as a precaution against being shot at by an air gun. It was a perfect assassin's weapon, powerful and silent, which Moran was to put to deadly use three years later.

Watson was alone on that evening of 24th April when Holmes walked into his consulting-room. Mrs Watson was away on a visit and he had settled down to spend the evening reading. He had not seen Holmes for several months, probably not since the Dying Detective case in November 1890, and may have assumed he was still in France, engaged on the important inquiry for the French government. Holmes' arrival was therefore totally unexpected. So, too, was his suggestion that Watson accompany him on a week's visit to the Continent although, as soon as Holmes explained the reason behind this request, the threat to his life posed by Professor Moriarty, Watson agreed without any hesitation. His practice was quiet and he knew Anstruther, his 'accommodating neighbour', would be willing to act as locum in his absence.

'You have probably never heard of Professor Moriarty?' Holmes inquires ingenuously. To which Watson replies, 'Never.'

This professed ignorance of Moriarty's existence, about which some critics have commented derisively, becomes perfectly explicable when the publication dates of the two accounts, *The Valley of Fear* and *The Final Problem*, are examined. *The Final Problem* was first published in the *Strand* and *McClure's* magazines in December 1893, two years and nine months after the events, whereas *The Valley of Fear* was not printed until much later in the *Strand*, in serial form between September 1914 and May 1915. Therefore at the time *The Final Problem* was published, Watson's readers knew nothing of either Moriarty or Holmes' encounter with him in 1888 during the Valley of Fear inquiry.

Watson's apparent ignorance of Moriarty when Holmes calls on him on that evening of 24th April 1891 is therefore nothing more than a literary device used deliberately by him to convey to his readers necessary information about both the Professor and his criminal activities. As a device, it is admittedly a little clumsy but, given the circumstances, there was not much else Watson as author could do to get round the problem. The only other alternative was for Watson to admit his knowledge of Moriarty but allow Holmes to give his account of the Professor and his career anyway, which would have been even more artificial. Watson has done his best in a difficult literary situation. Certain parts of Holmes' account printed in *The Final Problem* therefore belong almost certainly to a much earlier conversation between the two of them which took place during the 1888 Valley of Fear case and which Watson has transferred to the Final Problem inquiry of 1891.

Knowing he had probably been followed to Kensington, Holmes refused to stay the night as it might be dangerous for Watson and, when he left, he took the precaution of scrambling over the back garden wall into Mortimer Street,* where he

* There was no Mortimer Street in Kensington, a fact already pointed out in Chapter Ten.

hailed a hansom. It is not known where he went, perhaps to some small hotel or more probably to one of the five small refuges he had set up in different parts of London where he kept some of his disguises. The following morning, when Watson met him in their first-class carriage of the Continental express, he was disguised as an elderly Italian priest. He certainly did not return to Baker Street, where a fire broke out that night in his lodgings, although fortunately not a serious one. Mrs Hudson's reaction to this arson attack on her home is not recorded.

In the meantime Watson must have been busy packing for the trip abroad and sending his luggage in advance to Victoria station, as Holmes had instructed. He also had to make arrangements with Anstruther to look after his practice before setting off the following morning after breakfast for Victoria, carrying out Holmes' instructions about the journey to the letter, as he is careful to point out.

Despite these precautions, Moriarty discovered their destination, probably through their luggage, the one weak spot in the plan. If one of Moriarty's agents was watching Watson's house, it would have been easy enough for him to follow the messenger to Victoria station and then alert Moriarty who, by bribing the porter who loaded their luggage on the train, learned that it was booked through to Paris. There is no other explanation for Moriarty's sudden arrival just as the Continental express was drawing out of the station. He was too late to catch the train but not too late to follow them, as Holmes quickly realized. Moriarty, Holmes deduced, would do exactly what he would have done under the circumstances: that is, to engage a special train* and set off in pursuit.

Watson's suggestion, that they should arrange for Moriarty's arrest, was out of the question. This would alert the rest of Moriarty's gang who would then escape. Despite the threat he posed, Moriarty must be allowed to remain free. But if they were to elude him, Holmes had to make some last minute changes to his plans. His original destination was Paris. He had probably intended to travel to Dover where he and Watson would have

* It was possible for private individuals to hire trains for their own use. These were usually known as 'specials'.

159

caught the cross-channel packet to Calais, going on from there by train to the French capital.

Instead, he decided to go via the Newhaven–Ostend route to Brussels. And so, when the train stopped at Canterbury,* he and Watson alighted, abandoning their luggage, an inconvenience although Watson, who liked to think of himself as a seasoned traveller after his Afghan experiences, refused to be too annoyed at this loss. As Holmes pointed out, they could easily acquire a couple of carpet-bags and buy whatever they needed during the tour. He was also sanguine about what action Moriarty would take once he discovered he had been given the slip; oversanguine as events were to prove. He assumed that Moriarty would travel on to Paris, track down their luggage and wait at the depot for two days for them to arrive to collect it. In fact, as we shall see, Moriarty did no such thing.

Having alighted at Canterbury and watched from behind a pile of luggage as Moriarty's special train rattled through the station, Holmes and Watson then made their way cross-country to Newhaven, arriving in Brussels that same night, that is 25th April.

Their itinerary from then on can be established in some detail. They spent the following two days, 26th and 27th of April, in Brussels at an hotel, moving on Tuesday morning, 28th April, to Strasburg from where Holmes sent a telegram to Scotland Yard. Although the contents are unknown, he presumably asked for information about the arrest of Moriarty and his gang members which was due to have taken place the previous day, by which time Holmes must have assumed that Moriarty, having drawn a blank in Paris, would have returned to London. That same evening Holmes received an answer from Scotland Yard, informing him that Moriarty had escaped arrest but the rest of his gang had been rounded up. This latter piece of information was, however, incorrect and is an indication of Inspector Patterson's incompetence. In fact, three of Moriarty's gang had escaped, among them Colonel Moran.

Holmes was naturally bitterly angry at this failure on the part of the police and keenly aware of the danger to himself and

* See Appendix One.

Watson now that Moriarty was still at large. He tried in vain to persuade Watson to return immediately to England, but although they argued the matter over for half an hour in the hotel dining-room, Watson remained adamant. He refused to leave. Loyalty to Holmes and the promise of excitement proved too strong. That same night, 28th April, they left Strasburg for Geneva from where they set off on foot along the Rhône valley, branching off at Leuk and crossing the Alps by the still snow-bound Gemmi Pass to Interlaken before finally moving on to Meiringen, accompanied by a guide for at least part of their journey.

Watson thoroughly enjoyed the trip, which took a week. It was probably the first proper holiday he had had since returning to medical practice and, with his love of nature, he appreciated the beauty of the scenery, the green of the spring valleys below contrasting with the white snow of the mountains. Holmes, too, was in high spirits although he was also on the alert, conscious of the danger still posed by Moriarty. However, he remained determined that, once Moriarty was arrested, he would retire.

On 3rd May, they arrived at Meiringen, a picturesque Swiss village perched nearly two thousand feet up in the Bernese Oberland in the Hasli valley. There they stayed the night at the Englischer Hof owned by Peter Steiler who spoke excellent English, having spent three years as a waiter at the Grosvenor Hotel in London.

Although the route taken by Holmes and Watson can be established in detail, Moriarty's movements cannot be so easily traced. Presumably, on arriving at Dover on the special train and discovering neither man was on the Calais packet, Moriarty must have realized they had got off the train at Canterbury and had made their way to Newhaven. It must also have been evident to him that it was highly unlikely they would follow their luggage to Paris. But if not Paris, where else might they have gone? Brussels seemed a possible alternative. It was a capital city with a choice of routes fanning out across Europe. Holmes was not the only person intelligent enough to put himself in another man's shoes.

There was in fact no need for Moriarty himself to make the journey to Brussels. As his organization was international, he had merely to telegraph an agent in Brussels instructing him to make inquiries while he, Moriarty, waited in Dover for the reply. It may have been then that he also sent for Colonel Moran to join him. The evidence suggests that Moriarty was alone when he arrived at Victoria station. Holmes only mentions Moriarty while Watson saw only a tall man trying to push his way through the crowds.

The inquiries in Brussels need not have taken long. Both Holmes and Watson were apparently travelling under their own names; there is nothing in the canon to suggest otherwise. There would also have been a limited number of hotels in Brussels where they were likely to stay. In addition, they remained in the city for two whole days, which would have given Moriarty's agent enough time to track them down and discover their plans to move on to Strasburg and then to Geneva. He may even have booked into their Strasburg hotel and eavesdropped on their conversations. As we have seen, they discussed the matter of Watson's return to England openly in the hotel dining-room. Once their plans were discovered, it was simply a matter of telegraphing the information to Moriarty.

It is not known if Moriarty and Colonel Moran themselves travelled to Geneva and followed the two men on their ramble through the Rhône valley. Both were conspicuous figures, the Colonel with his huge, grizzled moustache and Moriarty, tall and thin with his professorial air. It is more likely that Moriarty employed a confederate, possibly the same Swiss youth who was to play such an important role in subsequent events, to stalk his quarry, while he and the Colonel remained at some convenient centre, awaiting further information on Holmes' and Watson's movements and following by road in a hired vehicle.

Holmes himself was aware of the danger. During the cross-country tour, he was constantly on the alert for any sign that he and Watson were being followed, scrutinizing the faces of every-one they encountered and once racing up to a ridge to look about him when a rock had fallen nearby. What is certain is that by the afternoon of 4th May, Moriarty and Colonel Moran had arrived in Meiringen or its vicinity and had been joined by a Swiss youth, one of Moriarty's agents, probably at a pre-arranged meeting.

That same afternoon, 4th May, on Herr Steiler's advice, Holmes and Watson set off to walk across the mountains to the small hamelt of Rosenlaui. It was clearly their intention to continue their walking tour. It was also on their landlord's advice that they made a small detour from their route to visit the Reichenbach Falls, a tourist attraction.

Watson has left a vivid description of the falls. The water, swollen by melting snow, plunged down into a deep, rocky ravine, hurling up spray as it fell. He has caught, too, the roar of the water and the sensation of vertigo both he and Holmes felt as, having followed the path which led to the top of the falls, they peered down into the chasm below. The path itself came to a dead-end. Once they had reached the head of the waterfall, there was no way out except to return the way they had come.

It was while they were standing there that a Swiss lad came running up to them with a letter ostensibly from Herr Steiler, asking Watson to return to the hotel to tend to an English lady who had only just arrived and who was dying of consumption. It was an artful appeal directed at Watson's compassion both as a doctor and a fellow compatriot although he was uneasy about leaving Holmes. However, it was agreed the Swiss lad would act as Holmes' companion and guide and that the two men would meet later that evening at Rosenlaui.

As Watson set off, he glanced back. Holmes was standing with his back against a rock and his arms folded, gazing down at the rushing water.

'It was the last that I was ever destined to see of him in this world,' Watson adds.

On his way back to the hotel, Watson passed a man dressed in black, walking very rapidly. But, failing to recognize him as the same tall man he had glimpsed at Victoria station, Watson took no further notice of him. As there was no sign of Colonel Moran, he was presumably keeping out of sight. And so they passed one another, Watson on his errand of mercy, Moriarty on his mission of revenge.

If Moriarty could have chosen the site for his final encounter with Sherlock Holmes he could not have picked a more dramatic setting. Its glistening black rocks, its roaring torrent, its immense chasm give the impression of a primeval landscape or a glimpse into hell itself, an impression enhanced by Watson's use of such words and phrases as 'abyss', 'boiling pit' and 'incalculable

163

depth', while the 'half-human shout' of the roaring water suggests the cries of souls in torment. It is elemental. In it, air and water are combined with earth in the form of the coal-black rocks, and with fire in the spray rolling up 'like smoke from a burning house'.

In such a setting, Holmes and Moriarty assume superhuman qualities, Holmes the angel of light engaged in a primordial struggle with the forces of darkness in the shape of Moriarty, a Satan-like figure who, although endowed, like Satan, by nature with phenomenal gifts, chose to use them in the pursuit of evil. John Milton has described such a setting in *Paradise Lost* in which he writes of a 'wild Abyss', composed

> Of neither Sea, nor Shore, nor Air, nor Fire
> But all these in their pregnant causes mixed
> Confusedly.

Holmes was expecting Moriarty. He had already guessed that the letter was a decoy, designed to lure Watson back to the hotel, and he was prepared for this final encounter, knowing it would be a fight to the death. For both men it was a matter of honour. Each was intent on fulfilling their own personal pledges, Holmes to free society of Moriarty's evil presence, Moriarty to bring about Holmes' destruction.

Honour played its part, too, in the conduct of that final encounter. It was no mere brawl but was carried out, like a duel, under gentlemanly rules, at least on Holmes' part. Holmes laid aside his alpenstock so that he would have no unfair advantage over Moriarty, who was unarmed. However, although Moriarty gave his 'courteous permission' for Holmes to write his farewell letter to Watson, he failed to mention that Colonel Moran was posted out of sight somewhere above the Reichenback Falls to act as long-stop in case Holmes escaped alive.

How far the actual contest was fair is questionable. Neither man had the advantage of height or weight as both were tall and of a similar build. But Holmes was certainly the younger and the fitter of the two. Against this should be set Moriarty's desperation. He was a man with nothing to lose, willing to risk everything on this last venture.

The site, a narrow path, the earth slippery with spray, favoured neither of them. It was largely a matter of chance which of them lost his footing first and plunged over the brink. But even in such a confined and dangerous setting, Holmes had one distinct advantage over Moriarty. He had studied baritsu,* a Japanese form of self-defence in which the techniques of balance and the use of arm and handholds are used against one's opponent.

As Moriarty rushed forward and gripped Holmes by the arms, Holmes was able to break free from his grasp, throwing his adversary off balance. A few seconds later, like Milton's Satan, Moriarty plunged screaming over the edge of the falls into the abyss below.

* Baritsu, or Bartitsu, a form of Japanese self-defence, was introduced into this country by E. W. Burton-Wright. The name was derived from the Japanese word 'bujitsu', meaning 'martial arts'.

CHAPTER TWELVE

THE GREAT HIATUS

4th May 1891–5th April 1894*

'A strange enigma is man.'

Holmes: *The Sign of Four*

Holmes' reactions as he watched Moriarty plummet to his death at the foot of the Reichenbach Falls have to be guessed as he has left no record of his emotions at witnessing this event. He must have felt enormous relief that it was not he but his mortal enemy who had lost that final battle. Moriarty's death was also his ulitmate triumph, the culmination of a lifetime's work dedicated to the fight against crime. But, judging by his subsequent actions, that sense of relief and exultation must have been tempered by other less triumphant thoughts.

With Moriarty now dead, there was nothing, in theory at least, to prevent him from walking back along the path by which he had come and returning to Meiringen to meet Watson who, as Holmes must have realized, would come hurrying back once he found out the letter delivered by the Swiss youth was a hoax. Instead, he decided to feign death and disappear.

Later, he was to tell Watson that this decision flashed into his mind in the space of a few seconds, even before Moriarty's body had time to crash to the bottom of the ravine. However, his explanation of his motives in coming to this decision, like his excuse for pretending to be mortally ill in the Dying Detective

---

* See Chapter Thirteen, page 184.

case, is, on examination, hardly tenable. He knew, he said, that three members of Moriarty's organization were still at large and had sworn to kill him, a revenge they would certainly not hesitate to carry out once they heard of Moriarty's death. But if they believed that he, Holmes, had also died at the Reichenbach Falls, they would become careless and his task of tracking them down and bringing them to justice would be made the easier.

But at the time he made his decision, Holmes could not have known that three members of Moriarty's gang had escaped arrest. According to the telegraph sent to him at Strasburg by Scotland Yard, all Moriarty's confederates had been rounded up. Holmes was not even aware of the fact that Colonel Moran was not only still at large but was at that very moment posted above the Reichenbach Falls, ready to make an attempt on his life, should he survive Moriarty's attack on him. His presence there, as Holmes himself later admits, came as a complete surprise to him.

Holmes could therefore have only learned of the escape of three of Moriarty's gang members at some later date, at which point he used the information to rationalize that split-second decision he claimed he made as Moriarty's body plunged into the ravine. Moreover, as soon as he encountered Colonel Moran, as he did shortly afterwards, he would have realized that Moran knew that he, Holmes, was still alive and would have informed his confederates of this fact. Holmes' excuse about wanting to deceive them into making mistakes by believing he was dead was therefore specious for this reason alone. In fact, Holmes' real motives for deciding to fake his own death and disappear were more complex than the simple and misleading account he was subsequently to give to Watson.

As we have seen, Holmes was at the time going through a period of psychological stress. Even before his encounter with Moriarty at the Reichenbach Falls, he was seriously considering giving up his career for a quiet, private life in which he would devote his time and energy to chemical research. It was only the continuing threat to society posed by Moriarty which prevented him from retiring. Moriarty's death had removed that barrier. Why, then, did Holmes not return to England and simply carry out this plan? Why decide instead to pretend he, too, had died?

Moriarty's death may well have been a greater emotional blow than even Holmes realized or was prepared to admit. He had, after all, devoted at least three years to gathering evidence about the man and his organization. It had formed the central point of his life, the focus of all his plans and aspirations, almost his *raison d'être*. And now it was gone.

As he stood on that ledge above the falls and watched Moriarty's body spinning into oblivion, Holmes may well have experienced an overwhelming sense of loss, if not of actual bereavement. With Moriarty gone, there was no one left of such superb intellect against whom he could pit his own intelligence. Compared to him, all other adversaries would seem unworthy of his efforts. Life without the Professor would indeed become 'humdrum' and 'commonplace'.

It should also be remembered that Holmes had prepared himself psychologically for death as he stood on that path above the falls face to face with Moriarty. Although he may have felt relief at having escaped alive, he may also have experienced a perverse sense of having been cheated.

The thought of his own death had been on his mind before the Reichenbach encounter. He had already toyed with the idea in the Dying Detective case in which he had deliberately used theatrical make-up to give himself the appearance of a man who was mortally ill. Although part of this pretence may be explained away by Holmes's love of the dramatic, there may well have been darker motives behind the adoption of the disguise. For someone like Holmes who tended to suffer from manic depression, the thought – what is it like to be dead? – may have already crossed his mind. This is not to suggest he ever contemplated suicide. Indeed, in the Veiled Lodger case, he was to round on Eugenia Ronder when she threatens to kill herself with the words, 'Your life is not your own. Keep your hands off it,' which suggests he was strongly opposed to suicide.* But the idea of pretending to be dead and actually disappearing as if he were dead, of assuming another identity and taking up a new life, coming at a time when he was considering retiring anyway and when he had lost

* It could, of course, be argued that Holmes had indeed contemplated suicide but had managed to overcome the temptation. If this is so, it might explain the vehemence of his response to Eugenia Ronder.

the one person, Moriarty, who had been the focus of several years' intensive work, may have proved irresistible.

Holmes himself may not have been aware of the complexity of the emotions which prompted this decision. But the act of disappearing is not uncommon. In this country alone, hundreds of people, suffering from some form of stress, disappear every year without trace although few go to the extent of faking their own deaths. Although part of this impulse may be the need to escape from the present and its insupportable pressures, there may also be a deeper, unacknowledged urge to run away from oneself and create an entirely new persona.

From a practical point of view, there were few obstacles to prevent Holmes from carrying out his decision. He had no dependants and, before leaving England, he had made arrangements with Mycroft for the disposal of his property in the event of his death. Presumably he also had enough money on him to pay for the rest of his Continental holiday and so was not without immediate funds, at least for the time being.

Although he had already seen Watson's reactions to his feigned illness only four months before in the Dying Detective case, it is doubtful if Holmes thought at all deeply of the devastating effect his apparent death would have on his old friend. His own unemotional temperament tended to make him insensitive to the feelings of others. There was also that callous streak in his character and, once he had made up his mind, a single-mindedness of purpose which amounted at times to ruthlessness. Watson would grieve, of course, but he would eventually recover.

Holmes was also aware that his apparent death would have to appear convincing, a challenge to his ingenuity as well as to his love of the dramatic. He therefore carried out his deception with meticulous care. It was vital his footprints were not seen returning along the muddy path and he considered reversing his boots, a trick he had used before. But, as this extra set of tracks might appear suspicious, he decided instead to attempt the ascent of the rock face above him which, although apparently sheer, presented, on closer examination, a few footholds. Leaving his alpenstock behind, together with his cigarette case and his farewell letter to Watson, written with Moriarty's permission before the fatal encounter, Holmes began the climb which was in itself a potentially fatal enterprise. In attempting it, Holmes was again risking his life as if, having escaped death once, he was challenging fate itself to a second duel. Or perhaps it was Moriarty he had in mind for, as he climbed, Holmes imagined he could hear his voice screaming at him from the abyss, like a voice from the depths of hell.

Reaching a grassy ledge, Holmes decided to wait there for Watson to return. It was a bizarre decision which seems to serve no useful purpose except, ostensibly at least, to prove to Holmes that Watson was indeed convinced of his death. One is left, however, with the disturbing feeling that Holmes wanted to witness something else as well – Watson's inevitable grief, a supposition which, if true, suggests not just a callous streak in Holmes' personality but a positively sadistic tendency, although Holmes himself may have seen it as nothing more than a natural curiosity, like wanting to be present at one's own wake.

And Watson was, of course, deeply distressed by Holmes' apparent death. After returning to the hotel and discovering the letter was a hoax, he immediately realized that the 'tall Englishman' who, Herr Steiler reported, had arrived shortly after he and Holmes had left, was Moriarty.

In a 'tingle of fear', as he himself describes it, he set off for the Reichenbach Falls but, despite his deep concern, he had the presence of mind to round up anyone in the village who might be of use in an emergency or to ask Herr Steiler to do so on his behalf. It is not known who they were. Watson does not mention them at all while Holmes refers to them only as Watson's 'following', a term which suggests a degree of contempt for their efforts. Presumably they were local men, possibly guides, who had knowledge of the terrain and some experience of mountain rescue.

Watson says nothing of his own feelings during the two-hour trek back to the falls, allowing his emotions to appear only after he and the others had arrived at the scene and he saw for himself the evidence which seemed to prove beyond doubt that Holmes was dead: no sign of Holmes himself, only his footprints leading up to the edge of the falls but not returning; the churned up mud, torn brambles and ferns at the edge of the ravine, indicating where the final struggle had taken place, and, lying nearby, Holmes' abandoned alpenstock, silver cigarette case and, last of all, his farewell letter. The sight of these objects, Watson reports, turned him 'cold and sick' and, 'dazed with horror' at the tragedy, he could do nothing except stand there, fighting to control his feelings.

And what was Holmes doing while Watson went through this agony of emotions? He was – and these are his own words – lying in 'most perfect comfort' on the ledge above, listening to Watson frantically shouting his name and observing with apparent amused detachment, like Jove from his Olympian throne, the 'sympathetic and inefficient' manner in which his old friend and his companions went about the painful task of examining the evidence of his own death.

It was by then almost certainly growing dusk and the search for the bodies was probably postponed to the following day. Holmes' body was, of course, not found. Neither was Moriarty's. A. Carson Simpson's theory that Moriarty had used one of his own inventions, an Atomic Accelerator, to blow himself into oblivion need not be taken too seriously. It is more likely that Colonel Moran returned later to the scene and, retrieving Moriarty's corpse from the ravine, buried it secretly somewhere in the vicinity. His bones may still be lying in their unmarked grave out there on the mountainside, perhaps within sound of the Reichenbach Falls, its raging torrent still appearing to echo, as it had seemed to Holmes, the voice of Moriarty, the Napoleon of crime, screaming out in terror as he plunged to his death into the abyss below. It might even be possible, using modern archaeological equipment, such as ground radar, to discover the burial place and to retrieve Moriarty's remains. His skull alone would be of immense interest to forensic pathologists. From it, they would be able to estimate the size of his phenomenal brain.

Once Watson and his colleagues had left, Colonel Moran soon made his presence known to Holmes, emerging from his hiding-place above the ravine from where he, too, had watched and listened to all that had been taking place below him. Some commentators have asked why he chose not to use his celebrated airgun to kill Holmes, a more sure and deadly weapon than the less certain method of hurling rocks at him from above. Holmes

171

was, after all, an easy target as he lay stretched out on the ledge. Moran may, of course, not have had the gun with him. Or in such a steep and rocky setting, the angle of fire might have been impossible. Alternatively, the light may have been too poor.

Night was certainly falling, as Holmes himself reports, and in the gathering darkness he could not make out even Moran's features clearly although he must have been familiar with his appearance. He describes seeing only a man's figure and a 'grim face' peering down at him. It was only later he realized his attacker had been Moriarty's Chief of Staff.

Although his way was barred upwards, the departure of Watson and his 'following' had left the path below empty and Holmes was able to scramble down the rock face, itself a difficult feat, and to land, cut and bleeding but alive, 'by the blessing of God', he adds, a rare example of Holmes openly expressing any religious convictions. Once safely on the path, he immediately took to his heels and made off across the mountains under cover of darkness.

Watson's own departure for England was probably delayed. There was evidently an official inquiry for he mentions 'an examination by experts' of the scene of the tragedy, possibly by the Swiss police, which almost certainly involved the search for the bodies already referred to. Whether or not an inquest was held either in Switzerland or in England or in both countries is not clear. English coroners are not obliged by law to hold an inquest on a British citizen who has died abroad unless they feel justice would be served by doing so. Certainly a trial was held, probably at the Old Bailey, of those members of Moriarty's gang whom the police had rounded up and against whom Holmes' evidence, contained in the blue envelope which he had asked Watson in his farewell letter to pass on to Inspector Patterson, was vital in bringing about their conviction.* Accounts of the trial were featured in the newspapers but, oddly enough, considering his international reputation, Holmes' death was not widely reported. Only three accounts were published, one in the *Journal*

* It is doubtful if Watson was called to give evidence against the Moriarty gang as he had no personal knowledge of their criminal activities, only indirect information learned from Holmes which, as hearsay evidence, would not have been admissible in court.

de Genève, and a Reuter's report which appeared in the press on 7th May, both condensed, and finally three letters from Colonel Moriarty, defending his late brother's name, which were printed some time after the events at the Reichenbach Falls.

But this was later. To return to the time immediately following Holmes' and Moriarty's last encounter on 4th May 1891, there was nothing Watson could do once the official inquiries in Switzerland were completed but to return to England and try to pick up the threads of his old life. It was not easy. Writing about these events two years later, Watson was still feeling an acute sense of loss which he describes as a void in his life.

One of the ways in which he tried to fill that enormous gap was by writing and publishing over the next three years accounts of all Holmes' cases with which he had been associated between October 1881, the suggested date of the Resident Patient inquiry, and the Naval Treaty investigation of July 1889, a period of nearly eight years. Up to that time, he had published only two accounts, *A Study in Scarlet* in December 1887 and *The Sign of Four* in February 1890. Readers are referred to the chronologies in Chapters Six and Ten in which the dates of all these first publications are tabulated. These chronicles were to establish Watson's reputation as an author both in this country and in the United States for some of them were published in the American magazines *Harper's Weekly, Collier's Weekly* and *McClure's.* They were later to be published in volume form as *The Adventures of Sherlock Holmes* in 1892 and *The Memoirs of Sherlock Holmes* in 1894. However, any pleasure Watson might have felt at having at last achieved literary success must have been overshadowed by the death of Holmes, the main protagonist in these accounts. Fame must have tasted very bitter indeed.

Although Watson may have already written down some of these narratives, it was nevertheless an immense undertaking, covering twenty-three cases in all, which included *The Adventure of the 'Gloria Scott'* and *The Adventure of the Musgrave Ritual,* two inquiries belonging to the period when Holmes was living in Montague Street, accounts of which he had narrated to Watson. Altogether these chronicles amount to about 150,000 words or the equivalent of over two full-length novels each averaging 70,000 words, a task which would daunt many full-time authors, which Watson, of course, was not. He was a busy GP with limited leisure, and even that could be interrupted by emergency calls which might take him away from home for hours at a time.

Quite apart from the physical labour involved in writing these accounts, Watson also had to deal with the mass of notes on the cases which he had accumulated over the years. It is small wonder, therefore, that he made mistakes over dates or other facts or that he failed on occasions to read through the proofs with sufficient care. Nor is it surprising that he postponed the publication of *The Hound of the Baskervilles* and *The Valley of Fear* until much later, the Baskerville case to 1901–2 and the Valley of Fear to 1914–5 when they appeared in serial form. He simply had not the time to write up accounts of these long and complicated investigations.

Watson cannot have needed the money. By then, he was a well-established GP with a flourishing practice. His needs were more emotional than financial. The act of writing and publishing these accounts not only helped to occupy his mind and his time but served also to keep green his memory of Holmes. They were Watson's memorial to his old friend.

Watson intended not to publish any more accounts after *The Adventure of the Naval Treaty*, which first appeared in print between October and November 1893. He was dissatisfied with the series, feeling it was 'incoherent' and 'entirely inadequate', an attitude which may have stemmed from Holmes' criticisms of his two earlier attempts as an author as well as from his own natural modesty. He certainly had no intention of making public any account of Holmes' last and fatal encounter with Moriarty at the Reichenbach Falls. Those events were still too close to his heart. His hand was forced, however, by Colonel James Moriarty, the Professor's younger brother, who wrote the three letters to the newspapers already referred to in which he defended his late brother's reputation. The last of these letters was such a distortion of the facts that Watson, always a stickler for the truth, felt obliged to put the record straight by publishing a correct version of the events. This account, under the title of *The Final Problem*, was published in December 1893, over two and a half years after Holmes' supposed death and only a month after the publication

174

of *The Adventure of the Naval Treaty*, the last intended account, appeared in print.

In undertaking the task of writing and publishing these accounts, Watson may have been assuaging another loss, that of his wife Mary, who died between April 1891 and March 1894; the exact date is unknown. It was not in Watson's character to describe his personal life in detail, much less to express openly his private grief, and the only comment he makes is in a passing remark in *The Adventure of the Empty House* in which he refers to his 'sad bereavement', a conventional phrase which barely hints at the enormous sense of loss her death must have caused him.

They had been married for only about three years and, although there were no children, theirs had been a happy and successful relationship. A warm-hearted and loving wife, Mary Watson had supported her husband during the difficult months in Paddington when he had struggled to build up the run-down practice. She had actively encouraged his friendship with Holmes, where another woman might have objected. She had tolerated without complaint the long hours of loneliness which any GP's wife has to endure as well as the occasions when Watson spent some of his limited leisure time, which might have been spent with her, in Holmes' company. Watson's grief at her death must have been overwhelming.

The cause of her death is not known. She was still a young woman, only thirty years old in 1891, and one suggestion that she died in childbirth, a common cause of death in women of childbearing age in Victorian times, is plausible although there is no evidence in the canon to support it. Another theory, that she was already suffering from tuberculosis, which was why Watson was so concerned to return to the Englishcher Hof to tend the Englishwoman dying of the same illness, and that Mrs Watson herself later died of the disease, is less supportable. In that period, tuberculosis was serious and potentially fatal. With no vaccines to prevent it and no antibiotics to cure it, the only treatment was rest and fresh air. And yet at the time Watson left with Holmes for the Continent, Mrs Watson was absent from home on a visit, an unlikely event if she was already a TB patient. Watson would not have allowed it nor would he have been as eager to accompany Holmes abroad had he known his wife was already suffering from consumption which, as a doctor, he would almost certainly have diagnosed.

Theories about the date of her death are as hypothetical as those regarding its cause. However, if she died in 1891, not long after Holmes' apparent death, this second loss coming so soon after the first, might have acted asa double spur to Watson to undertake the task of writing up these twenty-three cases in order to fill the long empty evenings he would have spent alone as a widower. As Holmes was later to remark, 'Work is the best antidote to sorrow, my dear Watson.'

Holmes' movements over the next three years can be established in broad outline from the account he subsequently gave to Watson, although many gaps remain in his narrative, some of which can only be filled by supposition.

Having eluded Colonel Moran and made off across the mountains perhaps for either Iseltwald or Grindelwald, both of which were about ten miles away, the distance he states he covered, he then travelled to Florence, where he arrived a week later. The time spent on the journey suggests he may have walked part of the way.

His destination was Tibet, although he is not specific about the exact route he took nor his method of travel. It must, however, have been a long and difficult journey necessitating a sea voyage to India, where he may have landed at Bombay, the port at which Watson had disembarked eleven years earlier in 1888 at the start of his military adventures in Afghanistan.

Before setting out on this journey, Holmes either wrote or telegraphed to his brother Mycroft, informing him of his survival and asking for money to be forwarded to him to pay for his travelling expenses, which must have been quite heavy. Mycroft also took it upon himself to retain Holmes' lodgings in Baker Street without his brother's knowledge. It is not known what prompted Mycroft to make this decision. He may have guessed that Holmes might eventually want to return or Holmes himself may have hinted as much in his letters. Nor is it known what excuse Mycroft gave to Mrs Hudson for keeping on his brother's rooms. Like Watson, Mrs Hudson believed Holmes was dead. As the Baker Street apartment must have been full of Holmes' possessions, including all his books and papers accumulated over the years, Mycroft may have told her that he preferred to leave them where they were rather than go to the trouble and expense of packing them up and putting them into storage. As long as the rent was paid regularly, Mrs Hudson would have had no reason to object to this arrangement.

Tibet was a difficult country for a foreigner to visit. Quite apart from its mountainous terrain, the Tibetans had closed their frontiers to outsiders, due largely to fear of the Russian and British empires along its borders. In the past missionaries, mostly Catholics, had managed to make their way to Lhasa, the capital, and later explorers had made the same attempt, among them an Englishwoman, Annie Royle Taylor, who, travelling in disguise, almost succeeded in reaching Lhasa before being discovered and expelled.

By assuming Norwegian nationality and the name Sigerson, Holmes would have avoided the hostility the Tibetans felt towards the English. His choice of nationality may have been prompted by the success of the Swede, Sven Hedin, who had already gained a reputation as a Far East explorer in 1885. Later Hedin was to travel extensively in Tibet and in 1905–6 published a detailed map of the country.

Holmes may have chosen Tibet because of its remoteness, its virtual inaccessibility and the fact that it was largely unexplored. It was, in short, a challenge. It was also a Buddhist country and, as we have seen, Buddhism was one of his interests. Reports of 'Sigerson's' travels in Tibet filtered through to the newspapers, probably via Mycroft, with whom Holmes remained in touch.

A. Carson Simpson, an expert on Tibet and author of *Sherlock Holmes' Wanderjahre*, has traced the probable route Holmes took. He has suggested that, having fitted out an expedition at Darjeeling, Holmes then trekked north, probably by pony, across the Teesta river through Kalimpong and Sikkim before beginning the steep climb through the Himalayas towards the Tibetan frontier, crossing by the Jelep La Pass. From there, he followed the mountain tracks to Lhasa, a distance of more than 210 miles. Or perhaps, like Alexandra David Neel, a Frenchwoman who visited Lhasa in 1923, the first white woman ever to enter the city, he crossed by the Sepo Pass and saw, like her, 'the immensity of the trans-Himalayan tableland' of Tibet stretching out before him, with its distant view of snow-capped peaks.

Holmes spent two years in Tibet, travelling about the country under the name of Sigerson and visiting Lhasa, where he spent two days with the head Lama (incidentally spelt incorrectly by Watson as 'Llama' in his original account). Sherlockian scholars disagree about who exactly Holmes meant by the term 'the head Lama'. It was probably not the Dalai Lama himself, who lived in seclusion, but either the Ta'shi Lama, in charge of spiritual affairs, or the Regent, who was also abbot of the Ten-gye-ling monastery in Lhasa, one of Tibet's most important religious centres.

A. Carson Simpson, who supports the Regent theory, has further suggested that Holmes was commissioned by him to investigate the stories concerning the Abominable Snowman, inquiries which took Holmes to the slopes of Everest, thus making him the first European ever to set foot on the highest mountain in the world. It is a fascinating theory. Unfortunately, there is no evidence in the canon to support it.

From Tibet Holmes journeyed on to Persia (modern Iran), a Muslim country and another potentially dangerous area. Like the Tibetans, the Persians regarded the English and the Russians with hostility, due to the political and economic rivalries between these two nations which had turned Persia into a semi-colonial state. As a consequence, anti-British and Russian riots had broken out.

Such potential danger need not have troubled Holmes for it is quite possible that for this part of his journey he adopted not only a new name and a new nationality, as he had done in Tibet, but also a new religion and appearance, passing himself off as either an Algerian or Moroccan Muslim. Such a disguise would have presented no problems for Holmes, an expert in changing his appearance. His dark eyes and hair as well as his lean features and hawk-like nose, which Watson several times compares to a Red Indian's, already gave him a cast of features not unlike an Arab's, a similarity which would have been enhanced by the deep tan he had acquired through exposure to the sun and wind during his travels in Tibet. Language would not have been a problem either. Both Algeria and Morocco were under French rule at that time and Holmes spoke French like a native. Nor would he have had any difficulty in conforming to Muslim religious practices. He had studied Buddhism and he may also have researched into Muhammadanism. Suitable clothing in the way of a burnous and an Arab head-dress would have been easily obtained in a local bazaar. As a French-speaking Algerian or Moroccan Muslim, Holmes could therefore have travelled quite freely through Persia and Saudi Arabia, even stopping off briefly at Mecca, a city sacred to Muslims as the birthplace of Muhammad and therefore forbidden to infidels, although he was prudent not to stay there long. He was later to tell Watson that he merely 'looked in' at Mecca.

From Saudi Arabia, he moved on to Khartoum in the Sudan where he paid a short visit to the Khalifa, its Muslim ruler. Edgar W. Smith in *Sherlock Holmes and the Great Hiatus* has pointed out that the Khalifa was not in Khartoum in 1893, the year Holmes visited the country, but at Omdurman, Khartoum having been largely destroyed in 1885 by Muhammad Ahmed, a Muslim leader, who had led a revolt against the Egyptians who then occupied it. But as Dr Ernest Zeisler has argued in *Baker Street Chronology*, the two cities were only two miles apart and, as Khartoum had been partly rebuilt by 1893, it was quite possible the Khalifa was in the city at the time of Holmes' visit.

Holmes was to report the results of his interview with the Khalifa to the Foreign Office, foreshadowing his later work as a Government agent. Like Persia, the Sudan had great political interest for the British.* Although nominally an Egyptian dependency, a British force, led by Watson's old hero, General Gordon, had been ordered into the territory in 1884 to quell the Sudanese rebels, an attack which led to Gordon's death at Khartoum the following year. In 1896, another force was to be sent to recapture the city and conquer the area, thus establishing British supremacy in the Sudan.

After his adventures in Tibet, the Middle East and Africa, Holmes moved nearer to home, settling for several months in the south of France where he carried out research into coal-tar derivatives at a laboratory in Montpellier, which Watson spells as 'Montpelier'.

* Readers are referred to the notes on Chapter Ten, Appendix One, under the entry for the Adventure of the Naval Treaty.

179

Some eminent Sherlockian scholars, among them Gavin Brend, have cast considerable doubt on Holmes' account of his activities between 1891 and 1894, the Great Hiatus, claiming that the whole story is fictitious and that Holmes was, in fact, in London during this period, secretly engaged in tracking down those members of Moriarty's organization who had escaped arrest. Gavin Brend in *My Dear Holmes* has gone so far as to suggest that Holmes actually joined the gang in disguise in order to bring about its final destruction. If he did so, he was singularly unsuccessful, as Colonel Moran together with at least one other gang member was still at liberty in the spring of 1894. According to another theory, Holmes was in America during the Great Hiatus, helping the police investigate the Borden case at Fall River, Massachusetts, in August 1892, in which Lizzie Borden was accused of murdering her father and stepmother.

Other more bizarre theories have suggested that Moriarty never in fact existed and that Holmes invented him in order to explain away some of his investigative failures, or that Holmes and Moriarty were one and the same person, while Monsignor Ronald Knox believed that Holmes indeed died at the Reichenbach Falls and that Watson made up the rest of the adventures, a theory shared by other Sherlockian scholars. Still yet another theory relating to this period suggests Holmes married Irene Adler while he was in Florence.* If he did so, it was a remarkably short marriage, the bride dying not long after the ceremony, for in *A Scandal in Bohemia*, published in September 1891, Watson refers to the 'late' Irene Adler.

All that can be said in rebuttal of this and any of the other theories is to repeat the statement that, ingenious though they are, there is no evidence in the canon to support them and, in the face of this irrefutable fact, one can only accept Holmes' statement as the truth: that Moriarty died at the Reichenbach Falls and that after his death Holmes did indeed travel to Tibet, Persia and the Sudan, arriving in late 1893 or early 1894 at Montpellier.

* Readers are reminded that in March 1889 Irene Adler had married Godfrey Norton, a young lawyer, in a secret ceremony at St Monica's church, Edgware Road, at which Holmes, disguised as a groom, had acted as witness. Unless Norton had died in the meantime, any marriage between Holmes and Irene Adler would therefore have been bigamous.

My only quarrel with Holmes' account, an objection with which many other commentators agree, is over the reason he later gave to Watson for his failure to inform him that he had survived his encounter with Professor Moriarty. It was the same excuse he had made in the Dying Detective case for not taking Watson into his confidence on that occasion: Watson was too honest and, had he known the truth, he might unwittingly have betrayed it. As Holmes expresses it, 'Several times during the last three years I have taken up my pen to write to you, but always I feared lest your affectionate regard for me should tempt you to some indiscretion which would betray my secret.' Like his explanation for feigning his own death, this sounds suspiciously like an attempt to excuse the inexcusable.

Although Holmes was prepared to admit he could be mistaken in some of his investigative deductions, he was not given to deep or critical self-examination and his first instinct when faced with the need to explain his own unacceptable behaviour was to look for something or someone else to blame, in this case, Watson's inability to dissemble. By doing this he could justify his conduct not only to Watson but also to himself. Holmes was probably unaware of this tendency of his. Certainly Watson, not given himself to subtle psychological inquiry and prone anyway to believe Holmes was usually right, accepted Holmes' explanation without question.

It was an aspect of their relationship on which Holmes relied when in the spring of 1894 he decided to return from the dead.

CHAPTER THIRTEEN

RETURN AND REUNION

5th April 1894

'I trust that age doth not wither nor custom stale my infinite variety.'

Holmes to Watson: *The Adventure of the Empty House*

Even before he learned of the Adair murder, Holmes was thinking of returning to England. His researches into coal-tar derivatives at the laboratory in Montpellier were completed and there was nothing to keep him in France. There may have been other considerations in his mind as well, among them shortage of money. His three years of extensive travel must have been expensive and presumably he had no opportunity to earn any fees while he was abroad. Nostalgia, too, may have played a part and while Holmes would never have admitted to such a sentiment, he may have felt homesick for London and the Baker Street lodgings. Certainly after his return, he speaks with pleasure of sitting once more in his old armchair in his familiar room.

During his time in Montpellier, Holmes had been reading the English newspapers with close attention, looking for any reports which might suggest Colonel Moran was back in England and had resumed his criminal career. For while Moran remained at large, Holmes' own life was in danger. There was nothing he could do to avert this risk. As there was no incriminating evidence against him, Holmes could hardly appeal to a magistrate for legal protection without proof of the man's guilt. Nor could he shoot Moran on sight without running the risk of being charged himself with murder.

The murder of the young aristocrat, the Honourable Ronald Adair, gave Holmes the opportunity he was looking for. As soon as he read the newspaper reports of the inquest on Adair and learned that a certain Colonel Moran had been playing cards with the victim only a few hours before his death, Holmes was convinced that Moran had committed the murder. And if he needed further proof, the fact that Adair had been shot through the head with an expanding bullet, the same ammunition used in Moran's celebrated airgun, would have provided it.

The Adair murder would have interested Holmes even if Moran's name had not been associated with it. It was a classic, locked-room mystery with no apparent motive. Adair, who appeared to have no enemies, was found murdered at 11.20 p.m. on the evening of Friday 30th March 1894 in his room on the second floor (American third floor) of his mother's house in Park Lane, after returning home at 10 p.m. from the Bagatelle Card Club, where he had been playing whist. His partner had been Colonel Moran, with whom Adair had played cards on other occasions, including one game a few weeks earlier in which they had won the considerable sum of £420.

As coins and banknotes totalling £37 10s were found on the table, together with a paper listing sums of money against the names of fellow club members, it was assumed that, at the time he was shot, Adair had been working out his gains and losses at cards. The door of the room in which his body was discovered was locked, no gun was found and no sound of a shot had been heard. There was no sign either of an intruder, although the window of the room was open. But it was more than twenty feet to the ground, with no means of ready access nearby such as a drain-pipe. Moreover, a bed of crocuses underneath the window was undisturbed.

As soon as he read the reports of Adair's murder, Holmes set off at once for London, a plan already in his mind for Moran's capture because on the journey he stopped off at Grenoble, where he commissioned the French artist, Monsieur Oscar Meunier, to model a wax bust of himself. This, at least, is the implication. Holmes would hardly have gone to the trouble and

183

expense of having the model made until he knew Moran's whereabouts and his association with the Adair murder case.

The exact date of Holmes' arrival in London is not known, Watson having for some inexplicable reason failed to record it, apart from a vague reference to an 'April evening'. One would have thought that, even if he were not keeping a journal at the time, the day of his reunion with Holmes would have been etched in figures of fire in his memory. But it must have been early April. Adair was murdered on 30th March and Holmes arrived not long after the inquest, which presumably took place shortly after the crime was committed. The date accepted by many Sherlockian scholars is 5th April, the weather on that evening being, according to Watson's description, 'bleak and boisterous', which agrees with the meteorological records for that date.

On first consideration, this would hardly have given time for the inquest to be held and reports of its findings to be published in the English newspapers, which would then have had to be sent to Montpellier by sea and rail. In addition, Holmes had to commission the bust from Monsieur Meunier, which took 'some days', possibly two, and to spend at least another two days travelling from Montpellier to Grenoble and then to Paris and from there to Calais to catch the cross-Channel packet to Dover. All of this could not have been accomplished in six days unless Holmes had prior knowledge of the facts. It is highly likely, therefore, that Mycroft informed Holmes by telegraph of Adair's murder and Moran's association with it on Saturday, 31st March, having learned of it through gossip among the members of his London club. Apparently, he failed to tell his brother that he had kept on his Baker Street rooms, for Holmes only learned of this fact on his arrival at his old lodgings.

On the matter of dating, the bed of crocuses underneath Adair's window has caused a few raised eyebrows among some commentators, who assert that these flowers bloom much earlier in the spring, usually in February, never in April. On this basis, D. Martin Dakin has argued that Watson was once again careless over dates and that Adair's murder took place on 30th January, Holmes returning during early February. Others have suggested that Watson was mistaken and that the crocuses were some other

184

spring flowers. However, according to the gardening books, there are different species of crocus, some flowering later than others, among them the *Crocus areus* which comes into bloom between late February and early April.

Holmes would have arrived from Dover by train at Victoria station, the same terminus from which he and Watson had set out three years earlier for their Continental tour. From there he went straight to Baker Street, arriving at 2 p.m., probably on the afternoon of Thursday, 5th April. He had already deduced that Moran would have 221B under surveillance. Colonel Moran was no fool and, once his name appeared in the newspapers in connection with the Adair murder, he himself would have realized that Holmes would be tempted to return to London. There was no need, therefore, for him to have had a watch kept on the house for the whole three years of Holmes' absence, as some commentators have suggested before scornfully dismissing it as so unlikely as to make this part of the account highly dubious, an example of setting up an Aunt Sally with the sole purpose of knocking it down. The surveillance would have lasted only a few days and Holmes' use of the word 'continuously' refers merely to the day and night observation kept on the house once his return was expected.

The man on watch when Holmes arrived was known to him and he immediately recognized him as Parker, a garotter* by profession and a player on the jew's harp in his leisure time, who had been a member of the late Professor Moriarty's criminal organization. As Holmes correctly guessed, Parker immediately hurried off to inform Moran of Holmes' return. In his turn, Moran, knowing his own life was in jeopardy now that Holmes was back in London, set about making his own plans to kill him, a stratagem Holmes also deduced although he was to be proved wrong in one important detail.

Holmes' movements on that first afternoon after his arrival in Baker Street can be established in some detail. Even before he set

* There had been an outbreak of garotting, principally in London, between 1861 and 1864. These attacks were usually carried out by three people, the 'choker' who attacked the victim from behind, his assistant who committed the robbery, and a lookout, often a woman. The frequency of these attacks caused much alarm and demands for more efficient policing.

foot inside his old lodgings, he would have noticed that Camden House*, directly opposite 221B, was vacant, an opportunity which was too good to miss. Once Mrs Hudson had recovered from her violent fit of hysterics at seeing Holmes returned from the dead and he had instructed her in the part she was to play in his plan, Holmes almost certainly set off for the estate agent whose name would have appeared on the 'Vacant' sign outside Camden House. No doubt pretending an interest in the property, he was able to obtain a key to the empty house.

That same afternoon he also visited Scotland Yard, where he warned the police that an attempt would be made on his life that night in Baker Street, a warning which Inspector Lestrade took so seriously that he decided to take over the case himself. Although the trap for Moran was now laid, Holmes had one more task to complete: a visit to 247 Park Lane in order to see for himself the site of Adair's murder.

What Holmes failed to do during that first afternoon in London was to inform Watson of his survival, an omission it is difficult to accept, even allowing for the fact that his chief concern at the time was setting in motion his plan for Moran's arrest. Watson was certainly in his thoughts. As he sat in his familiar armchair in the Baker Street sitting-room, Holmes wished Watson were occupying the chair opposite his. But that was as far as he went. If work was the best antidote to sorrow, it also served as a prophylactic against other emotions as well. Watson would have to wait. And yet it would have taken very little time or effort on Holmes' part to have written to Watson – and to Mrs Hudson, too, for that matter – or to have sent a note by messenger to warn them not only of his survival but of his imminent reappearance. Once again, Holmes' love of the dramatic overrode all thought of the effects his sudden return would have on them.

For his visit to Park Lane, Holmes disguised himself as an elderly bookseller, presumably as a precaution against Moran or one of his associates recognizing him in the street and killing him there and then.

At six o'clock that same evening, Watson also arrived outside the Adair residence. His presence there though coincidental was

* Readers are referred to Appendix Two.

not entirely fortuitous. His interest in crime, formed during his ten-year friendship with Holmes,* had not waned after Holmes's apparent death. Fascinated by the Park Lane Mystery, as the Adair murder was called, Watson had spent the day, as he drove round visiting his patients, turning the facts over in his mind and trying to use Holmes' methods to come to some conclusion about the case. Holmes was therefore still very much in Watson's thoughts and he regretted that his 'poor friend' was not there to take up the investigation.

Watson was, of course, unaware of the significance of Moran's name in connection with the Adair murder. As we have seen, Moran was recruited into the Moriarty organization only in early 1891, after the Professor had moved to London, having resigned from his university post. As Holmes had not confided in Watson his continuing interest in Moriarty and his gang, Watson had never heard of either Moran or of his position as the Professor's Chief of Staff. He was ignorant also of the Colonel's presence at the Reichenbach Falls and of his attempt there on Holmes' life. Watson's interest in the Adair murder arose therefore out of its inherent mystery, not from any known connection with Holmes' old enemy, Colonel Sebastian Moran.

So, having completed his medical duties for the day, Watson decided to walk from Kensington across Kensington Gardens and Hyde Park to Park Lane, where he joined the group of curious bystanders who had gathered outside the Adair house. Among them was a tall, thin man wearing tinted spectacles who, he deduced, was a private detective and who was expounding his own theories about the murder. As D. Martin Dakin has suggested, he was probably Barker, a private detective from Surrey and Holmes' rival, whom Watson was later to encounter in the Retired Colourman inquiry. Watson describes him then as 'a tall, dark, heavily moustached man' who wore 'grey-tinted sun-glasses'.

The man's conclusions were so absurd that Watson turned away in disgust. As he did so, he bumped into an elderly, bent man who was standing behind him in the crowd, causing him to

* I have not included the three years of the Great Hiatus when Holmes was absent and assumed dead.

drop the books he was carrying under his arm. Not recognizing the man as Holmes, Watson apologized and made his way back to Kensington.

Watson's inability to see through Holmes' disguise on this as on other occasions has caused much amusement among some Sherlockian commentators, who seize on it as another example of Watson's obtuseness, leading them to believe he was, quite frankly, not over-bright. However, when these incidents are analysed, it is seen that Watson had good reason to be deceived. Out of the seven occasions when he was fooled by Holmes' disguises, in one, the incident in Park Lane, he caught only a glimpse of his friend. On three others, he saw Holmes only in poor light, as happened in the opium den during the Man with the Twisted Lip inquiry. In the Final Problem, when he again failed to recognize Holmes as the elderly Italian priest, they were in the carriage of the Continental express which was stationary in the murky interior of Victoria station, while in the Dying Detective case, when Holmes made himself up to appear gravely ill, the weather was foggy, the room gloomy and Holmes was careful to keep Watson well away from the bed in which he was lying. When he appeared as an old master mariner in the Sign of Four case, Holmes was careful to cover most of his face with a scarf. The element of surprise played a part in the Lady Frances Carfax case, in which Watson was taken completely off-guard when Holmes came dashing out of a café in Montpellier dressed as a French workman, for he believed Holmes was in London.

Poor light may also be responsible when, having returned to his Kensington house from his inspection of the scene of Adair's murder, Watson again failed to recognize the elderly, white-haired bookseller who was shown into his study as Holmes. It was by then evening, the light was fading and, although the lamps may have been lit, the room was probably not brilliantly illuminated. Moreover, as in the Lady Frances Carfax case, the last person Watson expected to see was Holmes, whom he believed had died three years before at the Reichenbach Falls.

The shock of Holmes' sudden and unexpected reappearance was so great that, for the only time in his life, Watson fainted, a measure of the depth of his emotions at seeing his old friend once more. Even Holmes was taken aback by this reaction.

'I owe you a thousand apologies,' he told Watson, having brought him round and administered brandy. 'I had no idea you would be so affected.'

One would like to think that Holmes felt a twinge of guilt as well. His remark about his 'unnecessarily dramatic appearance' suggests that Holmes himself realized he might have gone a little too far on this occasion.

Watson describes him as 'even thinner and keener than of old', the 'dead white tinge to his aquiline face' suggesting that his life had not been a healthy one, remarks which have led some critics to believe that Holmes' accounts of his travels abroad were fictitious. If he had spent three years in Tibet and the Middle East, they argue, he would have been sunburnt. They appear to have forgotten that Holmes had spent the past three months in Montpellier working on his experiments on coal-tar derivatives, no doubt shut up in the chemistry laboratory for days on end.

In his joy and relief, it never occurred to Watson to reproach Holmes over his three-year-long deception any more than it had crossed his mind to protest at his pretence of being mortally ill in the Dying Detective case. And Watson was, of course, immediately willing to fall in with any plans Holmes had for that evening.

Having listened to Holmes' long account of his escape from death at Moriarty's hands and of his subsequent travels, and having in turn informed him, much more briefly one suspects, of the death of his wife, Watson then joined Holmes for dinner that evening before setting off by a circuitous route for Camden House. It was, as Watson says, just like old times to find himself once more in Holmes' company, embarking on a dangerous mission, with 'my revolver in my pocket and the thrill of adventure in my heart' – that same thrill which Watson had never been able to resist.

Holmes' plan was about to be put into action although, with his usual love of secrecy and, one suspects, that same urge for the 'unnecessarily dramatic', he omitted to explain this plan to Watson or to divulge even the name of his adversary. Like a stage magician, Holmes liked to keep his cards well up his sleeve.

In the same way that Holmes had been enticed back to London by Moran's name, a bait to which the Colonel had known Holmes would respond, so Holmes knew that Moran would be tricked into action by Holmes' own lure in the shape of Monsieur Meunier's wax bust which he had set up that afternoon on a pedestal table, draped with his own mouse-coloured dressing-gown, in one of the sitting-room windows of 221B Baker Street. Its position was such that, when the lamps were lit, its shadow was cast against the drawn blind. The lace curtains would have concealed the bust from any observer in the street during the day but it would have become visible when darkness fell and Mrs Hudson, as instructed, pulled down the blinds.

With regard to Mrs Hudson's part in the stratagem, it should be pointed out that, like Watson, she fell in with Holmes' plan with no apparent protest. Although no longer young, she readily agreed to crawl about on the floor on her hands and knees, turning the wax bust at intervals to make it appear that Holmes had moved in his chair. A very gallant and long-suffering woman, she had tolerated a great deal of inconvenience over the years from Holmes, whom Watson once referred to as the 'worst tenant in London'. Quite apart from his untidiness, his irregular hours, the stench from his chemical experiments and the constant stream of clients invading her house, she had put up with his peculiar personal habits, such as his using a jack-knife to skewer his correspondence to the mantelpiece, where he also kept the old dottles from his pipes, as well as with the actual damage done to her property. This included the bullet holes in the plaster of the sitting-room wall caused by Holmes' patriotic revolver practice, the arson attack on the night before Holmes left for the Continent with Watson, and the demolition of a window when Jefferson Hope had flung himself through it in a vain attempt to escape arrest at the end of the Sign of Four case. A window was about to be broken for the second time.

Inspector Lestrade also had his part to play in Holmes' plan, in readiness for which two policemen were stationed in a doorway in Baker Street while Lestrade concealed himself somewhere nearby. The trap was ready and was waiting to be sprung.

As Holmes had correctly deduced, Parker, Moran's associate who had been keeping watch on Holmes' lodgings, had informed the Colonel of Holmes' return, but Holmes was wrong in assuming that Moran, once tricked into thinking the silhouette was his old adversary's, would fire at it from the street. Like Holmes, Moran had noticed the empty property, Camden House, directly opposite 221B Baker Street, and had also decided to make use of it.

Having set out on the first part of their journey by hansom, Holmes, with his 'extraordinary knowledge' of London, then led Watson on foot from Cavendish Square through side streets and alleys into a back yard and from there into a house, using the key he had obtained from the agent. It was only when they were in the front room that Watson realized the house was in Baker Street. With obvious relish, Holmes drew his attention to the silhouette of himself on the blind of their old lodgings.

'We will see if my three years of absence have entirely taken away my power to surprise you,' Holmes remarks. He was never able to resist the opportunity to tease Watson and was no doubt well satisfied with his companion's cry of astonishment.

Watson, with his gift for words, has given a vivid description of the two-hour long vigil he and Holmes made in the empty front room of Camden House as they waited for Colonel Moran to show his hand, the light from the street lamps filtering dimly through the dusty glass of the window through which could be seen the figures of passers-by hurrying along the street on that 'bleak and boisterous night'. He has caught, too, Holmes' tension and impatience, which the years spent travelling abroad had not lessened. All the old nervous habits are still there, the tapping of fingers, the restless movements of the feet, the quick, excited intake of breath. And he was still inclined to show his exasperation when Watson was slow to understand how the silhouette had moved.

'Three years had certainly not smoothed the asperities of his temper, or his impatience with a less active intelligence than his own,' Watson reports a little ruefully. It was, indeed, just like old times.

The long vigil ended with the unexpected arrival of Colonel Moran at Camden House and, once more, Watson has conveyed the tense atmosphere in the darkened room as the sinister figure of Moriarty's Chief of Staff appeared in the doorway, 'a shade blacker than the blackness of the open door'. Unaware of Holmes' and Watson's presence, Moran crept across to push open the

191

sash window, the light from the street lamps falling on his features so that Watson was able to discern his 'gaunt and swarthy face, scored with deep, savage lines'. But it is the sounds which Watson has captured with particular vividness: the metallic noises as Moran assembled the gun, the sharp snap as he closed the breechblock and the man's 'little sigh of satisfaction' as, with the silhouette in his sights, he cuddled the butt of the rifle against his shoulder. It was followed by the 'strange, loud whizz' as the bullet was fired and then the 'long, silvery tinkle of broken glass'.

But if the old game hunter, whose bag of tigers remained unrivalled, thought he had picked off his prey, it was Holmes, the quarry, who sprang 'like a tiger' on Moran's back, a nice ironic reversal of roles on Watson's part as author. And in the ensuing struggle, it was Watson who dealt the final blow. As Holmes and Moran fought together on the floor, Watson with great presence of mind struck Moran over the head with the butt of his revolver.

A blast on Holmes' whistle brought Lestrade and the two policemen running to the scene and Moran was arrested. One trusts that Holmes had the grace to thank Watson for the part he played in the man's capture, and that the comment – 'I think you want a little unofficial help' – he made to Lestrade regarding three unsolved murders was tempered with a touch of his old mischievous humour, otherwise it could sound unpleasantly patronizing. Certainly he changed his criticism of Lestrade's handling of the Molesey Mystery into what passed as a compliment, although his remark, 'You handled it fairly well,' could be said to damn with faint praise.

In comparison, Lestrade's unreserved statement, 'It's good to see you back in London, sir', has a welcome ring of genuine pleasure at Holmes' return. Indeed, his manner towards Holmes is remarkably deferential. He had clearly missed having the advantage of Holmes' detective skills during his absence.

On the question of charges against Colonel Moran, Holmes chose not 'to appear in the matter at all', by which he apparently meant that he would refuse to act as a prosecution witness should Moran be charged, as Lestrade suggested, with attempted murder against himself. In the face of this refusal, the Inspector's hands were tied. Neither he nor the two policemen hiding in the doorway had seen Moran fire at the wax bust. All they knew was that someone had fired a bullet and, even though Moran was found with the airgun in his possession, there was no proof, the study of ballistics being then not even in its infancy,* that this was the weapon used, only a strong suspicion. The attack could have been made by any one of the enemies Holmes had made during his many years as a private consulting detective.

At the time he made his decision not to appear as a prosecution witness on the lesser charge of attempted murder, Holmes was confident that Moran would be found guilty of Adair's murder and would be sentenced to death. As subsequent events were to prove, it was a confidence which was to be badly shaken and Holmes must have bitterly regretted he had not agreed to give evidence against Moran.

It is difficult to understand the reasoning behind Holmes' refusal to co-operate with the police. It cannot have been out of reasons for security. With Moriarty dead and Moran under arrest, most of the Professor's old criminal organization had been broken up, although one member may still have been at large and was possibly behind the 'shocking affair' a few months later on board the Dutch steamship *Friesland* which so nearly cost Holmes and Watson their lives, an unrecorded case to which Watson refers in *The Adventure of the Norwood Builder*. In the absence of any explanation on Holmes' part one can only assume that during the three years spent abroad he had learned to appreciate the advantages of living incognito and now preferred to avoid publicity, an attitude which he was soon to show towards Watson's publication of accounts of their exploits together.

After Colonel Moran's arrest, Holmes and Watson retired to the sitting-room in 221B Baker Street, despite the draught from the broken window, to enjoy a cigar while Holmes gave Watson an account of Adair's murder and the motive behind it.

It would appear that Watson had not set foot in his old lodgings during the whole time Holmes was thought to be dead for he comments on the 'unwonted tidiness' of the room as if he had not seen it in this unaccustomed state before. But as Watson was

* It was not until 1910 that ballistic evidence was used by police forces in the investigation of crimes involving the use of guns.

a considerate man, it is difficult to believe that he never called on Mrs Hudson during those three years. He may well have visited her but preferred to remain in her downstairs parlour rather than mount the seventeen steps to the familiar sitting-room above, knowing that Holmes' possessions, his books, his chemistry table, his violin case, 'even the Persian slipper which contained the tobacco' were still in place, painful reminders of the many pleasant hours he had spent there over the years in Holmes' company. Or he may have invited her to visit him in Kensington, a kindness which Watson with his usual modesty omits to mention.

Holmes's account of the Adair murder seems straightforward enough on first reading. Several weeks before his death, Adair had won a lot of money playing whist at the Bagatelle Card club with Colonel Moran as his partner. Later, Adair suspected that Moran had cheated. On the day of his murder, or so Holmes believed, Adair had spoken privately to Moran and threatened to expose him unless he resigned from the club and promised never to play cards again. As this would have meant financial ruin for someone who earned his living as a cardsharper, Moran murdered Adair by shooting him through the open window of the young man's sitting-room in the Park Lane house.

According to this theory, the list of names, the money left lying on the table as well as the locked door could easily be explained. Adair had been calculating how much money he would have to return to those who had been cheated by Moran. Before beginning this task, he had locked the door so that no one could enter the room and ask what he was doing.

But on closer examination, there is one important omission in Holmes' account. Where was Colonel Moran when he fired the fatal shot? As Mr Percival White, among others, has pointed out, Park Lane faces Hyde Park and there are no houses opposite where Moran might have concealed himself. It is also highly unlikely that he fired from the street. Adair's window was on the second floor and was at least twenty feet from the ground. He also ran the risk of being seen. As Watson himself says, Park Lane was a 'frequented thoroughfare' with a cab rank only a hundred yards from the house.

Moran might, as Edgar W. Smith has suggested, have climbed

a tree in the park, using this as a firing position, and this seems the most likely explanation, despite objections that he still ran the risk of being seen. However, the murder was committed between 10 p.m., the time Adair returned home from his club, and 11.20 p.m. when his body was discovered. It was then dark and the number of passers-by in the street would have been considerably reduced, while Hyde Park itself would have been virtually deserted, apart from prostitutes and their clients, as well as poorly lit by gas lamps. In addition, Moran was, as Holmes himself states, 'the best shot in India' and an experienced 'shikari' Hindi for 'hunter'. He was used to stalking game and, as Holmes also points out, it was a usual practice for a big-game hunter to tether a young kid under a tree as live bait and then to hide among the branches for the quarry to arrive. Although elderly, Moran was still active enough to climb trees. Watson refers to his 'convulsive strength' as he fought with Holmes just before his arrest.

Holmes' remarks would seem to suggest that, with the exception of the live kid, this is exactly the method Moran used to murder Adair, firing at him from a tree directly opposite his window. The gun was silent so no one heard the shot and, as the window was open, there was not even the sound of breaking glass to attract attention. Having murdered Adair, Moran then climbed down from the tree, first making sure that no one was about, before escaping across the park.

It is also highly probable that Moran had set up an alibi for himself for the time of Adair's murder, a suggestion which may be linked to the fact that on the night he attempted to murder Holmes he was wearing full evening dress, attire which has struck some commentators as so unlikely as to be absurd. I can see no objection to this. Moran arrived at Camden House after midnight. He may well have spent the earlier part of the evening at the theatre or dining with friends as part of an alibi to cover his movements for that crime as well.

There still remains, however, one curious aspect of the Adair case which Watson fails to explain. This relates to Moran's trial. He was undoubtedly charged with Adair's murder and tried, the case probably being heard at the Old Bailey. But he was apparently found not guilty. He certainly escaped being hanged, the usual punishment at that time for murder, for he was still alive in September 1902, the date of the Illustrious Client case, when Holmes refers to him as 'the living Colonel Sebastian Moran'.

Faced with Watson's silence over the matter, one can only conclude that Moran was acquitted of the murder charge and set free, most probably through lack of evidence, despite Holmes' confident assertion that 'the bullets alone are enough to put his (Moran's) head in a noose'.

As has already been pointed out, ballistic evidence was unheard of, and the bullet which killed Adair was a soft-nosed, expanding bullet, usually fired from a revolver, which, in Watson's words, 'mushroomed out' on impact while the bullet fired at Holmes' bust had flattened itself against the wall. This in itself would have made comparison with other ammunition in Moran's possession impossible even if an attempt at making such a comparison occurred to Lestrade or any other of his Scotland Yard colleagues. Motive, too, would have been hard to prove. With Adair dead, there was no witness to confirm Holmes' theory that Adair had caught Moran cheating at cards and had threatened to expose him. If, as suggested, Moran also had an alibi for the night of Adair's murder, the case against him would have collapsed.

Holmes' decision not to co-operate with Inspector Lestrade over the charge of attempted murder against himself was therefore extremely foolish. Had he done so, Moran would have been found guilty on this lesser charge and sentenced to a long term of imprisonment.

By law, there was nothing to prevent the police, with Holmes acting as witness, to bring such a charge even after Moran was acquitted of Adair's murder. This is another curious aspect of the case, which Watson also fails to elucidate. For surely Holmes' objection to his name being associated with Moran would have been outweighed by the risk of letting a murderer like Moran escape justice? He was, after all, 'the second most dangerous man in London',* as Holmes himself states. However, if Moran

---

* Although Professor Moriarty was dead, Holmes probably ranked him as the first most dangerous man in London, the note on Moran's file in which he refers to the Colonel as the second most dangerous having been added by

disappeared after the Adair murder trial, possibly abroad, then any attempt by the police to arrest him would have been futile.

Moran's subsequent fate is unknown. He may have still been alive in 1914 for in *His Last Bow*, when Von Bork promises revenge, Holmes compares him to 'the late lamented Professor Moriarty', adding that Colonel Sebastian Moran had also made the same threats. But, in the absence of any qualifying adjective to suggest Moran was dead, the remark is ambiguous. If Moran were still alive, he must have then been in his late seventies or eighties.

After this, nothing more is heard of him and the old shikari, who was once Moriarty's Chief of Staff, passes at last into decent obscurity.

Holmes before the Final Problem, when he was still investigating Moriarty's criminal background.

CHAPTER FOURTEEN

RETURN TO BAKER STREET

April 1894–June 1902

'You know,' I answered, with some emotion, for I had
never seen so much of Holmes' heart before, 'that it is my
greatest joy and privilege to help you.'

Watson to Holmes: *The Adventure of the Devil's Foot*

It was at Holmes' request that Watson sold up his Kensington
practice and moved back to his old lodgings, where he was to
remain for the next eight years and three months. This must have
happened soon after Holmes' return to London in April 1894 for
by August of that year, the date of the Norwood Builder inquiry,
Watson was already installed at 221B Baker Street. In his account
of the investigation, Watson also refers to 'our months of partnership' during which two unrecorded cases had already taken
place, one concerning the papers of the ex-President Murillo,*
the other the 'shocking affair' of the Dutch steamship *Friesland*,
which so nearly cost them both their lives.

Watson sold his practice to a young doctor called Verner who,
to Watson's astonishment, paid the full asking price without
protest. It was only years later that Watson discovered that not
only had Holmes put up the money but that Dr Verner was a
distant relative of Holmes, presumably on his French grandmother's side of the family, as Verner sounds very much like an
Anglicized form of the surname Vernet.

* See Appendix One under the notes for **Wisteria Lodge**.

It was a generous gesture on Holmes' part and it was typical of him to keep the information secret for so long but his motives may not have been as disinterested as at first they seem. For it suited Holmes to have Watson living once more in Baker Street and, by using this subterfuge, he was certain of getting his own way. Although on the whole Holmes enjoyed his own company, there are signs that as he grew older – and he was now forty – he felt more in need of other people, a change of heart which the three years he had spent travelling alone may have helped to bring about. Watson supplied that companionship as well as serving other useful functions as assistant, amanuensis, confidant and, above all, appreciative audience.

Watson appears to have agreed with Holmes' suggestion without any overt protest. At least, he expresses none. And in many ways, the move may have suited him as well. He was now a widower and, although still only 42 or 43, was by the standards of the time already well into middle age. The first flush of enthusiasm at resuming his former career as a doctor may have passed. As we have seen in Chapter Ten, he found his practice 'not very absorbing' on occasions and, with the death of his wife, that feeling may have increased to the point at which the hard work and long hours no longer seemed worth the effort. While he was prepared to expend a great deal of time and energy on specific activities, such as making the Paddington practice a success or setting about the colossal task of writing and publishing the twenty-three accounts of Holmes' earlier investigations, he was always prone to take the line of least resistance and may well have allowed Holmes, with his more dominant personality, to make up his mind for him.

There were, of course, advantages from Watson's point of view. He needed companionship, more so than Holmes, and after the death of his wife must have felt particularly lonely. There was also the old lure of excitement and adventure which life with Holmes never failed to provide. But one would like to think that he felt a few pangs at selling his old home and parting with the furniture and other possessions which he and Mary had bought with so much pleasure when they had first set up house together in 1889, five years before, although no doubt he retained a few of the more personal items to take with him to Baker Street.

Although in some ways Watson may have welcomed his retirement from professional life, he may also have felt a little sad at selling up his practice. He was a good GP who had made a success of his medical career, and the decision to abandon it may not have come easily. However, although in the Red Circle case Holmes speaks of the time when Watson 'doctored', as if he were no longer actively practising, there is other evidence which might indicate that Watson continued to work as a GP if only on a more limited basis. In *The Adventure of the Veiled Lodger*, Holmes has to send a hurried note to Watson, summoning him back to Baker Street, suggesting he was absent for some reason. He may, of course, as some commentators have argued, have been merely visiting friends but it is possible, according to others, that he was acting as locum for a colleague. He may even have continued to treat a few of his more special patients, such as the Whitneys. Although he had sold his practice, he was still licensed and could therefore continue working as a doctor. Even after he had returned to Baker Street, he gave medical treatment when the need arose as, for example, in the Carfax case, when he revived Lady Frances Carfax with artificial respiration and an injection of ether. Some critics have commented a little derisively on the fact that Watson always seems to have his medical bag with him when it was needed. I find nothing unusual about this. As a doctor, Watson was used to snatching up his bag before leaving the house and experience would have taught him that any of Holmes' inquiries could end in someone getting hurt. In much the same way, Holmes always carried a magnifying glass about with him. Both the medical bag and the lens were part of their professional equipment.

However, Watson was certainly becoming out of touch professionally during this period as he acknowledges in *The Adventure of the Missing Three-Quarter* when he is introduced to Dr Leslie Armstrong, one of the heads of the medical school at Cambridge University, who had a European reputation in his particular branch of the science. 'It argues the degree in which I had lost touch with my profession that the name Leslie Armstrong was unknown to me,' Watson admits with perhaps a hint of regret. Nevertheless, he made an effort to keep abreast with some aspects of medicine. He was still reading up on surgery for in *The Adventure of the Golden Pince-Nez* he reports that he was 'deep in a recent treatise' on that subject and he was evidently interested in the comparatively new study of psychology* for in the case of the Six Napoleons, he speaks knowledgeably about monomania and the *idée fixe*.

If Watson did indeed continue to practise, if only on an occasional basis, it must have been out of professional not financial interest. He cannot have needed the money. Quite apart from any savings he may have made when a GP, the sale of his Kensington practice would have provided him with quite a large capital sum which he apparently invested in stocks and shares, the interest from which would have augmented his army pension. Holmes refers to such investments in *The Adventure of the Dancing Men*. In addition, Watson had earned other professional fees as an author on publication of the twenty-three accounts, already referred to in Chapter Twelve, which were published in this country and in America as well as appearing in volume form. But without Mary to keep a housewifely eye on the family budget, Watson reverted to his old, more extravagant bachelor habits, playing billiards with Thurston and betting on horses, the latter pursuit costing, as he himself acknowledges, 'half my wound pension'. At one point, the state of his friend's finances caused Holmes so much concern that he was forced to keep Watson's cheque book under lock and key in his desk.

Quite apart from the decision to sell his practice and move back to Baker Street, Holmes was to influence another aspect of Watson's life in his other professional role – that of author. Not to put too fine a point on it, Holmes positively forbade Watson to publish any more accounts, as Watson makes clear in *The Adventure of the Norwood Builder*, a case which occurred, as we have seen, in August 1894, not long after Holmes' return and Watson's move back to Baker Street. Holmes' 'cold and proud nature', Watson explains, 'was always averse' to 'anything in the shape of public applause' and 'he bound me in the most stringent

* Although the concepts of monomania (paranoia) and the *idée fixe* had been known since the beginning of the nineteenth century, the first serious research into abnormal psychology was carried out by J. M. Charcot at Salpêtrière, the hospital for nervous diseases outside Paris, where he studied patients suffering from hysteria. Sigmund Freud was one of Charcot's students in 1885.

terms to say no further word of himself, his methods, or his successes.'

This sounds like a case of special pleading on Watson's part. Holmes had not 'always', as he states, objected to publicity and, although he had admittedly criticized Watson's early efforts as an author, he had never issued such a strict ultimatum before. Indeed, on occasions he had positively relished the admiration which his enhanced reputation had brought him. It would seem that Holmes' attitude to publicity had changed during his three years spent travelling abroad incognito. He may also have been affected by the experience of coming so close to death at the Reichenbach Falls. Other people have undergone a similar change of outlook after a near-fatal event in which their whole philosophy of life is radically altered. In Holmes' case, it would seem he no longer desired the outward trappings of worldly success, an attitude which is seen in other aspects of his private and professional life. The work itself was its own reward, as he states in the Norwood Builder case; and in the inquiry into the missing Bruce-Partington plans, he declined Mycroft's offer of his name appearing in the honours' list with the words 'I play the game for the game's own sake,' although he accepted an emerald tie-pin from Queen Victoria in recognition of the part he had played in the recovery of the submarine plans. Later, in June 1902, he refused a knighthood for unspecified services which were probably performed on behalf of the government or the royal family. It also amused his 'sombre and cynical spirit' to allow the police to claim all the credit at the end of a successful inquiry as 'all public applause was abhorrent to him'.

Although one can sympathize with Holmes' attitude, there is nevertheless an element of selfishness about it. Watson had enjoyed enormous success as an author. What right had Holmes to deny Watson the opportunity to express this creative side to his nature or to deprive his many readers of the pleasure of seeing his accounts in print? There is, too, the suspicion that Watson was obliged to agree with the prohibition. Had he not done so, Holmes could have refused to allow him to accompany him on his investigations, thus depriving him of the very material on which his accounts were based. In short, there is the

202

unpleasant whiff of coercion about the veto which might even amount to a subtle form of blackmail.

To be fair to Holmes, the situation may not have been quite as bad as this. Watson may very well have agreed quite willingly with Holmes' decision. He had, after all, spent every hour he could spare over the past three years writing and publishing the twenty-three accounts already referred to and he may indeed have welcomed a break from his literary labours. Nevertheless, the suspicion still remains that Holmes used his more masterful personality to exert psychological pressure on Watson, as he may also have done over the sale of the Kensington practice. Part of Holmes' unwillingness to permit Watson to publish any more accounts stemmed from his dislike of Watson's style and approach to his material, an attitude he had already shown over the first two narratives to appear in print, *A Study in Scarlet* and *The Sign of Four*, as well as those he had read in manuscript. On his return to London after the Great Hiatus, Holmes undoubtedly read the further twenty-three accounts, published during his absence, and saw nothing in them to make him change his mind. Quite apart from Watson's habit of telling his stories 'wrong end foremost' and his tendency to put in too much 'poetry', by which Holmes meant descriptive passages, Holmes objected to Watson's 'fatal habit of looking at everything from the point of view of a story instead of as a scientific exercise'. It was a criticism Holmes had made before about Watson's narrative style and one which Watson countered with the same hurt and angry retort. 'Why do you not write them yourself?' he asked, with 'some bitterness'.

But Holmes' attitude was ambivalent. He evidently did not intend the prohibition to last indefinitely, for at the end of the Lady Frances Carfax inquiry, he comments that Watson might care to add the case to his annals, and he may have intended allowing Watson to write an account of his life after they both had retired from active practice, for on one occasion he refers to Watson as his 'trusted biographer'. He certainly had no objection to Watson keeping notes on the cases, for there are several references during this period to the 'extensive archives' Watson was accumulating and which were filed either in a 'long row of year books', which filled a whole shelf, or in dispatch cases, which probably included the 'battered tin dispatch box' with Watson's name and the words 'Late Indian Army' painted on its lid. This was crammed with papers, some of them relating to particularly sensitive inquiries, which Watson later deposited at his bank Cox and Co. at Charing Cross.

Towards the latter end of this period, Holmes lifted his veto to the extent of allowing Watson to publish *The Hound of the Baskervilles*, which appeared in serial form in the *Strand* between August 1901 and April 1902, and was also published in volume form in 1902. This, however, is the only account to appear in print between 1894 and 1902, although Holmes was to allow Watson to publish other chronicles in the following year, as we shall see in the next chapter. Any regret Watson may have felt over Holmes' prohibition against publication was no doubt mitigated by the number and importance of the cases in which he participated over the next eight years, some of which he was later to record. A suggested chronology of these inquiries is set out below. Readers are again referred to Appendix One for those cases for which the date is in question and for an analysis of the crimes involved.

Date	Case	First publication
April 1894*	Empty House	October 1903
April–August 1894*	(Murillo Papers; *Friesland* case)	(both unrecorded)
August 1894*	Norwood Builder	November 1903
November 1894*	Golden Pince-Nez	July 1904

(Other unrecorded cases for 1894: the repulsive story of the red leech and the terrible death of Crosby, the banker; the Addleton tragedy and the singular contents of the ancient British barrow; the Smith-Mortimer succession case; the tracking and arrest of Huret, the Boulevard assassin.)

March* 1895?	Wisteria Lodge	September–October 1908
April 1895*	(John Vincent Hardern)	(unrecorded)
April 1895*	Solitary Cyclist	January 1904

June? 1895*	Three Students	June 1904
July 1895*	Black Peter	March 1904
November 1895*	Bruce-Partington Plans	December 1908

(Other unrecorded cases for 1895; the sudden death of Cardinal Tosca; the arrest of Wilson, the notorious canary trainer.)

January 1896?	Second Stain	December 1904?
early 1896*	Veiled Lodger	February 1927
November* 1896?	Sussex Vampire	January 1924
January? 1897*	Abbey Grange	September 1904
March 1897?	(Colonel Carruthers)	(unrecorded)
March 16th 1897*	Devil's Foot	December 1910
Winter* 1897?	Red Circle	March–April 1911
December 1897?	Missing Three-Quarter	August 1904
July 1898?	Dancing Men	December 1903
August 1898?	(Two Coptic Patriarchs)	(unrecorded)
August 1898?	Retired Colourman	January 1927
January 1899?	Charles Augustus Milverton	April 1904
Summer 1899?	(Old Abrahams)	(unrecorded)
Summer 1899?	Lady Frances Carfax	December 1911
May 1900?	(Ferrers Documents; Abergavenny Murder Trial)	(both unrecorded)
May 1900?	Priory School	February 1904
May 1900?	(Conk-Singleton Forgery)	(unrecorded)
May* 1900?	Six Napoleons	May 1904
4th October* 1901?	Thor Bridge	February–March 1922
May* 1902?	Shoscombe Old Place	April 1927
June 1902*	Three Garridebs	January 1925

On reading through Watson's accounts of these investigations in sequence, several interesting and important factors emerge, one of which is Holmes' increasing involvement in cases concerning matters of state security which had European significance and which were to bring him into contact with international espionage, an experience which was to have important repercussions after his retirement. The inquiry into the missing Bruce-Partington plans was, as Mycroft pointed out, a 'vital international probem' in which Holmes had never had 'so great a chance of serving his country'.* In carrying out the investigation, Holmes would have the 'whole force of the State' at his back, should he need it. Mycroft was in a position to make such assurances, as he himself had enormous political influence, a fact which Holmes confided in Watson for the first time, adding the remark already quoted in which he states that on occasions Mycroft *was* the British Government.

The Second Stain inquiry also involved an important document, in this case a letter from a foreign ruler criticizing British colonial policy which, if it fell into the wrong hands, could cause a serious rift in Anglo-German relations, leading even to war between the two nations.[†] In fact, so serious was the situation that no less persons than Trelawney Hope, Secretary of State for European Affairs, and Lord Bellinger, Prime Minister, called on Holmes personally to ask him to take up the case (see p. 279). It is a mark of Holmes' growing influence that he was prepared to buy the letter back at any cost, even if it meant another penny on income tax.

He also continued to enhance his international reputation in France in 1894 by bringing about the arrest of Huret, the Boulevard assassin, for which he received the Legion of Honour, the only award he agreed to accept, as well as an autographed letter of thanks from the French President. The following year, 1895, the Pope again called on his services to inquire into the sudden death of Cardinal Tosca, a case which almost certainly necessitated his presence once more in Rome. He was also able to assist another religious body, the Coptic church[‡], in an inquiry involving two of its patriarchs, although Holmes appears to have conducted the investigation from Baker Street for he was engaged at the same time with the Retired Colourman case in Lewisham,

* After William II dismissed his chancellor, Bismarck, in 1890, he began enlarging the German navy. The theft of the Bruce-Partington submarine plans was almost certainly connected with the young Kaiser's naval ambitions, which so alarmed France and Russia that in 1894 they signed the Dual Alliance.

† See Appendix One.

‡ Members of the Coptic Church, which is based in Egypt, practise their own form of Christianity. The church is governed by bishops known as patriarchs.

south London. None of these foreign inquiries were recorded by Watson apart from references within the canon.

Despite his increasing fame, Holmes continued to charge his clients on a fixed scale, rarely claiming large fees and occasionally waiving payment altogether. However, although there are few references to his finances after 1894, he presumably earned enough to maintain his standard of living, although Watson reports that his tastes were 'frugal' and there are no references during this period to the epicurean little suppers and choice wines in which he had indulged himself and his guests in earlier years. But the remark he made to the Duke of Holdernesse – 'I am a poor man' – as he pocketed his Grace's cheque for £6,000, a huge sum in those days, is meant ironically, so too is the affectionate pat he gave to his notebook in which the cheque was placed. Taking the Duke's money was one way of making the man pay, quite literally, for his unjustifiable treatment of his young son, Lord Saltire.

There are subtle changes also in his attitude to Watson. Although Holmes refers to him as his 'friend and partner', he tends to treat him at times more as a secretary and even, on one occasion, almost as a bodyguard. In *The Adventure of the Norwood Builder*, Watson is requested to read a lengthy newspaper account out loud and is also expected to keep abreast of current affairs and inform Holmes of any interesting news items, as happens at the beginning of *The Adventure of the Bruce-Partington Plans*, while in the Norwood Builder case, Holmes declines Watson's help as there is unlikely to be any danger. Otherwise, he says, 'I should not dream of stirring out without you.'

Watson also had his uses as a research assistant when Holmes himself was too busy with more important matters. Holmes calls on his services in three cases: the Retired Colourman, the Solitary Cyclist and the Carfax inquiries. In the latter investigation, Watson is sent off to France to trace the whereabouts of Lady Frances Carfax. Watson's efforts were not always successful and he came in for criticism from Holmes over his methods, a response which not unnaturally angered Watson, who had done his best. But to be fair to Holmes, he gave praise where it was due and in the Retired Colourman case complimented Watson

207

on noticing the smell of paint in Josiah Amberley's house and remembering the number on the man's theatre ticket.

More significant still is Holmes' change of attitude towards such basic principles as law and justice, influenced no doubt by his increasing power and also by his near-fatal experience at the Reichenbach Falls which, as well as altering his opinion on publicity and public honours, brought about a fundamental shift in attitude towards certain moral issues. Holmes became more prepared to break the law when his own conscience told him justice was better served by contravening it. 'Once or twice in my career,' he declares to Watson in the Abbey Grange inquiry, 'I feel I have done more real harm by my discovery of the criminal than he had ever done by his crime. I have learned caution now, and I had rather play tricks with the law of England than with my own conscience.'

It was a tendency he had already shown earlier as, for example, in the Yellow Face inquiry when he suggested breaking into a cottage to discover the truth about its mysterious inhabitant, or in the Blue Carbuncle case when he allowed the thief, Ryder, to go free on the grounds that he will not steal again whereas, if he were sent to prison, he will become a 'gaolbird for life'. After the Great Hiatus, he was prepared to act even more as a maverick. He actually breaks into Amberley's house in the Retired Colour-man case, an illegal action he repeats even more spectacularly in the Charles Augustus Milverton inquiry when, equipped with a first-class, up-to-date burgling kit, probably bought specially for the occasion, Holmes, accompanied by Watson, forces an entry to Milverton's house in order to destroy the papers used by Milverton for purposes of blackmail. At first, Watson is horrified both by the illegality of the act and its consequences should Holmes be arrested. But once Holmes convinces him of the moral purpose behind the escapade, Watson, game as ever for a little excitement, eagerly joins in. He even makes the black silk masks which they wear during the burglary. 'Far from feeling guilty,' he remarks, 'I rejoiced and exulted at our dangers.'

Later, Holmes allows Milverton's murderer to escape justice even though he knows her identity, an act of leniency he also extends to Dr Sterndale for his murder of Mortimer Tregennis in the Devil's Foot case, while in the Three Students inquiry, he holds a 'private court martial' at the end of which both Bannister and Gilchrist are freed of any consequences arising from their attempt to cheat over the Fortescue Scholarship examination.

Holmes goes even further in the Abbey Grange inquiry when, with himself acting as judge and Watson as jury, they acquit Captain Croker of the murder of Sir Eustace Brackenstall, a drunken and violent brute, whom Croker has killed in a fight after Brackenstall struck his wife, Lady Brackenstall, across the face with his stick. Holmes justifies his decision with the comment that, unlike the police, he has the right to private judgement and, provided no one else is arrested for Brackenstall's death, Croker should go free.

Less justifiable, in my opinion, is Holmes' attitude at the end of the Priory School inquiry* when he agrees to withhold essential evidence from the police so that James Wilder, the Duke's illegitimate son, will not be charged with conspiracy to abduct the young Lord Saltire, on the understanding Wilder will emigrate to Australia. Wilder's crime has led to the murder of Herr Heidegger and the forcible imprisonment of a ten-year-old schoolboy under distressing conditions. Holmes' attempt to give the Duke marital advice by suggesting a reconciliation with the Duchess from whom he is separated is also difficult to accept for it shows a disturbing tendency on Holmes' part to interfere in other people's private lives, an inclination he has already shown in his behaviour towards Watson over the sale of the Kensington practice and his veto on publication.

The official police were, of course, ignorant of these occasions when Holmes withheld evidence or perverted the course of justice. Had they known, their attidue towards him might have

---

* In *The Adventure of the Blanched Soldier*, Holmes refers to 'the case which my friend Watson has described as that of the Abbey School, in which the Duke of Greyminster was so deeply involved.' This is clearly a mistaken reference to the Priory School inquiry, which involved the Duke of Holdernesse. I suggest this confusion arose over Watson's choice of pseudonyms for both the school and the Duke, designed to conceal their real identities. Watson may have originally, with Holmes' agreement, decided on the names of the Abbey School and Greyminster, but changed them, perhaps on the advice of his publishers, in order to avoid confusion with the Abbey Grange inquiry and the actual Duke of Westminster. Holmes must have been referring to his notes in which the original pseudonyms were indexed and had forgotten they had been changed.

been very different. As it was, there is a marked increase in respect and admiration, especially from Lestrade, who openly acknowledges the debt Scotland Yard owes to Holmes and his methods.

'We're not jealous of you at Scotland Yard,' Lestrade assures him at the end of the Six Napoleons case. 'No, sir, we are very proud of you, and if you came down tomorrow there's not a man, from the oldest inspector to the youngest constable, who wouldn't be glad to shake you by the hand.'

Holmes' own attitude to the police also improved, especially towards the more intelligent members of the force, such as Inspector Baynes of the Surrey Constabulary and Stanley Hopkins, a young Scotland Yard inspector, although Hopkins comes in for some criticism during the Black Peter investigation. Sadly, for Holmes genuinely liked the big Scotsman, there is no reference to Inspector 'Mac' MacDonald during this period. Perhaps he had been promoted and transferred to another force. Athelney Jones, who may have retired, also disappears from Watson's accounts.

But despite all these changes, much remained the same. Holmes still showed those manic-depressive tendencies which had been evident in his behaviour as a younger man, his 'hilarious manner' and 'spasms of merriment' which Watson observes during the Norwood Builder case alternating with more sombre moods when he was 'taciturn', not to say 'morose'. Even in his more lighthearted moments there was a 'sinister quality' about his cheerfulness which Watson has never remarked on before. In fact, the references to Holmes laughing or even smiling are much less frequent. One feels he has lost some of his sparkle and youthful zest although he still continued to be an active man who was physically very fit – more so than Watson who, in the Solitary Cyclist inquiry, had difficulty in keeping up with Holmes' faster pace. Of the two men, it was Watson who was beginning to feel his age, complaining of feeling 'rheumatic and old', in consequence of which he treated himself to the comforts of a Turkish bath. But he was no longer troubled by the wound to his leg which seems to have healed completely, and he was still agile enough to scale a six-foot-high wall at the end of the Milverton investigation.

There was no change either in Holmes' coldness of temperament and his indifference, amounting at times almost to callousness, towards other people, which Watson still had reason to deplore. He was particularly concerned over Milverton's housemaid, Agatha, to whom, under the assumed identity of Escott, a plumber, Holmes proposed marriage, solely for the purpose of gaining access to the house.

'But the girl, Holmes?' Watson cries on hearing of the engagement, to which protest Holmes responds by shrugging his shoulders. It is on this occasion that Holmes indulges in one of his rare fits of laughter, silent, inward merriment which does indeed have a sinister ring to it. Holmes' manipulation of the young woman's affections is hardly excused by the fact that she had another suitor vying for her hand. However, in the Veiled Lodger inquiry, Holmes does show compassion towards Eugenia Ronder, hideously disfigured by a circus lion.

And despite Watson's efforts to dissuade him, Holmes was still occasionally using cocaine. Although Watson had over the years 'gradually weaned him from the drug mania which had threatened once to check his remarkable career', he had not been entirely successful as he himself suggests in *The Adventure of the Devil's Foot*, in which he refers to those 'occasional indiscretions', which had helped to bring about Holmes' breakdown in health. Boredom was largely responsible for his use of drugs. Holmes was no better at dealing with tedium than he had been in the past. He himself refers to the 'insufferable fatigues of idleness' and compares his mind to 'a racing engine, tearing itself to pieces because it is not connected up with the work for which it was built.'

Nor had Holmes cured himself of another habit: that of overwork. He remained a workaholic, taking on too many cases and depriving himself of both food and sleep during some investigations. In the spring of 1897, the inevitable happened and he suffered another major breakdown in health, similar to the one he had already experienced in 1887. On the advice of his physician, Dr Moore Agar of Harley Street, who warned him that unless he rested he would never work again, Holmes, accompanied by Watson, travelled down to Cornwall where they rented a small cottage at Poldhu Bay. But even there, Holmes could not remain idle. Fascinated by the Cornish language, he had books on philology sent to him and, as happened during his earlier convalescence in Reigate, he became involved, despite Watson's objections, in an investigation, the case of the Devil's Foot, also known as 'The Cornish Horror', the outcome of which could have been fatal for them both had it not been for Watson's quick thinking and presence of mind.

When Holmes was not occupied with his professional work, there were still his hobbies to keep him busy. He continued to play the violin and to conduct his chemical experiments, long established interests of his to which he added several more: the music of the Middle Ages, the philology of the Cornish language, already referred to, and early English charters, research for which took both him and Watson to one of the university towns, almost certainly Oxford, his old Alma Mater*, where he made use of the library, probably the Bodleian. It was during this period that he found time, in the middle of the inquiry into the missing Bruce-Partington plans, to write his monograph on the polyphonic motets of Lassus, already referred to in Chapter Two.

He also maintained his interest in nature which, as we have seen, marked a change of attitude in the late 1880s when he was investigating Moriarty's criminal career. During the Black Peter case, he invites Watson to join him on a walk through the woods where they will 'give a few hours to the birds and the flowers'. As we have also seen, this interest in the countryside and the beauty of nature was linked to a longing for a quiet, private life and this was still very much in Holmes' thoughts. He was already making specific plans for his retirement for he speaks of a 'little farm of my dreams' and of devoting his 'declining years' to writing a textbook on the art of detection. Unfortunately, for it would have been of great general interest as well as of immense value to Sherlockian students, he apparently never found the time to complete this project.

But there were breaks in this punishing schedule of work. Holmes and Watson went on walks together round London, visited Covent Garden to hear a Wagner opera and also the

* See the entry for Chapter Two in Appendix One for the identification of the university that Holmes attended.

Albert Hall for a concert given by Carina, dined out at an Italian restaurant, Goldini's, and even went trout-fishing in Berkshire as part of their cover during the Shoscombe Old Place inquiry, the only instance of either of them showing any interest in this particular country sport. In 1895, at the end of the Black Peter inquiry, they both went to Norway for a holiday, a trip no doubt prompted by the Norwegian connections of the case although, with the investigation over, their visit was purely for pleasure.

Watson must have benefited from these social outings as much as Holmes for it cannot have been easy for him to share lodgings with someone of such exasperating habits and so volatile a temperament, especially as he had known the pleasures of owning his own home and following his own daily routine, however humdrum it may have seemed at times. Generally speaking, Watson tolerated it all with remarkable stoicism although there were occasions when even his patience was sorely tried and he expressed a not unnatural exasperation. These instances, however, are less frequent than they were in the earlier period (1881–9) when they shared lodgings.

On the whole Watson expresses far more admiration than criticism of Holmes, that 'extraordinary man', as he once refers to him. It was an admiration amounting at times to reverence. One of the reasons Watson agrees not to publish any accounts during this period is his fear that he might, by overburdening his readers, damage Holmes' reputation, 'a man whom above all others I revere'. Watson had always had a tendency towards hero-worship, seen in his admiration of General Gordon and Henry Ward Beecher and, as Holmes' reputation increased internationally, so Watson's regard for him grew proportionately. After the death of his wife, Watson also relied more and more on Holmes for that companionship for which he naturally craved. It was an attitude which left him vulnerable to criticism. However, although Holmes was still capable of hurting Watson's feelings, as for example during the case of the Three Students when he remarks that, as the inquiry is more mental than physical, it is unlikely to interest him, Watson was more than compensated by those other occasions when Holmes allowed his defences to drop and openly expressed his real feelings. This happened at the end of the Three Garridebs case when, thinking Watson was seriously

213

injured when Killer Evans fires at him, Holmes shows a genuine concern. 'It was worth a wound – it was worth many wounds – to know the depth of loyalty and love which lay behind that cold mask,' Watson remarks, adding that it was the first time he caught a glimpse of 'a great heart as well as a great brain'. Holmes shows a similar concern at the end of the Devil's Foot inquiry when his experiment with the West African poisonous root almost had fatal consequences, a response which prompted Watson's reply, quoted in the heading to this chapter.

This friendship and companionship, together with the opportunities for adventure and excitement which his association with Holmes afforded him, helped Watson to recover gradually from his wife's death. He had always been susceptible to female charm, and women in turn found him attractive. As we have seen, Holmes teased him sometimes on this subject, referring to the 'fair sex' as being his 'department'. But although Watson continued to feel concern for Holmes' female clients, going to the trouble, for example, of reporting that, after the conclusion of the Solitary Cyclist case, Miss Violet Smith inherited a large fortune and married Cyril Morton, her faithful suitor, it was not until the Abbey Grange inquiry in 1897 that Watson felt any real plucking at his heart strings at the sight of a beautiful woman. She was Lady Brackenstall, blonde, golden-haired, blue-eyed; very similar in colouring, in fact, to his late wife Mary, who was also fair-haired.

But when, towards the end of this period, Watson finally lost his heart and fell in love for the second time, it was with a young woman of an entirely different complexion. It was also an *affaire de coeur* which very nearly brought about an end to his friendship with Sherlock Holmes.

CHAPTER FIFTEEN

MARRIAGE AND PARTING

June 1902–October 1903

'I was nearer to him than anyone else, and yet I was always conscious of a gap between.'

Watson on Holmes: *The Adventure of the Illustrious Client*

The identity of the woman with whom Watson fell in love and whom he later married is not recorded. Watson himself makes no reference to her at all and our knowledge of the existence of the second Mrs Watson depends entirely on one single, brief statement made by Holmes in *The Adventure of the Blanched Soldier* in which he reports: 'The good Watson had at that time deserted me for a wife, the only selfish action which I can recall in our association.' To drive home the point, he adds, with a touch of self-dramatization, 'I was alone.' He quite clearly feels hard done by and sorry for himself.

Because of Watson's total silence about his second marriage, some commentators have doubted if it ever took place. Instead, they suggest that Watson's 'sad bereavement' during the Great Hiatus of 1891–4 refers either to the death of a child or to a serious breakdown in Mrs Watson's health, and they ascribe her disappearance from Watson's accounts after 1894 and his return to Baker Street to her long-term illness. She was, they argue, in a sanatorium where Watson visited her regularly. On her recovery, Watson went back to live with her: hence Holmes' reference to 'a wife'.

Quite apart from the lack of evidence to support these theories and their failure to explain satisfactorily Watson's silence over the matter, both Watson's and Holmes' choice of words alone would tend to refute them. If Mary Watson had been seriously ill, Watson would hardly have described this as a 'sad bereavement'. Nor would Holmes have referred to her as 'a wife'. If Watson had left him to return to Mary, whom Holmes knew quite well, it would be more natural to use the term 'his wife'. Other evidence within the canon also points to the existence of a second Mrs Watson. But who was she? Where and when did Watson meet her? When were they married? And why was Watson so careful never to refer to her in his accounts?

One theory suggesting she was Watson's housekeeper after he moved out of the Baker Street lodgings whom he married merely for practical reasons and was too ashamed to mention is not, in my opinion, tenable. Watson was a romantic man who was much more likely to marry for love than for such mundane considerations. And why should he go to the trouble of marrying her? Or, come to that, why should he even move out of Baker Street, where his material needs were well looked after by Mrs Hudson?

However, before any attempt is made to name the second Mrs Watson, it is important to try to establish the date of the marriage, if only approximately, for her identification depends largely on this factor.

It is clear that at the time of the Three Garridebs inquiry, a case which Watson positively assigns to June 1902, he was still unmarried and living in Baker Street. But by 3rd September 1902, the date of the Illustrious Client inquiry, Watson had already moved out of the Baker Street lodgings and was not only living in his own rooms in Queen Anne Street but was again practising as a doctor, facts which most commentators agree are connected with his second marriage. It is therefore often assumed that the wedding must have taken place between June and September 1902. However, as we shall see later in the chapter, Watson's marriage plans were probably more complex than this.

One fact at least emerges from the information set out above: Watson must have met the woman he was later to marry at some date before September 1902. This immediately rules out one candidate whom some commentators have put forward as the second Mrs Watson: Violet de Merville, who features in the

Illustrious Client case. Watson had already moved into Queen Anne Street and resumed his medical career before this investigation took place.

Other factors also mitigate against her. Violet de Merville was not the type of woman whom Watson would have found attractive. Young, rich and beautiful, she had fallen obsessively in love with Baron Gruner, a charming but highly undesirable suitor with a criminal past, whom Holmes suspected of murder and from whom her family was trying to separate her with Holmes' assistance. She was also self-willed, spoilt and, despite her passion for the Baron, a hard-hearted woman whom Holmes himself accused of 'supreme self-complaisance'. Watson preferred women of a softer and more agreeable nature. Neither would she, with her longings for a romantic lover like Baron Gruner, a wealthy man with an aristocratic and fascinatingly mysterious background, have been attracted to Watson, a middle-aged widower and a relatively dull and humble GP. The social conventions of the time would not have encouraged such a match either. Violet de Merville was the daughter of General de Merville who had friends in high places, including Sir James Damery, who asks Holmes to take up the case and who was, as Holmes himself says, 'a household name in society'. Sir James was acting on behalf of an even more illustrious client who, Watson hints, had ducal if not royal connections. It has even been suggested that he was none other than Edward VII. In short, Watson was not sufficiently wealthy nor of a high enough social rank to make such a marriage likely. There is no evidence either that Watson ever met her. When Holmes goes to her house to interview her, he is accompanied only by Kitty Winter, the Baron's former mistress. Watson is not present. Lastly, and I believe conclusively, Watson had, as stated earlier, already met the young woman whom he was later to marry. By the time of the Illustrious Client case, he had certainly moved out of Baker Street and was again in practice as a GP, two factors which, as we have seen, are generally accepted as related to his second marriage.

However, there is one young woman whom Watson had already met by June 1902 and who possessed many of the qualities he would have looked for in a prospective wife. Moreover, she was, like Mary Morstan, his first wife, a governess and therefore came from Watson's own middle-class background. There are also other similarities between the two women and Watson's feelings towards them which are too striking to be coincidental. This theory concerning her identity would also explain Watson's unprecedented silence about her, a reticence which he had not shown over his first wife, about whom he has given his readers a great deal of information in *The Sign of Four*, including an account of her background as well as details of his courtship of her and their subsequent married life together. The young woman in question is Grace Dunbar.

Watson first met her during the Thor Bridge investigation into the death of Mrs Gibson, the wife of Neil Gibson, the American gold millionaire. At the time Holmes took up the case, Grace Dunbar, governess to the Gibson children, had been arrested for the murder of Mrs Gibson, found shot dead on a bridge in the grounds of Thor Place, the Gibson family home, and was in Winchester prison awaiting trial. In fact, Watson was introduced to her in her cell. In a lengthy passage, as detailed as his account of his initial meeting with Mary Morstan thirteen years earlier, Watson describes her appearance and his reactions on seeing her for the first time. 'I had expected from all we had heard to see a beautiful woman,' he writes in *The Problem of Thor Bridge*, 'but I can never forget the effect which Miss Dunbar produced upon me.'

It was not only her beauty which captivated him. As with Mary Morstan, he was impressed by the sensitivity of her features which expressed 'a nobility of character' and was touched, too, by 'the appealing, helpless expression' in her dark eyes.

Although physically the two women were very different, Grace Dunbar being a tall brunette with a commanding presence, whereas Mary Morstan had been a small, dainty blonde, there are many similarities in the two descriptions. As well as Watson's immediate attraction towards them both, he also felt an urge to protect them combined with an admiration of their courage in facing life alone. Mary Morstan was an orphan who worked to support herself; Grace Dunbar had dependants who relied on her financially. In fact, Watson was so taken by Grace Dunbar that the short journey from Winchester to Thor Place seemed intolerably long to him in his impatience for Holmes to begin work on the case and prove her innocence, which Holmes eventually succeeds in doing.

At the end of the Thor Bridge inquiry, Holmes comments that, now Grace Dunbar has been cleared of the murder charge, it seems 'not unlikely' that she and Neil Gibson will marry. It is a curiously negative statement as if Holmes himself was not convinced of its likelihood. If he were aware, as seems highly likely, of Watson's feelings towards the young woman, the comment could be wishful thinking on Holmes' part for, if she married Gibson, it would place her beyond Watson's reach.

But a marriage between Gibson and Grace Dunbar is, I believe, out of the question. Gibson is a violent and cunning man, hated by his servants, one of whom, his estate manager, comes specially to Baker Street to warn Holmes about him. Gibson, the manager declares, is a brute and 'an infernal villain'. On Gibson's own admission, it is because of his ill-treatment of her that his wife, a passionate and neurotic Brazilian, was driven to commit suicide in such a way as to throw suspicion of murder on Grace Dunbar to whom Gibson had transferred his attentions. Far from welcoming his advances, Grace Dunbar had threatened to leave Thor Place and was only persuaded to remain by Gibson's assurances that he would stop pestering her. In addition, she had, as we have seen, dependants and, according to Gibson, she was convinced that, if she remained in her post as governess, she could influence him for the better.

None of this carries any weight in the argument that she later married him. At the time this happened, Mrs Gibson was still alive and any question of marriage between Grace Dunbar and the Gold King would not have arisen. It seems highly unlikely that, after Mrs Gibson's death and her own release from prison, Grace Dunbar, a woman of great strength and nobility of character, would have married a man whose brutal conduct had not only driven his first wife to commit suicide but had put her own life in jeopardy.

The date of the Thor Bridge inquiry is not known. Watson specifies the month only, which was October, but not the year. However, as the internal evidence makes it quite clear that Watson was still living in Baker Street, it must have occurred before September 1902 and Watson's move to Queen Anne Street.

D. Martin Dakin and Dr Zeisler, among others, suggest October 1901, a date with which I concur.

Although the rest of the theory is merely speculative, I also suggest that, after her release from prison, Grace Dunbar left Gibson's household. As she would then have been out of work, nothing would have been more natural for her than to come to London in order to visit one of the employment agencies which specialized in finding posts for governesses. Violet Hunter had made use of such an agency, Westaways, at the beginning of the Copper Beeches inquiry. And while she was in London, it would also have been quite natural for Grace Dunbar to pay a call on Holmes in Baker Street to thank him personally for his help in saving her from the gallows, an opportunity she had not had during the final stages of the Thor Bridge case. It was during this interview, I suggest, that Watson renewed his acquaintance with her, an occasion which led to further meetings and to their subsequent marriage.

This theory would also explain Watson's secrecy about the identity and even the very existence of his second wife. He would not want the general public, and in particular his patients and his readers, to know he had married a woman who had been in prison on a murder charge. Social conventions of the time would have inhibited him from publishing these facts. But there was an even more pressing reason for his silence. Gibson was a violent and revengeful man who even went as far as to threaten Holmes when he was at first reluctant to take up the case. In Watson's presence, he told Holmes, 'You've done yourself no good this morning, Mr Holmes, for I have broken stronger men than you. No man ever crossed me and was the better for it.' Had he known that Watson had married Grace Dunbar, the young woman whom he himself had hoped to marry, his desire for revenge would have been even stronger. He might have set about ruining Watson's career or even have threatened his life. Under such circumstances, it is hardly surprising that Watson omitted any reference to his second wife in the canon.

According to the evidence, Watson apparently failed to be totally frank with Holmes as well, although for entirely different motives. Knowing his old friend's strong aversion to marriage, Watson must have anticipated Holmes' reaction to the announcement that he intended marrying again. As it was, Holmes took the news badly, regarding it as a 'selfish action' on Watson's part, an attitude which reveals once more his strong urge to control other people's lives, Watson's in particular.

And from Holmes' point of view, Watson's decision to marry again was indeed selfish. At one stroke, Holmes was deprived of a friend, companion, assistant, amanuensis and all the other roles which Watson had filled over the years. It was no wonder he felt deserted and alone. Out of sheer necessity, he was forced to employ a man named Mercer, 'my general utility man who looks up routine business', as Holmes rather disparagingly refers to him in *The Adventure of the Creeping Man*. Mercer quite clearly carried out some of the duties Watson had once undertaken.* Nor is it surprising that Holmes failed to consider Watson's happiness or to appreciate that side of Watson which longed for domesticity and the love of a good woman. Watson was uxorious by nature; Holmes decidedly was not. Despite his own feelings for Irene Adler, Holmes had always scorned love as one of the softer emotions and, as he grew older, became, as many of us tend to do, less tolerant. In describing Watson's action as selfish, he was quite unaware that he himself was displaying a strong selfish disregard for Watson's needs.

Watson's second marriage was to have far-reaching repercussions. It led to a rift in his relationship with Holmes which lasted for about six months and which, even after their reconciliation, gave rise to a coolness between the two men for an even longer period. And it was to hasten Holmes' decision to retire from his professional career as a private consulting detective.

The means by which Watson set about the difficult task of informing Holmes of his intention to marry again were much more devious than is at first apparent. Although he had moved out of Baker Street by 3rd September 1902, he evidently did not inform Holmes of his second marriage until several months later,

---

* Holmes also made use of the services of Shinwell Johnson, a.k.a. Porky Shinwell, a former criminal, who, Watson reports in *The Adventure of the Illustrious Client*, had since the 'first years of the century', i.e. the early part of the 1900s, acted as Holmes' underworld agent, passing on valuable information about criminal activities. Holmes also had another useful contact, Langdale Pike, who was his 'human book of reference upon all matters of social scandal'.

after the Illustrious Client case had taken place, by which time, as we have seen, Watson was already installed in Queen Anne Street and was practising again as a GP. As the relationship between the two men was perfectly amicable during the Illustrious Client case, for they met at the Turkish baths in Northumberland Street at the beginning of the inquiry and dined twice together at Simpson's in the Strand during its investigation, one can only assume that at that time Holmes knew nothing about Grace Dunbar or Watson's feelings for her. We can, I believe, extend this theory and further assume that the marriage had not yet taken place.

It was not until five months later, in January 1903, that Holmes made his comment about Watson deserting him for a wife. The bitterness behind the remark suggests that Holmes had only recently discovered the existence of the second Mrs Watson. Moreover, Watson played no part in the Blanched Soldier inquiry which Holmes investigated on his own in January 1903 and an account of which he wrote and later published himself, an indication of a break in his relationship with Watson. In fact, it was not until June 1903 that Watson was to become involved in an investigation with Holmes, an account of which is told, curiously enough, in the third person under the title of *The Adventure of the Mazarin Stone*, the first instance within the whole of the published canon of the use of this narrative form. Indeed, its very unusualness has caused D. Martin Dakin among others to doubt if Watson wrote it, and its authorship has been variously ascribed to Watson's literary agent, to Dr Verner, who bought Watson's Kensington practice, and even to the second Mrs Watson. However, I believe that Watson was in fact the author and that he deliberately chose this narrative form in order to indicate a distancing in his relationship with Holmes. Although the breach was to some extent healed, a certain coolness remained between the two men, a state of affairs in which the use of the more impersonal third person seemed more appropriate.

Against this theory it could be argued that the nature of the material demanded this less intimate approach as many of the events in the Mazarin Stone case occurred when Watson was absent from the scene. Watson was himself aware of the potential difficulties of such a situation. As he states in *The Problem of Thor Bridge*, some of the unrecorded cases of which he had kept notes could only be told as if by a third person as he was 'either not present or played so small a part in them' to make the use of the first person viable. However, this had not prevented him in the past from invariably writing in the first person, relying on Holmes to narrate in the form of direct speech those events which Watson himself had not witnessed. Good examples of the use of this technique are seen in *The Adventure of the 'Gloria Scott'* and *The Adventure of the Musgrave Ritual*, both accounts of cases which occurred before Watson met Holmes and in both of which almost the entire narratives are given by Holmes through direct speech.

There is evidence within the account of the Mazarin Stone case to support this theory of a cooling off between the two men due to Watson's second marriage. Watson has quite clearly not been inside the Baker Street rooms for some considerable time. It has, in fact, been so long that he looks about the room, familiarizing himself again with such well-known objects as Holmes' violin case and chemistry bench. He has not seen anything of Holmes either, for he has to ask Billy the page-boy about Holmes' state of health, evidence that Holmes has not visited Watson in Queen Anne Street. There is an edginess, too, about their conversation, at least at the beginning of their meeting for, although Holmes expresses pleasure at seeing Watson again in his 'old quarters', he goes on to add, as he indicates the gasogene, that he hopes alcohol is permitted and that Watson has not learned to despise his, Holmes', pipe and 'lamentable tobacco', remarks which I take to be a sardonic comment on the possible influence of the second Mrs Watson on her husband's tastes and habits in the intervening months since the two men had met.

Nevertheless, after this initial sarcasm, Holmes quickly relents and the conversation between the two men soon assumes its former, easy familiarity with Holmes teasing Watson and referring to him as 'my old friend', although there is a valedictory ring to one of his later comments. When Watson declares that he cannot leave Holmes alone with Sam Merton, a dangerous and desperate man, Holmes replies, 'Yes, you can, Watson. And you will, for you have never failed to play the game. I am sure you will play it to the end.'

At that period, the acknowledgement that someone had 'played the game' was one of the highest compliments one Englishman could pay to another. In praising Watson in this manner, Holmes seems to be looking back over his shoulder, as it were, at Watson's role in their relationship and, while endorsing Watson's outstanding qualities as a friend, is also signalling that the time for parting has almost come.

And yet, despite this resumption of their relationship, some lingering reserve remains. It is still evident, I believe, as late as September 1903 at the time of the Creeping Man inquiry, in his account of which Watson admits outright that 'the relations between us in those latter days were peculiar'. Watson goes on to explain that Holmes had come to regard him as a habit or an institution, like his violin and his shag tobacco. Although Watson had his uses, Holmes was nevertheless exasperated by a 'certain methodical slowness in my mentality' which served to 'make his own flamelike intuitions and impressions flash up the more vividly and swiftly'. 'Such', Watson adds with a touch of sadness, 'was my humble role in our alliance.' There is a similar quality of valediction about these remarks, particularly the last one, as if Watson is also standing back from his relationship with Holmes and seeing it clearly for the first time.

But if Holmes was exasperated by Watson's slowness of mentality, Watson, too, was annoyed at times by Holmes' behaviour to an extent which he has not expressed in quite so critical a manner since the early days of 1881–9 when they had first shared the Baker Street lodgings. It was caused by the demands Holmes was making on his time.

His new practice in Queen Anne Street was 'not inconsiderable', as he himself describes it. It was also in a fashionable part of the West End and in the heart of London's most exclusive medical district, centred on Harley Street where all the best and most expensive specialists had their consulting rooms. Holmes' own physician, Dr Moore Agar, had his practice in Harley Street. Situated not far from Portland Place and within walking distance of Regent's Park and the gardens of Cavendish Square, Queen Anne Street, which crosses Harley Street, remains much as Watson knew it at the turn of the century, apart from some modern redevelopment. Architecturally, it is more interesting than Baker Street. The tall houses of four or more storeys with their narrow basements are built in a variety of styles from the classic simplicity of the eighteenth century with its preference for plain brick or half-stuccoed façades and simple sash windows to a more exuberant taste for decorated bays, mansard roofs and imposing balustrades.

This third practice must have cost Watson more than the run-down one in Paddington or the smaller one in Kensington, and it is a minor mystery, given his mishandling of his personal finances and his weakness for betting on horses, how he managed to afford it. Grace Dunbar, with dependants relying on her for support, cannot have contributed much from just her governess's salary, unless Gibson presented her with a cheque when she left his employment as compensation for all she had suffered through his conduct. Watson had, of course, the capital from the sale of the Kensington practice as well as his fees as an author, which he may have augmented by a lucky win at the races or shrewd investment in stocks and shares. However he managed it financially, the move to Queen Anne Street was a step up the professional ladder and there is every sign that, as a newly-married man, Watson threw himself as enthusiastically into making this practice a success as he had at Paddington when he and Mary had first set up home together.

He was certainly kept busy. After he has given medical treatment to Baron Gruner in the Illustrious Client case, Watson has to hurry away as he is 'overdue', presumably for one of his own patients. These professional commitments made him less tolerant of the demands Holmes made on his time. Summoned to Baker Street by one of Holmes' 'laconic messages' at the beginning of the Creeping Man inquiry, Watson was disappointed to discover that the apparent purpose behind the request for his presence was to discuss dogs, about which Holmes was thinking of writing a monograph. 'Was it for so trivial a question as this that I had been summoned from my work?' Watson asks himself, not without justification. Although amusing, the contents of Holmes' message, 'Come at once if convenient – if inconvenient come all the same', sound peremptory and also show scant regard for Watson's professional duties.

Watson expresses a similar impatience during the Creeping

Man inquiry, in which Holmes expects him to spend several days at one of the university towns, helping him to investigate Professor Presbury's strange behaviour. It was, Watson points out, 'an easy task on the part of Holmes, who had no roots to pull up, but one which involved frantic planning and hurrying on my part, as my practice was by this time not inconsiderable.' Holmes' thoughtlessness is inexcusable as he was perfectly well aware of Watson's professional commitments. In *The Adventure of the Mazarin Stone*, he remarks that Watson bears 'every sign of a busy medical man, with calls on him every hour.'

And yet, despite these occasions when Watson's tolerance was sorely tried, he still remained a loyal and caring friend. When he heard of the murderous attack on Holmes during the Illustrious Client case, a 'pang of horror' passed through his 'very soul' and, for the next six days, he visited Holmes regularly. He was also willing to spend a great deal of time learning about Chinese ceramics at Holmes' request even though Holmes, with his love of secrecy, failed to tell him to what purpose this acquired knowledge would be put. 'By long experience I had learned the wisdom of obedience,' Watson remarks resignedly as he sets off to borrow a book on the subject from the London Library in St James's Square where, incidentally, the sub-librarian, Lomax, is a friend of his.

To return to the subject of Watson's marriage, I believe that, given the evidence set out above, we can, by making reasonable assumptions, chart out the events leading up to this event. Having met Grace Dunbar again after the end of the Thor Bridge inquiry, Watson continued to meet her clandestinely, keeping all knowledge of their developing relationship secret from Holmes. At some time between June and September 1902, they agreed to marry but Watson, knowing what Holmes' reaction would be, decided to approach this delicate matter circumspectly. His first action, therefore, was to move out of Baker Street into his own apartment in Queen Anne Street and to resume his medical career. It is not known what excuse he gave to Holmes. It may have been financial; he needed the money. Or he may simply have expressed a desire to return to active practice as a GP.

Although Holmes cannot have been pleased with Watson's decision, he apparently took it philosophically. As we have seen, there is no indication of any break in their relationship during the Illustrious Client case. The rift came not long before January 1903 when Grace Dunbar and Watson married, probably quietly in a registry office,[†] and Holmes realized the full extent of Watson's so-called desertion. In fact, they did not see one another again until June 1903, after which, as has already been observed, there still remained a certain reserve between them.

In setting out the suggested chronology of the cases belonging to this period, I have inserted in italics this other information regarding Watson's second marriage and its effect on his relationship with Holmes in order that this pattern of events is made quite clear. Readers are again referred to Appendix One for an explanation of the dating of some of the cases and an analysis of the crimes involved. Some of these cases have already been set out in the chronology in Chapter Fourteen. Because of their relevance to the events described above, I have repeated them here.

Date	Case	First publication
October* 1901?	Thor Bridge	February–March 1922
	Watson meets Grace Dunbar	
May* 1902?	Shoscombe Old Place	April 1927
June 1902*	Three Garridebs	January 1925
	Between June and September Watson moves to	
	Queen Anne Street and resumes his medical career	
September 1902*	Illustrious Client	February–March 1925
	December 1902 or early January 1903 Watson	
	marries Grace Dunbar	
January 1903*	Blanched Soldier	November 1926
	Told by Holmes.	
	Reference to Watson's marriage.	
	Rift between Holmes and Watson.	
June 1903?	Mazarin Stone	October 1921
	Told in the 3rd Person.	
	Relationship between Holmes and Watson resumed.	

† Mr Hilton Cubitt married his American bride, Elsie Patrick, at a registry office ceremony. See *The Adventure of the Dancing Men*.

| July 1903* | Three Gables | October 1926 |
| September 1903* | Creeping Man | March 1923– |

It should be pointed out that several commentators, among them D. Martin Dakin, have questioned the authenticity of some of these accounts. As readers may see from the chronology, all the dates of first publication belong to a much later period, 1921 to 1926, and for this reason I propose dealing with this contentious subject in the epilogue, which covers that stage in Holmes' and Watson's lives, although one aspect of it relating to *The Adventure of the Three Gables* must be examined now as it has a direct bearing on Holmes' state of mind at this particular time.

This account has evoked much criticism largely because of the racist attitude Holmes shows towards Stevie Dixon, the Negro boxer. Two of his remarks are especially offensive: 'I shan't ask you to sit down for I don't like the smell of you' and his retort, as he reaches into his pocket, that he is looking not for his gun but for his scent bottle. Holmes has not shown such overt racism before. In fact, in the Yellow Face inquiry, he treats Mrs Munro's little half-caste daughter, the product of her marriage in America with John Hebron, a Negro, with sympathy and makes no disparaging comment either about the child or Mrs Munro's first husband. Nor does he remark on Daulat Ras, the Indian undergraduate, in the Three Students inquiry. However, Holmes was a product of his age and it should be pointed out that the Victorians tended to regard uneducated people of non-white races as uncivilized.

It should also be pointed out that Stevie Dixon is a thoroughly unpleasant character, a 'bruiser' whom Holmes suspects of killing a young man called Perkins outside the Holborn Bar. In dealing with any violent or brutal men, as for example Neil Gibson in the Thor Bridge case or Dr Roylott in the Speckled Band inquiry, both of them white, Holmes shows no compunction in expressing his dislike of them. Nevertheless, it must be admitted that, until the Three Gables case, Holmes had never before shown his contempt for another human being in quite so blatant a manner. The remarks are unworthy of him.

If it is any defence, which I doubt, it should be added that Holmes had an 'abnormally acute set of senses', to quote his own words in *The Adventure of the Blanched Soldier*, and his sense of smell was quite clearly offended by Dixon's lack of personal freshness, although this does not excuse his sneering references to it.

Another reason for Holmes' exceptional rudeness may be attributed to his mental health at this particular period. He was showing definite signs of stress, brought on by many years of over-work and almost certainly exacerbated by Watson's departure from Baker Street and his second marriage. Watson himself describes the 'gap of loneliness and isolation which surrounded the saturnine figure of the great detective'. In that loneliness, Holmes had reverted to using drugs again as Watson reports in *The Adventure of the Creeping Man* in which he refers obliquely to 'less excusable habits' in which his old friend was indulging. He was also not eating properly and had lost weight to such an extent that Billy, the page-boy, was anxious about his health. It is clear that Holmes was close to another breakdown.

There are signs, too, that he was becoming more eccentric in his behaviour. In the Mazarin Stone inquiry, having recovered the stolen gem, Holmes slips it into Lord Cantlemere's pocket, much to that elderly peer's bewilderment. Holmes tries to pass off this bizarre behaviour as an 'impish' example of his love of practical jokes. But Lord Cantlemere is much nearer the truth in describing it as 'perverted'. He seldom laughed either, as Watson, or rather the anonymous narrator, remarks in his account of the same case, and his periods of abstraction were becoming more extreme. Having summoned Watson to Baker Street at the beginning of the Creeping Man inquiry, Holmes sits huddled silently in his armchair for half an hour as he ponders over the problems of the case, quite oblivious of Watson's presence in the room.

It is therefore not surprising, even if it is still inexcusable, that given the stress Holmes was under and these signs of growing eccentricity, those quirks of personality which had always been apparent, such as his outspokenness and his disregard for other people's feelings, should be accentuated to such a degree that his behaviour became at times socially unacceptable.

His work was also suffering. In the Creeping Man inquiry, Holmes castigates himself for missing vital clues which would

229

have led to an earlier solution of the case. In fact, only a few weeks* after this investigation, which occurred in September 1903 and which Watson reports was one of the last cases Holmes was to undertake, Holmes decided to retire. 'It is surely time that I disappeared into the little farm of my dreams,' he tells Watson.

Holmes, whose sense of the dramatic was one of the strongest features of his personality, knew when to quit the stage, although this was not to be his final curtain call.

* See Chapter Sixteen for the theory regarding the date of Holmes' retirement.

SUSSEX AND QUEEN ANNE STREET

October 1903–July 1907

'. . . since he [Holmes] has definitely retired from London
to Sussex and betaken himself to study and bee-farming
on the Sussex Downs, notoriety has become hateful to
him . . .'.

Watson: *The Adventure of the Second Stain*

Although the precise date of Holmes' retirement from active
practice is unknown, we have already established that it was not
long after September 1903, the date of the Creeping Man case. I
suggest it took place in early October, a theory which will be
explained in detail later in the chapter when the publication dates
of some of Watson's accounts are more fully examined.

It is not known either why Holmes chose Sussex as the place
to which to retire. One reason could have been his familiarity
with the area. He knew it well, having visited it during at least
four investigations: the Musgrave Ritual, the Valley of Fear, the
Sussex Vampire and the Black Peter inquiries. In fact, it was the
location of the third case Holmes was called on to investigate, the
Musgrave Ritual affair, during which he came to the decision to
become a professional private consulting detective and, although
sentiment played little part in Holmes' personality, he may have
remembered the area with particular affection. Certainly he was
struck by the beauty of its countryside for during the Black Peter
case he took time off from his inquiries to walk with Watson in
the 'beautiful woods' to admire the birds and the flowers.

From a practical point of view, Sussex was an ideal setting for retirement. It was not far from London and, had Holmes wished, he could have travelled easily by train to Victoria station and from there to the Albert Hall, Covent Garden or St James's Hall to attend concerts and the opera, although there is no evidence in the canon of his having done so. But as he no doubt took his gramophone and records with him when he retired, as well as his violin, he could still enjoy the pleasure of listening to and making music.

Sussex is also a coastal county, with a long shoreline facing south towards the English Channel, where in the past fishing ports such as Hastings and, more recently, popular seaside resorts, for example Brighton and Eastbourne, have grown up. But, despite the development of some of these resorts and other urban areas in more modern times, Sussex still remains an agricultural county given over largely to sheep and arable farming. In Holmes' time, it was even more rural and parts of it, as can be seen from the isolated setting of, for example, Ferguson's house in the Sussex Vampire case, which was situated at the end of a long, winding lane, remained unspoilt.

The house which Holmes bought for his retirement was in such an undeveloped part of the county. Although not far from Lewes, the county town of East Sussex, a picturesque place of historic buildings and steep, narrow streets, it was isolated from any near neighbours. Standing alone on the southern slope of the South Downs, a continuation of the broad chalk uplands which extend from the borders of Hampshire to Beachy Head, it had views over the cliffs to the sea beyond and was within walking distance of the beach, which was reached by a steep path. The setting was superb.

Although attempts have been made by some Sherlockian scholars to identify the house, its exact location will probably never be established. Holmes valued his privacy and, in the same way that Watson altered certain details so that 221B Baker Street could not be precisely located, Holmes deliberately included false information in his description of the setting of his house to throw potential sight-seers off the scent. The names of the nearest village, Fulworth, and Fulworth Cove on which it was built, are inventions, for no such places exist. Little is known either of its physical appearance. It is variously described by both Holmes and Watson as a house, a villa and a farm, but as the adjectives most often applied to it are 'small' or 'little' it is safe to assume that it was a modest building with some land attached to it and may have originally been what is usually referred to as a smallholding.

Holmes was happy there. As he himself expresses it, 'I had given myself up entirely to that soothing love of Nature for which I had so often yearned during the long years spent amid the gloom of London.' He describes with obvious pleasure the 'thyme-scented Downs' and the beauty of the coast with its long shingle beach, extending for several miles, broken only by Fulworth Cove and by the rock pools, scattered along its length, which were filled by each new tide with sea-water as clear as crystal and which served as convenient bathing pools for Holmes and other residents in the area.

As we have already seen, this love of nature had begun to develop before the Great Hiatus when Holmes, tired of London and exhausted by the heavy demands made on him by his professional career, turned to a contemplation of nature for solace and relaxation. After his retirement, he benefited both psychologically and physically from the change in environment and lifestyle and, as the signs of stress which had marked his latter months in Baker Street gradually disappeared, he became more sociable and relaxed. His daily routine was simple and healthy. He went for walks, he swam regularly every morning, he read, and he tended his bees, a new interest, the relevance of which in connection with his childhood and his relationship with his mother has already been referred to in Chapter One, although, as was pointed out there, Holmes himself may not have been aware of the symbolic significance of the queen bee.

He was, however, conscious of another parallel. The bee-hive with its 'little working gangs' reminded him of London's criminal underworld, an unusual comparison which suggests the wide gulf which now existed between this new Holmes and his former self as a private consulting detective. No longer involved emotionally or professionally in the world of crime, he could now stand back and regard it with an aloof detachment.

Watson's reference to bee-farming, quoted in the heading to

this chapter, could imply that Holmes' apicultural activities were not confined to keeping a few hives for his own use and he may have been running a small commerical enterprise, selling honey to local shopkeepers and residents. The thyme, growing wild on the Downs, would have given the honey a pleasantly distinctive flavour.

Writing still remained one of his interests. During his retirement, Holmes wrote and published his *Practical Handbook of Bee Culture, with some Observations upon the Segregation of the Queen*, the 'fruit of my leisured ease', as Holmes himself describes it, and the *magnum opus* of his latter years. He was obviously proud of this product of 'pensive nights and laborious days' for, when he finally had the opportunity to show it to Watson, he declares, 'Alone I did it.' No doubt he intended the remark to be a wry reminder that so much of his life had been chronicled, not by himself, but by his old friend and former close companion. It was a small book, bound in blue with the title printed in gold across the cover. Unfortunately, no copies of it have survived. Nor apparently was he to find the time to produce the other volume he had intended writing, his textbook on the art of deduction, referred to in Chapter Fourteen. Perhaps, once he had retired, he no longer wished to be reminded of the life he had left behind.

There were other hobbies and interests to fill his time. He remained an 'omnivorous reader' as he himself states, and he took his books with him from Baker Street which presumably included his encyclopaedias, his commonplace books of newspaper cuttings as well as all the other records of the hundreds of cases he had investigated during the twenty-three years he had been in active practice in London. There were so many volumes that some had to be stored in the attic of his house which, Holmes reports, was 'stuffed with books'. Others, the ones he needed for more regular reference, were no doubt kept on shelves in the main rooms. He also mentions a bureau, almost certainly the desk fitted with pigeon-holes which used to stand in the sitting-room of 221B Baker Street and which he took with him when he moved. Other furniture was presumably bought especially for the Sussex house, as Mrs Hudson owned the contents of Holmes' old lodgings. Knowing Holmes' ascetic tastes, the house was probably furnished very simply with only the barest essentials.

Another new interest was photography. In the Lion's Mane inquiry, a case which occurred in July 1907, Holmes was evidently skilful enough at this particular hobby to produce an enlarged photograph of the injuries to Fitzroy McPherson's back, the victim of a mysterious and apparently murderous attack. Holmes may very well have developed and enlarged the print himself. He had the necessary knowledge of chemistry to carry out the process and the equipment was available for amateurs. If so, he must have set up his own dark-room on the premises. Photography may have replaced his earlier interest in chemical experimentation for there is no reference to any such research during his retirement.

Apart from these activities, there were social contacts as well. Although Holmes reports that 'the good Watson had passed almost beyond my ken', Watson travelled from London occasionally for weekend visits, presumably alone as there is no reference to his wife accompanying him on these trips. There were also other friends and acquaintances to visit and who paid calls on Holmes, in particular Harold Stackhurst who owned a private school, The Gables, half a mile away, where about twenty young men were coached for entry into various professions by a staff of several teachers.

Holmes met Stackhurst soon after he retired to Sussex and struck up an immediate friendship with him on such good terms that the two men called on one another in the evenings without waiting to be invited, another indication of Holmes' more relaxed attitude to life. When he was living in London, he would not have encouraged such easy-going informality on so short an acquaintance and the calls he made even on Watson, a long-standing friend, were infrequent. To a certain extent, Stackhurst replaced Watson as Holmes' companion. Like Watson, Stackhurst was a cheerful, athletic man, a former well-known rowing Blue, who shared Holmes' pleasure in walking and swimming. A graduate of either Oxford or Cambridge University, Stackhurst was also an excellent all-round scholar, a distinction to which Watson, with his less academic education, could not hope to aspire. Holmes also had contact, although not so close, with some members of Stackhurst's staff, including Fitzroy McPherson, the science master, with whom he would also have had common interests, and he became acquainted at least with the more unsociable Ian Murdoch, the mathematics coach, a taciturn man who made no friends.

Holmes was also on good terms with the local policeman, Anderson, whom he describes as a 'big, ginger-moustached man of the slow, Sussex breed', a breed which, Holmes hastens to add, 'covers much good sense under a heavy, silent exterior.' This tolerant attitude is a far cry from the exasperation he had shown towards Watson's 'methodical slowness' of mentality in the months prior to his retirement.

Inevitably, despite his dislike of publicity, Holmes' reputation as a private consulting detective had followed him to Sussex. Anderson was aware of it. So, too, was Inspector Bardle who, when called in to inquire into the death of Fitzroy McPherson, refers to Holmes' 'immense experience' in criminal investigation, while Stackhurst, in pleading with Holmes to use his powers when a similar attack is made on another of his staff, Ian Murdoch, speaks of his 'world-wide reputation'.

But not every facet of Holmes's personality was altered on his retirement, as is made evident during the Lion's Mane inquiry. He was still prone to secrecy. When Inspector Bardle asks him if he has any idea what has caused the strange weals on McPherson's back, Holmes replied enigmatically, 'Perhaps I have. Perhaps I haven't.' He was also willing to take the law into his own hands when necessary, suggesting that Murdoch's rooms should be secretly searched in his absence, a clandestine operation in which, incidentally, Stackhurst collaborates, in much the same way as Watson has assisted in the past with some of Holmes' other illegal activities.

And Holmes was still subject to exaggeration on occasions. In the opening sentence of his account of the case, *The Adventure of the Lion's Mane*, he describes the mystery of McPherson's death as being as 'abstruse and unusual as any I have faced in my professional career' and one which, as he states a little later, brought him to the limits of his powers. This is an overestimation of the importance and difficulty of the inquiry. Compared to such

236

earlier cases as the Hound of the Baskervilles or the Second Stain, the Lion's Mane inquiry is relatively straightforward, its unusualness depending solely on the means by which McPherson met his death.

In carrying out the investigation, Holmes shows a distinct waning of his skills, perhaps through lack of use. It was almost four years since he had last undertaken a major inquiry. Or increasing age may have blunted his former mental agility; he was fifty-five. It took him over a week to realize the significance of McPherson's dying words, 'the lion's mane', and to relate them to a passage he had once read in the book *Out of Doors* by J. G. Wood, a copy of which was in his attic. A younger Holmes, with his capacity for storing information and recalling it at will, an ability referred to in Chapter One, would not have taken so long to remember the relevant passage with its detailed description of *Cyanea capillata*.*

Holmes himself may have been aware of this diminution in his mental powers for he compares his mind to 'a crowded box-room with packets of all sorts stored therein—so many that I may well have but a vague perception of what was there.' This is in sharp contrast to the description he had given to Watson before the Study in Scarlet inquiry twenty-six years earlier, in which he speaks of a man's brain as being like 'an empty attic' which each individual has to stock as he or she chooses. It was the fool who kept the lumber. The wise man stored only that knowledge which was useful to him, discarding everything else.

But in one significant area of his life, Holmes underwent a fundamental change of heart which, like his increased forbearance and sociability, shows a more sympathetic response to other people. This was his attitude to women. Even before his retirement, he was already becoming less intolerant of them. In 1902, during the case of the Illustrious Client, he had expressed concern for Violet de Merville. Although exasperated by her pride and

---

* *Cyanea capillata* or the Lion's Mane jellyfish is fairly common off the British coast. It has many fine tentacles which hang down from a reddish-brown bell and which may extend for several yards. The bell can grow to 40 inches or 100 centimetres in width. Although its sting is dangerous, it is not usually fatal unless the victim is suffering from a weak heart, as is the case with Fitzroy McPherson.

supreme self-complaisance, he was sufficiently moved by the thought of her fate, should she marry Baron Gruner, to remark: 'I was sorry for her, Watson. I thought of her for the moment as I would have thought of a daughter of my own.'

He was even more affected by Maud Bellamy whom he met during the Lion's Mane inquiry. 'Women have seldom been an attraction for me, for my brain has always governed my heart,' Holmes writes, 'but I could not look upon her perfect clear-cut face, with all the soft freshness of the Downlands in her delicate colouring, without realizing that no young man would cross her path unscathed.' Later, he adds, 'Maud Bellamy will always remain in my memory as a most complete and remarkable woman.'

Not since his brief acquaintance with Irene Adler eighteen years earlier had Holmes' emotions been so moved by a woman's beauty and strength of personality. There is, too, in these remarks a note of uncharacteristic wistfulness as if Holmes were regretting the daughter he had never had or were mourning his lost youth when he might have met and fallen in love with someone like Maud Bellamy, if only his heart had not been ruled by his head. But it was too late.

Holmes was cared for by an elderly housekeeper whom he does not name. It has been suggested by some commentators that she was none other than Mrs Hudson who had given up the Baker Street house to look after Holmes in his retirement. I consider this unlikely. Had the housekeeper been Mrs Hudson, Holmes would have referred to her by name. Nor was it in Mrs Hudson's nature to indulge in gossip, as Holmes' Sussex house-keeper obviously does, to the extent that he was obliged to discourage such conversations. Through her long relationship with Holmes, which had lasted for nineteen years,* Mrs Hudson knew better than to try to engage her gentleman lodger in idle chat. The impression one has of the anonymous Sussex house-keeper is of a garrulous local woman, possibly a widow, who had lived all her life in the area and whom Holmes employed after his retirement.

* In calculating the length of time Holmes was acquainted with Mrs Hudson, I have discounted the three years of the Great Hiatus.

While on the subject of housekeepers, it is worth looking ahead to the events of August 1914 in which Martha, another elderly housekeeper, was to play a part. It is unlikely that Martha, whom Holmes introduced as his agent into the household of Von Bork, the German spy, was either Mrs Hudson or the Sussex house-keeper although the description of her as 'an old, ruddy-faced woman in a country cap' with her knitting and her cat might better fit the anonymous Sussex lady than Mrs Hudson with her London background. However, the Sussex housekeeper, with her predilection for gossip, hardly seems capable of acting as Holmes' undercover agent, while Mrs Hudson, apart from the one occasion when she helped Holmes to bring about Colonel Moran's arrest by turning the wax bust in the sitting-room window of 221B Baker Street, had never played any active role in assisting him in any of his other inquiries. In addition, Holmes arranges to meet Martha at Claridges Hotel in London for a debriefing after the case has been successfully concluded, an unnecessary rendezvous if she had been Mrs Hudson for he could have interviewed her more conveniently at 221B Baker Street, or, if she were his Sussex housekeeper, waited until they had both returned home. I suggest, therefore, that the three women are quite separate individuals and that Holmes recruited Martha, possibly through an employment agency, to act as Von Bork's housekeeper, having interviewed her personally and coached her in her role.

Less is known about Watson's activities during this period. Presumably he was kept busy with his Queen Anne Street practice although, as we have seen, he found time to spend an occasional weekend with Holmes in Sussex, where no doubt he accompanied Holmes on his walks across the Downs and may also have joined him in his early morning expeditions to the beach, although there is no evidence in the canon that Watson could swim. He was probably also introduced to Holmes' new friends, in particular Harold Stackhurst. Knowing Watson's kind and generous nature, it is unlikely that he felt any resentment towards them but welcomed the fact that Holmes had found some like-minded companions.

Despite his busy professional life, Watson still found time for writing. In September 1903, the month of the Creeping Man inquiry, according to Watson one of the last cases which Holmes undertook before his retirement, Holmes lifted the ban on publication which he had imposed on his return to England in April 1894 after the Great Hiatus, although, as we have seen, it had been partially lifted in 1901 when Watson was permitted to publish *The Hound of the Baskervilles* in serial form between August of that year and September 1902.

Watson made the most of this new authorial freedom. Between September 1903 and December 1904, he published both in this country and in America thirteen accounts of his earlier exploits with Holmes, beginning with *The Adventure of the Empty House*, in which he chronicled Holmes' return to London in April 1894 and which was first published, not in the *Strand* but in the American magazine *Collier's Weekly*. The series ended with *The Adventure of the Second Stain*, which first appeared in the *Strand* in December 1904 and in *Collier's Weekly* in January 1905. Readers are referred to the chronology set out in Chapter Fourteen for the titles and publication dates of the other eleven accounts. All thirteen were published in 1905 in volume form under the general title of *The Return of Sherlock Holmes*.

The date of the first publication of *The Adventure of the Empty House* and the choice of *Collier's Weekly* rather than the *Strand* in which to launch it are, I believe, significant clues to the date of Holmes' retirement. In his account of the case, Watson states that it was only 'at the end of nearly ten years' after the events that Holmes allowed him to publish it, that permission being granted on the 'third of last month', that is 3rd August 1903, the month before it appeared in *Collier's Weekly*. This suggests that Holmes was making positive plans to retire and may already have found that 'little farm' of his dreams in Sussex by August of that year. Knowing his retirement was imminent, Holmes therefore lifted his veto and allowed Watson to publish his account of the Empty House case on the understanding that it appeared first in the States and that the English publication in the *Strand* magazine was delayed until October, by which time Holmes had given up practising as a private consulting detective and had left Baker Street.

However, even when the embargo was lifted in September 1903, Watson's problems were far from over. Holmes still continued to exercise editorial control over his publishing activities, as Watson makes clear in *The Adventure of the Second Stain*. Because of Holmes' objections to the publication of this latter account, Watson had intended to end the series with *The Adventure of the Abbey Grange*, which first appeared in print in September 1904. This decision was made, he explains, not through any shortage of material, for he has notes on many hundreds of cases never alluded to, nor out of a lack of interest on the part of his readers, either in Holmes' 'singular personality' or the 'unique methods of this remarkable man'. But, on thinking the matter over, he decided that an account of the Second Stain inquiry would form a more appropriate climax to the sequence. He had, moreover, given his word that he would place this case before the public. The problem was persuading Holmes to allow its publication. To quote Watson's own words, he states: 'It was only upon my representing to him that I had given a promise that *The Adventure of the Second Stain* should be published when the time was right, and pointed out to him that this long series of episodes should culminate in the most important case which he has ever been called upon to handle that I at last succeeded in obtaining his consent that a carefully guarded account of the incident should at last be laid before the public.'

Watson does not specify to whom he gave this promise. It may have been his literary agent, if he had one, or possibly the proprietors of the *Strand*, who published his accounts and with whom he may have discussed projected subject-matter. They would have had a keen interest in Watson's literary output as his chronicles of Holmes' exploits were very popular with their readers. They may also have felt that, in view of the international situation in 1904, publication of *The Adventure of the Second Stain* was particularly apt. At that time, Great Britain was anxious, in the face of growing German expansionism and increased rearmament, to end its policy of 'splendid isolation'* which had marked Queen Victoria's reign and the premiership of Lord Salisbury.

* The term 'splendid isolation' was first used in the Canadian House of Commons in 1896. However, the description is misleading for, although Great Britain tended to keep aloof from international politics, she did sign alliances with some European countries when these were to her advantage. Readers are referred to the entry for *The Adventure of the Naval Treaty* (Appendix One).

With Victoria's death in 1901 and Salisbury's retirement in 1902, a new foreign policy was adopted and Britain began to cast around for European allies. In 1904 Edward VII made a state visit to Paris in order to patch up Britain's relationship with its old enemy, France. Despite anti-British feeling, exacerbated by the Boer War (1899–1902),* Edward VII was able finally to win French support and an Entente was signed in 1904.

Although the Second Stain case dealt with events which had probably happened about eight years before,* nevertheless it was relevant to the political situation of 1904 in which Great Britain, aware of the growing threat posed by the Kaiser's foreign policy, was attempting to hold the balance in Europe by signing the Entente with France, thereby preventing the scales of power falling too heavily in Germany's favour, points which the prime minister at the time, Lord Bellinger, put to Holmes during the course of that inquiry. Indeed, the contents of the stolen letter, which Lord Bellinger had been so anxious to retrieve and which had criticized Great Britain's colonial policy, probably towards South Africa in 1895 before the outbreak of the Boer War, were also applicable to the 1904 situation after the Boer War, which had aroused strong anti-British feeling in Europe, particularly in Germany. Readers are reminded of the telegram sent by the Kaiser in 1896 congratulating the Boers and offering them friendship, an action seen by the British at the time as decidedly hostile.* Publication of *The Adventure of the Second Stain* would therefore have been seen as an opportunity to put forward the British side of the situation and also to warn of the danger still posed by Germany.

These continuing difficulties in obtaining Holmes' permission to publish certain accounts must have caused Watson considerable frustration as an author. It also placed him in an embarrassing situation with regard to his readers, to whom he felt he owed some explanation. But he could hardly blame Holmes outright for exercising this form of editorial control without placing his old friend in a poor light. In the end, Watson compromised by deliberately blurring the issue.

* See the entry in Appendix One, Chapter Fourteen, under *The Adventure of the Second Stain*.

'The real reason,' he writes in *The Adventure of the Second Stain* in an attempt to explain the situation, 'lay in the reluctance Mr Holmes has shown to the continued publication of his experiences. So long as he was in actual professional practice the records of his successes were of some practical value to him; but since he has definitely retired from London and betaken himself to study and bee-farming on the Sussex Downs, notoriety has become hateful to him, and he has peremptorily requested that his wishes in this matter should be strictly observed.'

This sounds like an apologia for Holmes' conduct. Readers will note that Watson makes no reference to the April 1894 ban which extended, with the exception of the publication of *The Hound of the Baskervilles*, until September 1903, a period of nearly nine and a half years when Holmes was, in fact, in active practice. Nor was the ban imposed, or rather re-imposed, immediately on Holmes' retirement as Watson implies in his statement. Holmes was already living in Sussex when the majority of Watson's thirteen accounts were published. Indeed, Holmes only decided that notoriety was 'hateful' to him fifteen months after his retirement when *The Adventure of the Second Stain* was first printed in the *Strand* in December 1904. Having belatedly made up his mind to avoid publicity, Holmes then re-imposed his veto on publication and Watson was silenced again until September 1908, a period of almost another four years. This aspect of Watson's career as an author will be examined in more detail in the next chapter.

However, although Watson gives Holmes' hatred of notoriety as the reason for his refusal to allow publication, there may have been a subconscious resentment on Holmes' part towards Watson's success as an author. Despite his own literary achievements, for example his monograph on the motets of Lassus and 'The Book of Life', these were minor triumphs compared to Watson's much greater output and widespread popularity. Holmes' remark regarding the publication of his treatise on bee-keeping—'Alone I did it.'—could indicate such a resentment, while another comment made by him in *The Adventure of the Lion's Mane*, which Holmes himself wrote, has all the hidden suggestiveness of a classic Freudian slip. In it, Holmes refers to 'all my chronicles' of past cases, as if claiming authorship of Watson's accounts. If such an interpretation is correct, it might help to explain Holmes' need to control not only Watson's right to publish but other aspects of his life as well. By doing so, Holmes was asserting his authority over Watson who, in his eyes at least, was assuming authorial control of his own life by acting as his chronicler, a role which Holmes, with his dominant personality, found unacceptable on occasions.

Watson was under other publication restraints in addition to those imposed by Holmes. Because of the delicate nature of the case involving the blackmailer Charles Augustus Milverton, Watson had to wait until the 'principal person' in the inquiry, presumably the titled lady who shot Milverton, was herself dead before he could publish his account, and even then he deliberately withheld the date and other information in order that she should not be identified. As we have seen, he also had to be 'guarded' in his account of the Second Stain case, refraining from divulging all the facts because sensitive international issues were involved.

The subject of Watson's writing and publishing activities between September 1903 and December 1904 gives rise to several other notable factors. Firstly, in none of these accounts, and not even in those which were to be published towards the end of Watson's life, is there any reference to his second wife, an omission which has been commented on earlier. One suspects that, as the years passed, this was not so much out of a need to suppress the old scandal surrounding his wife's past nor fear of Neil Gibson's revenge, both of which would have faded with time, but from a continuing anxiety on Watson's part about Holmes' reaction should any reference to this second marriage remind Holmes of his, Watson's, so-called desertion and perhaps cause him to extend his ban on publication even further. One assumes the marriage was happy. There is no evidence in the canon to suggest otherwise.

With regard to Holmes' objections to publicity, Watson must have discussed the whole matter with him either on his weekend visits to Sussex or by letter, a fact which is made evident by those comments already quoted from *The Adventure of the Empty House* and *The Adventure of the Second Stain*.

Thirdly, and more importantly, although Holmes now lived in

Sussex he was still exercising a degree of control over Watson's life even from a distance, a state of affairs which Watson apparently accepted without protest. At least, he voices none. From this, we may reasonably assume that when the two men met, if only infrequently, their relationship almost certainly continued on much the same footing as before, Holmes acting as the dominant partner in the friendship, Watson deferring to his wishes.

One final fact emerges concerning Watson's life during this period from September 1903 to December 1904: the punishing work schedule he had set himself. Despite the calls made on him as a practising GP, he nevertheless managed to find the time to write on average one account a month, a total of about 100,000 words over fifteen months, an output which many professional full-time writers would find taxing and one which Watson himself had not surpassed since the time of the Great Hiatus, when he also produced over 100,000 words.

It should also be noted that, during both these exceptionally productive periods in Watson's career as an author, Holmes was absent. During the first, he was travelling abroad; during the second, he had retired to Sussex. It is a sad but significant reflection on their friendship that, when Holmes was present, such were the demands he made on Watson's time that the latter's writing activities were considerably curtailed. As an author, Watson found himself in a classic double-bind situation. Without Holmes, he had no material on which to base his accounts. But when Holmes was there, he had scant opportunity to record it.

CHAPTER SEVENTEEN

HOLMES AND WATSON: THEIR LAST BOWS

July 1907–2nd August 1914

'Tut, my dear sir, we live in a utilitarian age. Honour is a mediaeval conception.'

Baron Von Herling: *His Last Bow: The War Service of Sherlock Holmes*

Very little is known about Holmes's and Watson's lives over the next seven years. In consequence, some commentators, unable to tolerate the silence, in much the same way as Nature is said to abhor a vacuum, have put forward their own theories in an attempt to fill this gap. Holmes, they suggest, was acting as a spy for the British authorities throughout this period. They even claim that, in this capacity, he was responsible in 1917 for handing over to the United States government the Zimmerman note which proposed an anti-American alliance between Germany, Mexico and Japan should America remain neutral. It was the discovery of this note which led to America's declaration of war against Germany shortly afterwards.

My own theory seems prosaic by comparison. I suggest he remained quietly in Sussex, tending his bees and enjoying all those other activities such as reading, swimming and walking over the Downs which had given him so much pleasure in the first four years of his retirement. The fact that he was reluctant to leave Sussex to undertake an important mission on behalf of his country and was only persuaded to do so by the personal intervention of no less a person than the prime minister tends to support this conclusion.

But he was not idle for it was probably during this period that he wrote and published his book, *Practical Handbook of Bee Culture, with Some Observations on the Segregation of the Queen*, already referred to in the previous chapter.

Presumably he also kept up his friendship with Harold Stackhurst and other members of the staff at The Gables. But he and Watson seem to have drifted apart for, when they finally met in August 1914, it is quite clear that they have not seen each other for some considerable time. Watson's comment that he has 'heard' of Holmes 'living the life of a hermit' among his bees and his books on a small Sussex farm is, of course, like his apparent ignorance of Professor Moriarty's existence when Holmes came to visit him in Kensington at the beginning of the Final Problem, merely a literary device intended to inform his readers of Holmes' activities during his retirement. The account in which he makes this comment, *His Last Bow: The War Service of Sherlock Holmes*, was first published in the *Strand* in September 1917, while *The Adventure of the Lion's Mane*, which Holmes himself wrote and in which he set out details of his life in Sussex up to July 1907, was not published until November 1926, nine years later. Watson was therefore obliged to fill in some background information about Holmes when he came to write his own account. His remark also tends to support the theory that Holmes remained in Sussex during those intervening years.

Like *The Adventure of the Mazarin Stone*, *His Last Bow* was written in the third person, a choice of narrative form which was largely dictated by the material. As we have already seen, Watson was aware when he published *The Problem of Thor Bridge* that some cases in which he was either not present or had played too small a part 'could only be told as by a third person'. This is certainly true of *His Last Bow* which opens with a long discussion between Von Bork and Von Herling, witnessed by neither Holmes nor Watson. One can only assume either that Watson learned the details of this conversation from Von Bork himself after he was arrested and taken to Scotland Yard for questioning or that he was later given access to the report of the interview by one of the police officers. Watson's choice of the third person may also reflect that loss of contact between himself and Holmes, already referred to, which he may have thought was better indicated by the use of a less personal narrator.

This is not to suggest there was any serious rift in the relationship between Holmes and Watson between 1907 and 1914. When they finally meet, they greet one another with obvious pleasure. Their lack of contact is due more to a slow drifting apart, brought about by the physical distance between them, rather than through any specific alienation. Both were busy men, absorbed in their own very different lives and, as can happen in even the closest friendships, they found they had less and less in common as the years passed and there were fewer opportunities to meet.

Despite his work as a GP, Watson still found time for writing although to a lesser extent than before. Once again, Holmes lifted his veto on publication in September 1908 when Watson was allowed to publish *Wisteria Lodge* which appeared in print in the *Strand* in two parts during September and October of that year. It was the first of only six accounts which he published in the seven years between 1907 and 1914, the last being *The Adventure of the Dying Detective* which first appeared in *Collier's Weekly* in November 1914 and in the *Strand Magazine* the following month. Readers are referred to the chronology in Chapter Fourteen for the titles and publication dates of the other four accounts.

This diminution in literary output may have been partly caused by the demands made on Watson's time by his professional duties although difficulties in gaining Holmes' permission to publish were largely to blame. As Watson makes clear in *The Adventure of the Devil's Foot,*it was because of Holmes' 'aversion to publicity' and not through any lack of interesting material that has caused him 'of late years to lay very few of my records before the public'. In fact, he wrote his account of the case only after receiving a telegram from Holmes containing the message: 'Why not tell of the Cornish Horror – the strangest case I have ever handled.' Watson himself had no idea what had prompted Holmes to make this suggestion but he immediately set to work to look out his notes on the case and to begin writing them up before Holmes could change his mind and send another telegram cancelling the arrangement. It would seem that, in withholding and granting permission, Holmes was acting largely on whim. Although there are no signs that he continued to suffer from those periods of manic depression which he had experienced as a younger man, he remained mercurial by nature. As an author, Watson must have found this behaviour frustrating. However, Watson was evidently given permission to write an account of the Birlstone tragedy which had occurred in the late 1880s and in which Professor Moriarty and his gang had played such a significant role. As well as the six short accounts already referred to, Watson must have also written this novel-length narrative, *The Valley of Fear*, during this same period, for it was published as a serial in the *Strand* between September 1914 and May 1915. It was issued in volume form in the latter year.

One detail of Watson's private life is, however, recorded for this period. He learned to drive, a useful accomplishment for a busy GP. In the past, he had either walked or taken a cab when visiting his patients. But he was now in his fifties, no longer a young man, and the convenience of driving himself round his practice, especially in bad weather, must have made life a great deal easier for him. It is also a tribute to Watson's adaptability and continuing sense of adventure that he was willing to learn this new skill at a relatively late age. The car he owned was a modest Ford and he evidently became a capable driver for during the Von Bork inquiry it was only his expertise which prevented a collision with Von Herling's larger and more powerful limousine. Apparently, Holmes never learned to drive but with his simple Sussex life-style he would have had less need of transport.

But at some time in 1912, Holmes' quiet way of life was to be disrupted as the international situation worsened and he was called out of retirement to serve his country for the last time.

The strained relations between Germany and Great Britain have already been commented on (pp. 205–06 and 277–79) in relation to the Second Stain case in which, as we have seen, Great Britain, alarmed by the growing power of the Triple Alliance, formed by Germany, Austria-Hungary and Italy, patched up its old differences with France and signed the Entente in 1904. This was followed three years later by the Anglo-Russian agreement, thus forming the Triple Entente to counterbalance the Triple Alliance.

Great Britain also reorganized and rearmed its fleet, the supremacy of which had been challenged by Germany's expansion of its own navy in the late 1890s under Bismarck. In 1907 the first of the new 'Dreadnought' class of battleships was launched, followed by eighteen more between 1909 and 1911. Weighing 17,900 tons and capable of 21 knots, these Dreadnought battleships, armed with ten 12-inch guns, were the largest and best equipped in the world. The British army was also reorganized, a Territorial Force set up and Officer Training Corps (OTCs) established in all public and secondary schools in order to prepare a young officer class should relations with Germany worsen and war break out.

It was because of this heightening of tension that in 1910 Germany decided to send one of its most experienced spies, Von Bork, to England in order to gather information and to assess Great Britain's state of war-readiness. Von Bork was an ideal choice for the task. A young and wealthy aristocrat who spoke excellent English, he was also a sportsman. His prowess on the polo and hunting fields and skill at yachting and driving a four-in-hand,* guaranteed him entry to English upper-class society from which were drawn top-grade officials in the diplomatic corps and Foreign Office as well as higher-ranking army and naval personnel. He even boxed with some of the younger officers. These social contacts would have provided him with the opportunity to listen to conversations between these members of the Establishment. Such conversations could be 'amazingly indiscreet', as Baron Von Herling, Chief Secretary to the German Legation in London, with whom Von Bork was working in close liaison, discovered for himself during a weekend spent at a cabinet minister's country house where Von Bork had also been a guest.

Through his own contacts, Von Herling was able to assure Von Bork that, as far as he could ascertain, Great Britain was quite unprepared for war. It was a situation similar to that of 1939, just before the outbreak of the Second World War when, compared to Germany's state of military rearmament under Hitler, Great Britain was ill-equipped to take part in a major conflict.

* A carriage drawn by four horses. Prince Philip, the Duke of Edinburgh, is an expert at driving a four-in-hand.

Von Bork owned his own country residence, a large mansion in Essex overlooking Harwich harbour where he played the part of the country squire. He also adopted another personality, that of the 'hard-drinking, night-club, knock-about-town, devil-may-care young fellow' which would have endeared him to the raffish circle of friends with which the pleasure-loving Edward VII surrounded himself. So good was his cover that Von Bork was confident that no-one suspected him of espionage.

'They are not hard to deceive, these Englanders,' he was to tell Von Herling. 'A more simple, docile folk could not be imagined.'

In coming to this conclusion, Von Bork had seriously misread the signals, assuming Great Britain would be unwilling to declare war, a mistake Hitler was to make when in 1933 the Oxford Union, the university debating society, passed the motion: 'That this country refuses in any circumstances to fight for King and Country' by 275 votes to 153. Six years later some of those young men would be fighting in France.

In his information gathering, Von Bork paid special attention to naval installations, harbours and the movement of shipping, particularly after 1912 when the British navy was transferred from the Mediterranean to patrol the North Sea, the Atlantic and the English Channel as a precaution against possible German aggression. During his time in England, Von Bork also built up a highly successful spy-ring which, by 1914, consisted of at least five active agents, including Steiner and Hollis and an American citizen, Jack James.

By 1912 fighting had already broken out in Eastern Europe in an area which today is still politically unstable. In 1908 Austria-Hungary, encouraged by the disintegration of the Turkish empire, had taken the opportunity to seize Bosnia and Herzogovenia, former Turkish possessions. This had led to the first Balkan war of 1912 in which the inhabitants of other parts of the area, in particular the Serbs, rose against the Turks, whom they defeated. The following year, they rebelled again in an attempt to free Bosnia from Austrian domination. An event which occurred in Bosnia on 28th June 1914, as we shall see later in the chapter, was to trigger the outbreak of the First World War.

Holmes must have been aware of the tense international situation which preceded this event. Although it is not known if he possessed a wireless set, he had always been an avid reader of newspapers and, while he may not have scanned them quite so eagerly as in the past for reports on crime, he cannot have failed to notice at least the headlines as the crisis deepened.

In 1912 the British Government decided to ask for his help when it was realized by those same men with whom Von Bork had gone drinking, hunting and sailing that a spy-ring was operating virtually under their noses, although they apparently were not yet aware of the identity of the man who was controlling it. Holmes had already served his country on at least three occasions in the past: the inquiry into the missing Naval Treaty in 1889 which was not connected with international espionage and, more importantly, with two further investigations in the 1890s, the Bruce-Partington Plans affair and the Second Stain investigation. Both of these had involved foreign agents: the first Hugo Oberstein, almost certainly German, and the second Eduardo Lucas, probably of Italian origin. In both cases, Holmes had been specifically asked to undertake the investigations either by Mycroft Holmes, acting on behalf of the British Government in the Bruce-Partington affair, or, more directly in the Second Stain inquiry, by the Prime Minister and the Secretary for Foreign Affairs. As we have seen, Holmes was offered a place, which he refused, in the honours list for the part he played in the Bruce-Partington case. He had also been offered a knighthood which he had again refused. Readers are referred back to Chapter Fourteen and to Appendix One for more detailed accounts of these two inquiries and the part Holmes played in their successful conclusion.

In addition, Holmes had worked for the French Government on a 'matter of supreme importance' during the winter of 1890 and the early part of 1891, not long before the Final Problem, and, during the Great Hiatus, had travelled to the Sudan where he had visited the Khalifa, reporting the results of that interview to the Foreign Office in London. His credentials were therefore impeccable.

The decision to recruit Holmes in 1912 for the task of infiltrating the German espionage-ring and identifying its spy-master may have originated with Mycroft. The two brothers must have kept in touch during Holmes' retirement and may have met on

252

occasions either in Sussex or in London. Although Mycroft may have himself officially retired by 1912, by which date he was sixty-five, it is unlikely that his connections with the British Government had been entirely severed and he would almost certainly have gone on meeting his former ministerial colleagues at the Diogenes Club or elsewhere in the capital. Mycroft may even have approached Holmes himself with the suggestion that he came out of retirement to serve his country for the last time.

But whoever made the initial move, Holmes was at first reluctant to agree even when the Foreign Minister intervened. His hesitation is understandable. He was fifty-eight, happily retired for the past nine years and fully occupied with his own interests and activities. Although strongly patriotic, he had no wish to sacrifice all of these hard-won advantages and return to active practice. He may also have been aware after the Lion's Mane inquiry that his old expertise had rusted through lack of use, a realization to which he himself would never admit but which nevertheless may have played a part in his decision to refuse the mission. It was only when the Prime Minister* himself made the journey from London to visit him in his Sussex house and plead with him personally that Holmes finally relented.

Holmes has given no details of that extraordinary and unprecedented interview apart from referring to the 'strong pressure' which was brought to bear on him. But one may imagine what that pressure comprised: the appeals to his sense of patriotism, the emphasis on the dangers facing his country, the declaration that there was no one else who possessed the necessary skill and experience to undertake such an important mission. Holmes had always been susceptible to flattery and if this last appeal was made to his ego, it may well have persuaded him at last to accept the challenge.

The idea of infiltrating him into the German spy network as an American supporter of the Irish Republican movement was a brilliant ploy and may have come from Holmes himself. Although

* The Prime Minister in 1912 was H. H. Asquith, who led a Liberal Government from 1908 to 1916 and whose cabinet included Lloyd George and Winston Churchill.

he had had no direct contact with the Republicans during his professional career, he cannot have remained in ignorance of Irish politics nor the attempts by the more radical supporters of Catholic emancipation to free themselves from British domination.

The Irish Problem, as it was euphemistically called, had its roots far back in history. Alarmed by the existence of a Catholic country so close to Protestant England which could be used as a base for attack by Spain, Elizabeth I had tried but failed to control it four hundred years earlier. Similar fears during the French Revolution that Ireland might become a centre for this new and terrifying form of radicalism had led to the abolition of the Irish Government and the passing of the Act of Union in 1801 which made Ireland part of the United Kingdom, governed from Westminster. The struggle of the Catholic Irish to free themselves from British rule intensified, exacerbated by the potato famines of the 1840s in which over a million Irish, mostly impoverished Catholic tenants of Protestant landowners, died of starvation. Another two million emigrated to America.

It was to these disaffected emigrants and their descendants that the Republican movement in Ireland, dedicated to Catholic emancipation and the repeal of the Act of Union, looked for advice and support. As the international situation grew worse, the old British nightmare recurred. If war with Germany became inevitable, Ireland might become a German base, especially for submarines, operating against the British fleet in the North Sea and the Atlantic. The Irish-American community was also seen as a potential recruiting ground for German spies.

It was this cover which Holmes was to adopt. It was an inspired choice. Holmes, with his ability to assume a variety of different personalities, would have no difficulty in taking on the identity of an Irish-American with strong anti-British feelings. The part needed no elaborate disguise, while the accent was not difficult to imitate. In addition, Holmes already had useful contacts in the States although there is no evidence that he called on their services. Nevertheless, should he have needed them, he was already acquainted with Leverton, an agent from the Pinkerton National Detective Agency whom Holmes had helped in the Red Circle case in the late 1890s. He also knew Wilson

Hargreave of the New York Police Bureau. Holmes had cabled him for information about Abe Stanley during the Dancing Men investigation. In turn, Hargreave had made use of Holmes' knowledge of London crime on more than one occasion.

Holmes' quick ear for languages was another advantage. Once in the States, he picked up both the accent and the slang so convincingly that he was able to pass himself off as an Irish-American with no difficulty, although such terms as 'sucker', 'mutt' and 'nitsky' sound strange coming from his lips.

It is not known precisely when in 1912 Holmes set sail for America on what was probably his first visit to that country although, as we have seen, some commentators have suggested he was there in the 1870s, touring with the Sasanoff Shakespearean Company and, more recently, in 1893 during the Great Hiatus when it is claimed he assisted the Falls River police in the investigation of the Borden murders.

He was probably there for just over a year. The whole mission took two years to complete or, as Holmes expresses it, 'It has cost me two years,' a remark which suggests that, although he was totally committed to the undertaking, some lingering resentment at the loss of time, which might have been spent more agreeably in Sussex, still remained.

He went first to Chicago, where presumably he laid low, learning the accent and perfecting his cover as Altamont. It was while he was there that he may also have grown the goatee beard which was part of his disguise and which gave him a striking resemblance to Uncle Sam. This was a nice touch, typical of Holmes' impish sense of humour.

From Chicago he moved on to Buffalo, where he joined an Irish secret society which may itself have sent him to Skibbareen, a town on the south coast of Ireland, in order that Holmes could play a more active role in the Republican movement. The fact that he clashed with the Irish Constabulary suggests that he was involved in overt political action. As intended, this brought him to the notice of one of Von Bork's subordinate agents, who recruited him into the German spy-ring and sent him on to England. Here, Holmes was introduced to Von Bork, who was so impressed by this 'tall, gaunt man of sixty' with his Irish-American antecedents and his experience in the Republican movement, motivated by his bitter hatred for the British, that he took Holmes into his confidence. Holmes, however, was clever enough not to appear too idealistic in his role as Altamont. He expected to be paid, and paid well. And, under his disguise, he preserved some of his old qualities – his love of good wine and his enjoyment of a cigar – to add authentic details to his assumed identity. In his guise as one of Von Bork's agents, he adopted yet another cover, that of a 'motor expert', using such words as 'sparking-plugs' and 'oil-pumps' as part of a code with which to communicate with Von Bork.

Holmes had already had connections with two members of Von Bork's family. Von Bork's cousin Heinrich was imperial envoy in 1889 when Holmes investigated the Scandal in Bohemia case, in which Irene Adler and the king of Bohemia were so intimately associated. Holmes had also saved the life of Von Bork's uncle, Count Von und Zu Grafenstein, his mother's elder brother, when the Nihilist Klopman attempted to murder him. Had Von Bork known Altamont's real identity, his new agent's name and reputation would have been familiar to him.

At this stage, Holmes had successfully completed the first part of his mission. Not only had he identified the man at the centre of the German espionage network but he had penetrated the actual spy-ring.

Once this had been achieved, the mission took on the qualities of a subtle and dangerous game played on four different levels. Holmes was able to feed Von Bork disinformation, a counter-intelligence ploy which is still used today. So, for example, he passed on to him false plans of the location of mine-fields in the Solent as well as incorrect reports on the speed of British cruisers and the size of naval guns. Holmes was also able to warn the British authorities about the information Von Bork and his agents had already gathered so that counter-measures could be put into operation. Steps were taken to change the codes once the Admiralty were told of Von Bork's knowledge of naval signals. Holmes was also responsible for the arrest and imprisonment of all five of Von Bork's agents. Lastly, he introduced his own agent, Martha, the elderly housekeeper, into Von Bork's household. Her task was to report to Holmes on Von Bork's visitors and to take note of the letters he sent and received.

Time, however, was not on Holmes' side. International events were moving swiftly and war was imminent.

On 28th June 1914 Archduke Francis Ferdinand, the heir to the Austrian Emperor, the elderly Francis Joseph, was on an official visit to Sarajevo, a town in Bosnia which was then part of the Austro-Hungarian empire. He was driving with his wife towards the town hall when a bomb was thrown at their car by a young Bosnian Serb who hated the Hapsburg domination of his country. Although the bomb missed and the Archduke and his wife escaped injury, a second assassination attempt made not long afterwards was successful when another young Bosnian Serb, Gavrilo Princip, mounted the running-board of their car and shot them both dead at close range.

In reprisal, Austria sent an ultimatum to the Serbian Government, which it accused of complicity in the assassination, making some of the demands so harsh that the Serbs refused to agree. Using this as an excuse, Austria, with Germany's support, declared war on Serbia on 28th July. Determined to maintain its position in the Balkans and to protect the Serbs, Russia in turn began to mobilize its forces, refusing to comply when Germany demanded it should put a halt to these preparations. Consequently, on 1st August, Germany declared war on Russia, following two days later with a declaration of war against France, Russia's ally. On the same day, 3rd August, on its way to attack Paris, the German army invaded Belgium, having been refused free passage through that country. The next day, 4th August, the British Parliament, which had guaranteed Belgium's neutrality, declared war on Germany. The First World War, which was to last four years and cost ten million lives, had begun. As Sir Edward Grey, the Foreign Minister, was to write: 'The lamps are going out all over Europe; we shall not see them lit again in our lifetime.'

On 2nd August, two days before Britain's declaration of war against Germany, Von Bork was making hurried preparations to leave England. His wife and members of his household, with the exception of Martha, had already left for Flushing, taking some of his less important papers with them. He, too, was planning to leave as part of the personal suite of Baron Von Herling, the Chief Secretary to the German Legation in London. As such, both he and his baggage containing his more important documents would have had diplomatic immunity. In fact, Von Herling had driven down from London to Von Bork's house in Harwich on the evening of the 2nd August to discuss with him the final arrangements for Von Bork's arrival at the German legation the following morning. In a few hours, he would be immune from arrest.

Holmes' plans, however, were in place. He himself had telegraphed Von Bork, arranging to meet him that same evening and to hand over to him the new naval codes. Martha had been instructed to signal the departure of Von Herling by extinguishing her lamp. Holmes had also wired Watson, asking him to meet him in Harwich with his car, an invitation which Watson eagerly accepted. He was now sixty-one or two, an 'elderly man' who had put on weight and whose hair had turned grey. But his devotion to Holmes and his love of adventure had not diminished. Indeed, some of that enduring spirit of youth prompted Holmes to comment that Watson was 'the same blithe boy as ever'.

Apart from the 'horrible goatee', Watson found Holmes little changed physically although it was several years since they had last met. He would also have recognized some of the quirks in Holmes' character which had not changed either with the passage of time: his sense of humour, for example. Instead of handing over to Von Bork the expected naval codes, he gave him a copy of his own book, *Practical Handbook on Bee Culture*. He was also still prepared to act outside the law. Having chloroformed Von Bork and bound his arms and legs, Holmes removed the documents from his safe and then, with Watson's help, bundled him into his old friend's small car to drive him back to London to be questioned at Scotland yard.*

Before setting off, the two friends lingered for a few minutes on the terrace, looking out over the moonlit sea. Holmes was in a thoughtful mood.

'There's an east wind coming, Watson,' he remarked.

* Holmes assumed that Von Bork, after he was questioned at Scotland Yard, would be allowed to join Von Herling's suite and leave England although, in view of his espionage activities, this seems unlikely. His subsequent fate is unknown.

Watson, with characteristic obtuseness, failed to take the point.
'I think not, Holmes. It is very warm.'

There is affectionate amusement in Holmes's reply.

'Good old Watson! You are the one fixed point in a changing age.'

Holmes was right in his prediction. Within a month, the Germans had swept through Belgium and invaded France, where they met the French army and a small British expeditionary force at the battle of the Marne in September 1914. The lamps were indeed beginning to go out, extinguished by that cold east wind which would sweep across Europe from Germany, just as Holmes had foreseen when he and Watson stood side by side on that warm evening of 2nd August, gazing out towards the harbour lights of Harwich.

EPILOGUE

That occasion on 2nd August 1914 when Holmes and Watson stood in Von Bork's garden gazing out towards the lights of Harwich, two days before Great Britain declared war on Germany, is the last glimpse we are afforded of the two old friends together. On that warm, summer evening they both took their last public bows and the curtain finally descended.

But while they might have left the stage, their lives continued behind the scenes for at least another thirteen years. Some of their activities can even be traced, although the references are few and scattered.

Soon after returning to London after Von Bork's arrest, Watson rejoined his old regiment, presumably the Berkshires with which he had served in Afghanistan in 1880. It is unlikely at his age, for he was sixty-one or sixty-two in 1914, that he was sent to France. More probably he was allocated a post at a home-based hospital, perhaps even at the Royal Victoria at Netley where he had trained as an assistant surgeon thirty-four years before and where he himself had received treatment for the wounds he had received at Maiwand before being invalided out of the army with a pension. If he was sent to Netley, he would have seen the casualties from the battlefields of France arriving by boat at the specially constructed landing-stage. His own experience of active service as well as his skills as a surgeon and a general practitioner would have been useful wherever he was sent. It is not known what happened to his Queen Anne Street practice during his absence but he may well have found a locum willing to take care of it until peace was declared in 1918.

Holmes' career during the war is not recorded. He may have returned to Sussex to resume his interrupted retirement although, given his specialized knowledge of espionage and the activities of the Irish Republican movement,* it is possible he remained in London, acting as a Government adviser, or travelled to and from Sussex to attend ministerial meetings. He may even have made use of his old rooms at 221B Baker Street, if they remained vacant and if Mrs Hudson had not herself retired in the meantime.

Mycroft, too, may have come out of retirement to return to his former post as Government adviser and to contribute his own expertise towards the war effort. Although he was sixty-seven when the war began, it is hard to believe that his great intellectual powers were in any way diminished. Indeed, both brothers may even have served on the same Whitehall committee, an intriguing if speculative thought.

Despite his army service, Watson still managed to continue writing. Between September 1914, only a month after the outbreak of the war, and May 1915, he published *The Valley of Fear*, much of which, as has been suggested in Chapter Seventeen, was almost certainly written before 1914, while in 1917, possibly when he was still serving as an army doctor, *His Last Bow: The War Service of Sherlock Holmes* appeared in print.

There then followed a gap of four years when he published nothing. No doubt he spent these years after the war and his demobilization building up his London practice once again. But in 1921 he resumed his writing career and *The Adventure of the Mazarin Stone* which, like *His Last Bow*, is told in the third person, appeared in print in this country and America. However, compared with his earlier efforts, his literary output was low and he only succeeded in publishing one account a year over the next two years, *The Problem of Thor Bridge* in 1922 and *The Adventure of the Creeping Man* in 1923, drawing on his extensive notes, some of which he kept in his old tin dispatch-box. At some time he had gone to the precaution of depositing this box in the safety of the vault of his bank, Cox and Co, at Charing Cross, perhaps during the war when the German zeppelins were making bombing raids on London. Or an event which happened not long before the publication in 1927 of *The Adventure of the Veiled Lodger* may have

* See Appendix One.

prompted this decision. Watson is too discreet to reveal the full facts but, reading between the lines, it is apparent that an attempt was made 'to get at and destroy' certain of his more confidential papers, presumably in the course of a burglary at his rooms in Queen Anne Street. Watson knew the identity of the person involved and, with Holmes' permission, issued a warning at the beginning of the Veiled Lodger account that 'if these outrages' continued, 'the whole story concerning the politician, the light-house and the trained cormorant will be given to the public.' He adds ominously, 'There is at least one reader who will understand.'

It is an intriguing story and one wishes Watson had revealed more. In the absence of further details, one can only assume that the papers concerned some intrigue involving a member of His Majesty's government which, if revealed, would have caused scandal in high places, although what part the lighthouse and the trained cormorant played in the events can only be imagined.

The Problem of Thor Bridge dealt, of course, with his first meeting with Grace Dunbar who, if my theory is right, became his second wife. The publication of the account may mark an acceptance on Holmes' part of Watson's so-called desertion in 1902 or 1903, although Watson was still careful not to refer directly to his marriage and, as far as his readers were concerned, the identity of the second Mrs Watson remained unknown.

The year 1924 was more productive, with the publication of three more accounts of earlier cases: the Sussex Vampire, the Three Garridebs and the Illustrious Client inquiries. The last two first appeared in the American magazines *Collier's Weekly* and *Liberty* and were not printed in the *Strand* until January and March of 1925.

Holmes was partly responsible for Watson's low literary output, although his ban on publication during this period arose not so much out of his own aversion to publicity as from a concern to protect the right to privacy of some of his former clients, as Watson makes clear in the opening paragraph of *The Adventure of the Veiled Lodger*. In his many year books and dispatch-cases filled with papers, Watson states, were notes and documents of cases undertaken by Holmes which concerned 'the social and official scandals of the late Victorian era.' Evidently Holmes had received many 'agonized letters' from relatives of those involved in these inquiries, begging him for the sake of their family honour, not to reveal the details of these old scandals. Watson was able to reassure them.

'The discretion and high sense of professional honour which has always distinguished my friend are still at work in the choice of these memoirs, and no confidence will be abused,' he promises them a little sententiously.

It was this concern for the reputation of one of his former clients which prompted Holmes to ban publication of an account of the Illustrious Client case until 1925 although Watson had been pleading for permission since 1915. Publication of *The Adventure of the Creeping Man* was also postponed until 1923 when, over twenty years after the events, 'certain obstacles' were removed, almost certainly a discreet reference to the death of Professor Presbury whose bizarre behaviour had featured so largely in the case. Even then, it was only a desire to dispel 'the ugly rumours' circulating round the university about the professor which finally persuaded Holmes to allow Watson to publish an account of the case. The use of the first person plural in Watson's statement 'Now we have at last obtained permission to ventilate the facts', is almost certainly not a reference to himself and his wife but to himself and his publishers.

Watson published nothing in 1926. Instead, Holmes took up his own pen, writing and publishing two accounts of his own, *The Adventure of the Blanched Soldier* and *The Adventure of the Lion's Mane*. Watson had been pressing him for some time to turn author and to 'write an experience' of his own. During the composition of the Blanched Soldier account, Holmes, reminded of Watson's second marriage which had taken place shortly before that particular investigation, allowed some of that old resentment at Watson's 'selfish action' to resurface. It was perhaps not a wise choice of subject-matter for it had opened up old wounds. But they soon healed for in *The Adventure of the Lion's Mane*, also published in 1926, Holmes was able to refer to his former companion affectionately as 'the good Watson'. They may have still met for an occasional weekend together in Sussex although, with the passage of time and their own advancing years, these meetings would have become more difficult and therefore less frequent.

Several critics, among them D. Martin Dakin, have questioned the authorship of some of the accounts published in this 1921-7 period. Their doubts include the two accounts written by Holmes, which they consider are unworthy of him and which they have attributed to Watson or even to the second Mrs Watson. Some of them go as far as to claim that she wrote the whole of these last twelve chronicles which were later published in volume form in 1927 under the general title, *The Case-Book of Sherlock Holmes*. Others have attributed them to Dr Verner, who bought Watson's Kensington practice, or to an anonymous author, possibly Watson's literary agent, who managed to acquire the doctor's notes on the cases.

Those chronicles which are considered the most doubtful are *The Adventure of the Mazarin Stone*, *The Adventure of the Creeping Man* and, in particular, *The Adventure of the Three Gables*, the last one largely because of the racism shown by Holmes in that account, an attitude which has already been examined in Chapter Fifteen.

To present a detailed review of the arguments for and against the case put forward by these critics who doubt the authorship of some at least of these chronicles would require another whole chapter. Those readers who are interested in following up the pros and cons of the dispute may do so on their own account. For my own part, I wish to add only two points to the discussion. The first concerns Holmes' authorship of the two narratives relating to the Blanched Soldier and the Lion's Mane inquiries which, critics argue, show none of that 'severe reasoning from cause to effect' which Holmes advocated and the lack of which he had so deplored in Watson's own accounts. But, while it is easy to criticize, it is more difficult, when one turns author oneself, to put those precepts into practice. As we have already seen, Holmes himself found this out, as he ruefully admits in *The Adventure of the Blanched Soldier*. 'Having taken my pen in my hand,' he writes, 'I do begin to realize that the matter [*i.e. the material*] must be presented in such a way as may interest the reader.'

The second point concerns the general reduction of literary standards shown in some of these later chronicles, whether written by Holmes or by Watson. It should, however, be remembered that both men were growing older and that, by the time these disputed accounts were published in the 1920s, they were in their seventies. The fall in quality could therefore be as easily attributed to their increasing age as to the assumed participation of some anonymous third author.

Readers are again referred to the chronologies in Chapters Fourteen and Fifteen for the publication dates of these last twelve accounts.

With the publication of *The Adventure of the Blanched Soldier* and *The Adventure of the Lion's Mane* in 1926, Holmes finally passes from the records. He was seventy-two. Watson, however, remained active for another year, publishing three more accounts, *The Adventure of the Retired Colourman*, *The Adventure of the Veiled Lodger* and *Shoscombe Old Place* which appeared in the *Strand* between January and April 1927, when he was seventy-four or seventy-five.

After this, the rest, as Hamlet says, is silence.

The dates on which Holmes and Watson died are not known. No obituary was ever published on either of them, an extraordinary omission when one considers their reputations. For the twenty-three years he had been in active practice as a private consulting detective, Holmes had gained worldwide renown, numbering among his clients kings and cardinals, millionaires and prime ministers, as well as many hundreds of ordinary men and women. As his chronicler, Watson had, over his long and successful career as an author, made their names household words.

One can only assume that, for their own different reasons, both men preferred their deaths to pass unnoticed, Holmes out of his hatred of publicity, Watson through his own natural modesty. While still alive, they must have left instructions that no one outside their immediate family and friends was to be notified. The funerals were therefore private and unreported.

Holmes is almost certainly laid to rest in the graveyard of Fordham church, wherever that may be, in good Sussex soil and within sound of the sea, as he himself no doubt had wished.

265

Watson may also have retired from London to spend his last years, like Holmes, in the quiet of the English countryside which he had loved and which he had described with such deep affection. He, too, may be buried in some peaceful village churchyard. If that is so, the location of his grave will remain unidentified.

In the absence of any known memorial to those two remarkable friends, one can do no better than to quote Holmes' own words to Watson as their final tribute: 'You have never failed to play the game. I am sure you will play it to the end.'

APPENDIX ONE

Chapter One

Page 14: Holmes' date of birth has been assigned to various years between 1852 and 1858, one commentator dating it as late as 1867. However, as the statement that Holmes was a man of sixty in 1914 has no qualification attached to it, the year 1854 seems the most likely, as many commentators agree. The month of his birth is variously ascribed to January or June, with January 6th or 7th suggested as his actual birthday. Other commentators have claimed Yorkshire, Shropshire or Surrey as his place of birth. There is, however, no conclusive evidence in the canon to support any of these theories.

Page 22: Dorothy L. Sayers bases her theory on the fact that in *The Man with the Twisted Lip*, Mrs Watson addresses Watson as James, not John. She suggests that the initial 'H' in Watson's full name stands for Hamish, the Scottish form of James, which was given to him by his mother who was of Scottish descent. Mrs Watson uses 'James' as a pet name, in preference to calling her husband John, which had unpleasant associations in her mind with Major John Sholto who betrayed her father, Captain Arthur Morstan.

Page 24: Some commentators have suggested that Watson was married three times, the first occasion before 1887, the possible date of the Five Orange Pips case, which Watson assigns to September 1887 and in his account of which he refers to his wife. But if, as many commentators agree, this date is incorrect and the inquiry took place in 1889, not 1887, then the suggestion of three marriages is no longer supportable.

Chapter Two

Page 26: Dorothy L. Sayers argues for Cambridge on the grounds that, as dogs were not allowed in colleges, Holmes must have been bitten in the street on his way to chapel from lodgings in the town. But as Oxford undergraduates spent their first two years in college whereas Cambridge students lived in town lodgings, Holmes must therefore have gone to Cambridge. However, as other commentators have pointed out, rules were often broken and Trevor may well have kept a dog on college premises.

Page 27: There is much disagreement among Sherlockian scholars over the date when Holmes entered university and the number of years he spent as a student. For example, Gavin Brend considers he entered Oxford in 1871 and left in 1875. William S. Baring-Gould, among others, claims Holmes was a student at both Oxford and Cambridge between 1873 and 1878.

Page 30: The *Gloria Scott* case is variously dated between 1872 and 1876. D. Martin Dakin, whose chronology I have largely but not always followed, assigns it to July-August of 1874.

Page 30: The internal dating of the events which took place on board the *Gloria Scott* is confusing, largely due to the reference to the Crimean War. I am inclined to agree with D. Martin Dakin that this was a later interpolation by Watson, who wanted to add a little historical colour to the narrative but muddled up the dates. Once the reference to the Crimean War is removed, the rest of the dating adds up satisfactorily to thirty years.

Page 30: The Musgrave Ritual case is variously assigned to 1878, 1879 and 1880, D. Martin Dakin opting for 1879.

Chapter Three

Page 47: In *The Adventure of Shoscombe Old Place*, an account which is set in Berkshire, Watson speaks of his 'summer quarters' as having been situated near there. This may be a reference to his time at Netley, training to be an army surgeon, when candidates were sent on field exercises. If this is so, then Watson may have entered Netley in April 1879, not October, after having served as a house surgeon at Bart's for less than a year. He would therefore have qualified as an army surgeon in September 1879, not March 1880. As a result, his subsequent military career would have been five months longer than the nine months suggested in Chapter Three, amounting in all to a year and two months up to the time he was invalided out of the army, and would better justify his claim to be 'an old campaigner'. Shoscombe in Berkshire should not be confused with the village of Shoscombe in Wiltshire, near Bath, now part of Avon.

Chapter Six

Page 85: Various theories have been put forward by Sherlockian scholars in an attempt to assign these undated cases to specific years. While it is impossible to refer to them all in detail, the following much shortened versions will give the reader some idea of the range of the hypotheses and the arguments on which they are based. Readers may make up their own minds as to the validity of the arguments.

The Adventure of the Resident Patient. This case clearly took place in October and is dated by many commentators to 1887 on the grounds that the Worthington gang, referred to in the account, were arrested in 1875 and sentenced to fifteen years' imprisonment. Allowing the three and a half years' remission to which Holmes also refers, they would have been released in 1887. However, when the account was first published (August 1893) Watson explains that, while he cannot be sure of the date because he had mislaid some of his memoranda, the case must have occurred 'towards the end of the first year during which Holmes and I shared chambers in Baker Street'. This would place the case in October 1881. This sentence is omitted from later versions of the account.

The Adventure of the Yellow Face. This case took place in spring, probably April and possibly in the year 1882. As Mrs Munro's first husband died of yellow fever in Atlanta, many commentators take this as a reference to the epidemic of 1878. We are also told that she was married to her first husband for three years and that there was a gap of just over six months between the two marriages. This evidence would date the case to 1882. Other commentators disagree and assign the case to various years between 1882 and 1889.

In *The Adventure of the Yellow Face*, Watson refers to 'the affair of the second stain' as one of the half-dozen cases in which, although Holmes 'erred' in his inquiries, the truth was nevertheless discovered. Quite clearly, this cannot be a reference to the adventure of the Second Stain, referred to in *The Adventure of the Naval Treaty* which occurred, Watson states, in the July 'which immediately succeeded my marriage', that is in July 1889. Nor can it refer to the published account, *The Adventure of the Second Stain*, which is deliberately undated by Watson for reasons of state security and which, far from being a case in which Holmes 'erred', was successfully concluded by him. The title of 'Second Stain' is one which Watson evidently liked and used on more than one occasion, possibly on three: firstly, for the unrecorded case of the 1881–9 period; secondly, for the case which occurred in July 1889; and thirdly, for the published but undated case which involved the theft of a highly confidential state document.

The Adventure of the Copper Beeches. This case is particularly difficult to date because in it Holmes refers to various cases which took place between 1888 and 1889. On this evidence, most commentators have dated it to 1890. However, this is after Watson's marriage and yet he is clearly living in Baker Street. I am inclined to agree with D. Martin Dakin's theory that Holmes's remarks regarding the cases were made at a later date and Watson has mistakenly inserted them into this account whereas they should belong to a later publication.

The Adventure of the Beryl Coronet. Watson refers to deep snow, weather conditions which Dr Ernest B. Zeisler in his *Baker Street Chronology* has traced through meteorological records as applying to Friday, 23rd February 1886.

The Valley of Fear. Watson himself assigns this case to the 7th January 'at the end of the eighties'. As Watson is living in Baker Street, it must be before his marriage in 1888/9. However, the year 1888 does not agree with the dating of the Vermissa Valley narrative, which would suggest the much later date of 1895. This, however, is out of the question as Moriarty, who features in Watson's account of the case, died in 1891. Mr William S. Baring-Gould and others have suggested that Watson's dating was incorrect and that the trial of the Scowrers took place in 1865, not 1875, and is another example of either Watson's bad handwriting or a mistake in calculation.

The Adventure of the Greek Interpreter. This case took place in summer and must have occurred after the publication in December 1887 of *A Study in Scarlet* as Mycroft Holmes refers to Watson as Holmes' chronicler. Some commentators prefer to assign it to an earlier date on the grounds that Holmes would not have waited seven years before introducing his brother to Watson. However, as Watson himself refers to his 'long and intimate acquaintance' with Holmes, the word 'long' would tend to support the later date of 1888.

The Adventure of the Cardboard Box. This case occurred in a particularly hot August before Watson's marriage. The August of 1888 seems the most likely and is supported by Dr Zeisler's researches into the meteorological records which show that on Saturday, 10th August, the temperature reached 87.7 degrees Fahrenheit, close enough to Watson's remark that the thermometer stood at 90. However, in the account, Holmes refers to the Sign of Four case which did not take place until later, September 1888. This is probably another instance of Watson's placing a comment by Holmes out of its correct context. If Watson recorded Holmes' conversations in a separate notebook but failed to date them precisely on every occasion, this explanation would account for the mistake.

The Adventure of Silver Blaze. It is generally accepted by most commentators that this case occurred in the autumn of 1888. As Holmes speaks of Watson's memoirs, he must be referring to *A Study in Scarlet* which was published in December 1887.

The Hound of the Baskervilles. This is another case which presents great problems over dating and has been assigned by different commentators to dates as early as 1886 to as late as 1900. It took place in autumn and the internal evidence from the date of 1884 inscribed on Dr Mortimer's walking stick, a gift from his colleagues at Charing Cross Hospital, suggests the late 1880s, a dating confirmed by Mortimer's medical record quoted by Watson from his copy of the Medical Directory. As Watson is unmarried and still living at Baker Street, Holmes' remark that Mortimer left the hospital five years before, which might suggest the year 1889, must therefore be wrong and he should have said four years, thus assigning the case to the autumn of 1888.

Despite the evidence put forward by such distinguished Sherlockian scholars as Dr Zeisler, Mr Gavin Brend and others in support of the year 1899, I am inclined to agree with that other great Holmesian expert, William S. Baring-Gould, that 1888 is the correct date. The fact that Watson's leg wound was troubling him in 1888, which he refers to in *A Sign of Four*, also dated to September 1888, and that he could not therefore have run the great distances he covered in the Baskerville inquiry need not disprove this theory. As I point out in Chapter Eight, Watson walked from Baker Street to Camberwell to visit Miss Mary Morstan, a distance of some twelve or fourteen miles there and back, without any apparent discomfort.

Chapter Eight

Page 111: Although Watson does not specifically state the year in which the Sign of Four case occurred, there are two references within the account which establish it as 1888. Mary Morstan states that her father disappeared on 3rd December 1878, 'nearly ten years ago', and that the advertisement appeared in *The Times* 'about six years ago – to be precise on 4th May 1882'. The only problem arises over the month when the events took place. Mary Morstan states that she received a letter 'that morning' asking for the meeting outside the Lyceum theatre, the envelope of which Holmes notes is postmarked July 7. However, Watson states that the meeting took place on a 'September evening'. As all the descriptions of the weather point to autumn rather than summer, most commentators accept the September dating. The reference to July is therefore either a mistake on Watson's part which he failed to correct, or on the printer's which went unnoticed and uncorrected.

Chapter Ten

Although several cases for this period can be dated without any difficulty, the following are problematic:

A Case of Identity. Watson supplies no date but there is a reference in his account to the Scandal in Bohemia inquiry. As Holmes also speaks of Mary Sutherland (*A Case of Identity*) in *The Red-Headed League*, the investigation must therefore have occurred between March 1889 and October 1890. D. Martin Dakin dates the events of *A Case of Identity* to September 1889 as there is a reference to a fire burning in the Baker Street sitting-room, suggesting autumn weather. However, the fire could as easily indicate early spring. As Holmes has recently received the gifts of the snuff-box and the ring from his royal clients for the services he had rendered them in March of that year, April 1889 would seem the more likely date as neither of them would have waited over six months before sending Holmes these tokens of their gratitude.

The Adventure of the Naval Treaty. Watson dates this case to the July immediately succeeding his marriage, that is July 1889. However, some commentators have dated it to July 1887, before his marriage, because of the connections with the Triple Alliance, signed in 1882 between Germany, Austria-Hungary and Italy, a pact which was intended to isolate France after the Franco-Prussian war (1870–71). Although Great Britain, which preferred to follow an isolationist policy with regard to Europe, refused to join the Alliance, Lord Salisbury, then Prime Minister, did sign two secret Mediterranean Agreements with Italy and Austria in 1887. The first promised British support for Italian interests in Libya against French ambitions in that area in return for Italian support for British interests in the Sudan and Egypt. It was therefore vital that the stolen naval treaty, which dealt with Great Britain's policy in the event of the French fleet gaining ascendancy in the Mediterranean, was recovered before it could be sold to France and Russia, traditional enemies of both Great Britain and Germany. In 1893, France and Russia signed the Dual Alliance in an attempt to counterbalance the power of the Triple Alliance. These alliances were to play a significant role in the events leading up to the First World War.

The Five Orange Pips. Watson ascribes this case, as well as the five unrecorded cases, to the year 1887, obviously a mistake as he is married at the time of these investigations. The mistake could have easily arisen through a badly-written 9 being mistaken by the printer for a 7 and left uncorrected by Watson. However, this theory causes problems with the internal dating of Joseph Openshaw's death, which should have occurred four years and eight months before, not two years and eight months as stated in *The Five Orange Pips*. I am inclined to agree with D. Martin Dakin's suggestion that, once the mistake over the year remained uncorrected, someone, possibly the printer or even Watson himself, altered the figures relating to Openshaw's death to make it accord with the incorrect year, 1887. On meteorological evidence, Dr Zeisler assigns the case to 24th September, a particularly stormy day which matches Watson's description of the weather.

The Boscombe Valley Mystery. As Holmes states that 'Monday last' was 3rd June, most commentators date this case to June 1889, when 3rd June was on a Monday. However, in the light of the evidence, referred to in the footnote to page 147 about Anstruther, I am inclined to date this case to June 1890 and to relate it to Watson's move to Kensington because in June 1889 Watson was still living in Paddington, as is made clear in accounts of the Stockbroker's Clerk and the Man with the Twisted Lip inquiries.

The Red-Headed League. The year is undoubtedly 1890 as, in his account which was published in August 1891, Watson states that he called on Holmes in 'the autumn of last year', ie 1890. It is the references to the months which are confusing, Watson referring to 27th April, the day on which the advertisement appeared in *The Morning Chronicle*, as being 'two months ago' while Jabez Wilson speaks of eight weeks having passed since he read the advertisement. Both references would suggest June which is hardly autumn. However, the Red-Headed League was disbanded on 9th October, according to the notice pinned up on the door of its premises. D. Martin Dakin has offered a brilliantly simple explanation for this tangle of dates, suggesting Watson's hastily scrawled Aug 4th for the date of the newspaper advertisement was incorrectly read by the compositor as Ap. 27, for April 27th. Once this theory is accepted, the other dates fall into place.

Of the thirteen recorded cases for this period, 1889–91, four involved no crime, three involved theft or burglary and six involved murder or attempted murder, two of which, the Dying Detective case and the Final Problem, concerned attempts on Holmes' life.

Chapter Eleven

Page 160: There is some confusion over which Continental express Holmes and Watson caught that morning and what precisely was Holmes' intended destination. According to Mr Bernard Davies, who has studied *Bradshaw's Monthly Railway Guide* for April 1891, there were three morning boat trains: the 8. 30a.m. and the 11a.m., both bound for Calais and neither of which stopped at Canterbury, and the 10 a.m. for Ostend which did stop at Canterbury. As Watson had to present himself at the far end of the Lowther Arcade at precisely 8.45 a.m., this suggests that both he and Holmes caught the 10 a.m. Ostend train, a supposition confirmed by the fact that they got off at Canterbury. Why, then, was their luggage labelled for Paris? I suggest it was part of a plan by Holmes to throw Moriarty or one of his agents off the

275

scent should one or other of them attempt to follow. Holmes may have intended either waiting at Dover for the packet which connected with the 11 a.m. Paris boat train from Victoria or, alternatively, taking the Dover–Ostend packet and travelling to Paris from Ostend to collect his and Watson's luggage. However, once he realized that Moriarty was following them, Holmes dropped this plan and decided to abandon the luggage and travel instead by the Newhaven route to Brussels, assuming Moriarty would track their bags to Paris, where he would wait two days before returning to London. According to this assumption, Moriarty should have arrived back in London on Monday 27th April on the same day Inspector Patterson was supposed to arrest the Professor and the members of his gang.

Some commentators have gone so far as to suggest that the whole Continental trip was an elaborate ruse on Holmes's part to lure Moriarty abroad and so give Holmes the satisfaction of either arresting or killing him himself.

Chapter Fourteen

Page 204: Although some of the cases from April 1894 to June 1902 can be dated without difficulty, the following present problems:

Wisteria Lodge. Watson assigns it to the end of March 1892, clearly a mistake as in 1892 Holmes was still abroad during the Great Hiatus. D. Martin Dakin, who has disputed the date of Holmes' return, preferring to place it in early February 1894, not April, has opted for March 1894 as the date of the Wisteria Lodge case. As evidence, he has used the reference in the Norwood Builder inquiry, dated to the summer of 1894, to the case involving the papers of ex-President Murillo, one of the unrecorded investigations which occurred soon after Holmes' return. I see no problem with this. As Miss Burnett, a.k.a. Signora Victor Durando, makes clear at the end of the Wisteria Lodge inquiry, usually dated to March 1895, she and others had banded together into a secret society several years before to hunt down Murillo after the murder of her husband. They may well have stolen some of Murillo's papers in 1894 in an attempt to prove his guilt,

276

a case which Holmes was asked to investigate at the time, although I agree it is curious that Holmes makes no reference to this earlier inquiry during the Wisteria Lodge investigation. I have therefore assigned the Wisteria Lodge inquiry to March 1985, a date which other commentators have suggested.

The Adventure of the Sussex Vampire. Watson dates this case to 19th–20th November but omits to state the year. D. Martin Dakin, together with other Sherlockian scholars, has assigned it to 1896 as Holmes was fully occupied with other cases in the Novembers of other likely years.

The Adventure of the Second Stain. Watson has deliberately withheld the date of this case apart from a reference to autumn. Most commentators, among them D. Martin Dakin, have assigned this inquiry to a year before November 1895, the date of the Bruce-Partington case, because in the account of the Second Stain inquiry Holmes refers to Oberstein as one of only three spies capable of stealing the missing document. Oberstein is therefore clearly still at liberty whereas, at the end of the Bruce-Partington affair, Hugo Oberstein is arrested and sent to prison for fifteen years.

However, despite this evidence, I have dated the Second Stain case to January 1896 on the grounds that the international situation described by Watson in his account relates better to this year than to the period before November 1895. The reference to Oberstein as being still at liberty is therefore either a mistake on Watson's part, who misheard Holmes' remark or muddled up his notes, or, more probably, a deliberate attempt on his part to mislead his readers over the dating of the case. His reference to 'autumn' could also be intended to mislead.

The contents of the stolen document, which had been written by a 'foreign potentate', without the knowledge of his ministers, criticized Britain's colonial policy in such provocative terms that, had they become generally known, would have aroused such hostility in Great Britain that it might have led to war, especially if the document was sent to any of 'the great chancelleries of Europe'. This is a clear reference to Germany, partners with Austria-Hungary and Italy in the Triple Alliance.

There was only one area of British colonial policy which aroused such severe criticism during this period and this was in regard to South Africa, where events in late 1895 and early 1896 did indeed cause strong anti-British feeling in Europe, especially in Germany.

Briefly, the situation was this. In 1886, gold was discovered in the Transvaal, one of two states in South Africa founded and governed by the Boers, the original Dutch settlers of the area. The other Boer republic was the Orange Free State. With the discovery of gold, miners and developers poured in to the Transvaal, mostly British settlers from the Cape Colony, a British possession. These 'Uitlanders', or outsiders, soon outnumbered the Boers, who resented their presence. As a consequence, Paul Kruger, President of the Transvaal, refused to allow them certain civil rights, including the right to vote, and taxed them heavily, a policy deeply resented by the Uitlanders. Cecil Rhodes, Prime Minister of the Cape and founder of Rhodesia after his conquest of the native territory, Matubeleland, decided to take up the Uitlanders' cause and use the situation as an excuse to seize the Transvaal. With the assistance of a close colleague, L. S. Jameson, whom Rhodes had appointed administrator of former Matubeleland, Rhodes planned to stage an uprising in the Transvaal among the Uitlanders to which Jameson would respond by sending in an armed force to attack the Boers under the pretext of protecting British interests. The plot, however, misfired. The uprising failed to take place but Jameson, unaware of this, sent in his force which was defeated by the Boers in December 1895. When the plot was uncovered, it caused a great outcry not only abroad but also among Liberal MPs in the British Parliament, which led to Rhodes' resignation as Prime Minister of the Cape Colony. Anti-British feeling was particularly strong in Germany. In January 1896 Kaiser William II sent a personal telegram to Kruger, congratulating him on his success over the Jameson raid and promising the Boers friendship, a gesture which the British regarded as decidedly hostile. The situation eventually persuaded Great Britain to look for European allies and to sign an Entente with France in 1904 and an Anglo-Russian agreement in 1907, thus forming the Triple Entente which counterbalanced the Triple Alliance of Germany, Austria-Hungary and Italy.

The situation in the Transvaal also led to the Boer War of

1899–1902 in which James Dodd and Godfrey Emsworth took part (*The Adventure of the Blanched Soldier*). In 1909, after the end of the Boer War, the Union of South Africa was formed, uniting the separate states.

In dating *The Adventure of the Second Stain* to January 1886, I am therefore linking the case with the events which took place between December 1895 and January 1896, including the Jameson raid and the dispatch of the Kruger telegram by the Kaiser. In addition, I suggest that the document criticizing British colonial policy was also written by the Kaiser, without his ministers' knowledge. Had it found its way to the German Chancellery, it might have been made public and further exacerbated the hostility already aroused by the Kruger telegram.

This theory would positively identify Lord Bellinger with Lord Salisbury, Prime Minister at the time. Watson's description of Lord Bellinger as 'dominant' and 'eagle-eyed' would fit Salisbury, a large, bearded man with an imposing presence. As Salisbury also served as Foreign Minister, I suggest Trelawney Hope, the Secretary for European Affairs, was, in fact, Joseph Chamberlain, Salisbury's Secretary of State for the Colonies, who was indeed a 'rising statesman in the country', as Watson describes him. Chamberlain was also 'elegant', invariably sporting a monocle and an orchid in his buttonhole.

The Adventure of Abbey Grange. Watson assigns this case to 'the winter of '97'. Dr Zeisler suggests late January 1897 as this accords with the meteorological records of that date.

The Adventure of the Red Circle. A difficult case to date as Watson only mentions the season, which was winter, while his reference to a Wagner night at Covent Garden confuses rather than clarifies the situation. As H. W. Bell has pointed out, there was a Wagner season in January 1897 but it was at the Garrick Theatre, while a Wagner season at Covent Garden was held in October 1897. On the assumption that Watson has confused the theatres, D. Martin Dakin has opted for February 1897.

The Adventure of the Missing Three-Quarter. Watson gives the month as February but university rugby matches were played in

279

December. He also states that the events occurred 'seven or eight years ago', i.e. before publication of the account, which was in August 1904. This would therefore place it either in December 1896 or December 1897. However, Watson states that Oxford won by a goal and two tries but in December 1896, Oxford won two goals to one, while in December 1897, Oxford won by two tries. D. Martin Dakin has opted for December 1897, a date with which I concur.

The Adventure of the Dancing Men. This case is undated by Watson apart from a reference by Hilton Cubitt to his visit to London 'last year' for the Jubilee. This could mean either the Jubilee of 1887 or the Diamond Jubilee of 1897. Cubitt also refers to a letter he received 'about a month ago, at the end of June'. Most commentators assign the case to July 1897.

The Adventure of the Retired Colourman. Watson has given no date for this case but internal evidence suggests August 1898. Amberley retired in 1896 and married early in 1897 but his wife left him 'within two years'. There is also a reference to the 'hot summer'.

The Adventure of Charles Augustus Milverton. This case is deliberately undated by Watson apart from a reference to a 'cold, frosty winter's evening'. Some commentators assign it to the late 1880s, before Watson's marriage. However, the references to the electric lights in Milverton's Hampstead house suggest a later date, as electricity was not brought to that part of London until 1894. Although some commentators have argued that Milverton could have had a private lighting system installed, as must have happened at Baskerville Hall, Mr William E. Plimentel has pointed out that these early installations were equipped with press-buttons to turn lights on and off whereas Watson refers to a switch which makes a 'sharp snick', a later system. Mr William S. Baring-Gould has therefore suggested January 1899 as the date for the Milverton case, a theory with which D. Martin Dakin agrees. The meteorological records support this date.

The Disappearance of Lady Frances Carfax. Watson has failed to date this case. It must have occurred after 1889 as Holy Peters had his ear bitten off in a fight in that year. As Watson is clearly living in Baker Street at the time, it must also have taken place after Holmes' return in 1894. It is assigned to various dates between 1894 and 1903. The fact that Holy Peters spent some time sitting on the verandah suggests it was summer. D. Martin Dakin has suggested the summer of 1899 as a possible date.

The Adventure of the Priory School. Watson has dated the disappearance of Lord Saltire to Monday 13th May but failed to give the year. In 1901, 13th May was indeed on a Monday and this is the year most favoured by commentators. However, there was a full moon on the night the young lord disappeared and there was no full moon on Monday 13th May 1901. Dr Zeisler has therefore suggested the case took place on Monday 14th May 1900 when the moon was indeed full.

The Adventure of the Six Napoleons. The case is undated by Watson. However, Beppo was last paid on the 20th May the year before. Assuming he was paid on a Saturday, the most likely year when 20th May fell on a Saturday was 1899. This would then date the case to 1900. William S. Baring-Gould has suggested the inquiry took place between 25th and 29th May. If this dating is correct, Holmes was particularly busy during May 1900 for, as well as the Priory School and the Six Napoleons investigations, he was also involved with the Conk-Singleton forgery case, the affair of the Ferrers documents and the Abergavenny murder trial.

The Problem of Thor Bridge. Watson states the case took place on the 4th October but has failed to give the year. Although some commentators have assigned it to 1900, others, including D. Martin Dakin have opted for 1901. Holmes refers to 'a month of trivialities and stagnation' which would apply to 1901 as Watson records no other cases for that year.

Shoscombe Old Place. Watson only gives the month, which was May, but not the year. Both Dr Zeisler and William S. Baring-Gould, taking into account the date of the Derby and the phases of the moon, theories too long and complex to be explained here, have chosen 6th May 1902, a date with which D. Martin Dakin concurs.

Out of the thirty recorded cases which occurred between April 1894 and September 1903, fourteen concerned murder or attempted murder, including one old murder case which had taken place several years before and one attempt on Watson's life. Three cases involved manslaughter or had mitigating circumstances which might have prevented a murder charge being brought. Four were cases of fraud or theft, or attempted fraud or theft. Of the rest, three involved no crime, four if one includes the Thor Bridge case, which was a suicide (although the attempt to make it appear a murder had criminal intent). The remaining three involved malicious wounding, an attempted abduction and a failure to register a death.

Chapter Fifteen

Readers are referred to the entries under Chapter Fourteen for the dating of the Thor Bridge, Shoscombe Old Place and the Three Garridebs inquiries.

The Adventure of the Mazarin Stone. This case is told in the third person and no date is given, apart from a reference to 'the evening of a lovely summer's day'. But as Watson has moved out of Baker Street and is practising as a GP, the case must have occurred after June 1902 but before Holmes' retirement in the autumn of 1903. The case must therefore have taken place in the summer of 1903, possibly in late June of that year, as D. Martin Dakin suggests.

The Adventure of the Three Gables. This case is also undated and some commentators have doubted its authorship. However, as Watson is not living at Baker Street, it must, like the Mazarin Stone inquiry, belong to the period between June 1902 and the autumn of 1903. The reference to 'geranium beds' indicates it took place in the summer. I have therefore assigned it to July 1903.

The Irish problem continued to trouble British politics. The Liberal Government, which needed the support of Irish MPs in order to keep in office, tried between 1912 and 1914, to pass a Home Rule Bill, giving Ireland self-government. This, however, was opposed by Protestant Ulster which feared that a majority of Catholics would dominate an Irish Parliament. Ulster's resistance to Home Rule was supported by Sir Edward Carson, a Protestant MP, who spoke against the bill and encouraged the formation of the Ulster Volunteers, a military organization which tried to import arms from Germany. The Ulster Volunteers were challenged by the rapidly growing Sinn Fein movement which also opposed Home Rule, preferring instead complete independence from Britain. In turn, they set up their own military force, the Irish Volunteers, which also tried to acquire German arms. The situation was extremely volatile and, had the Home Rule Bill been passed, might have led to civil war in Ireland. However, the outbreak of the First World War in 1914 led to its postponement.

Although many Irishmen, both Catholic and Protestant, remained loyal and enlisted in the British army, an uprising did take place at Easter 1916 when a force of about 2,000 Sinn Feiners, some equipped with German guns, took part in an armed rebellion in Dublin and, having seized some public buildings including the Post Office, declared an Irish Republic. After five days of fighting, the Republicans were defeated and their leaders executed, among them Roger Casement who, for his attempt to gain German support for the Republican cause, was found guilty of treason and hanged.

Holmes' direct knowledge of Irish politics in the years 1912–14 would have been extremely useful to the British Government during World War I, especially with regard to events leading up to the Irish Uprising of Easter 1916. Under his cover as Altamont, he may even have become personally acquainted with some of the leading figures in the Irish Volunteers and the Sinn Fein movement.

APPENDIX TWO

THE SITE OF 221B BAKER STREET

Various theories, too numerous to describe in detail, have been
suggested for the site of 221B Baker Street. These include, among
others, 21, 27, 49, 59, 61, 63 and 66. Mr James Holroyd's claim for
number 109, based on evidence in *The Adventure of the Resident
Patient*, was apparently supported by Dr Chandler Brigg's discovery that the house opposite, number 118, was actually called
Camden House and must therefore have been the same house
from which Holmes and Watson kept watch on 221B Baker Street
in *The Adventure of the Empty House* (1894). Unfortunately, it has
since been shown that Camden House was then in use as a
private school and would therefore not have been empty.

Mr Bernard Davies's claim for number 31 seems more likely.
Basing his theory on a large-scale map of Baker Street, he
demonstrated that number 34, opposite number 31, fitted the
description of the Empty House, having rear access through a
mews and a yard, its front door to the right when faced from the
road, and no street lamp nearby. Number 31 has since been
demolished to make way for a block of flats.

However, according to the street directory for the period, in
1894 number 34 was occupied by Arthur Canton, a dentist and
surgeon, and therefore would also be ineligible as the Empty
House.

Wherever 221B was situated, it was almost certainly on the east
side of Baker Street, facing west, for in *The Adventure of the
Cardboard Box*, Watson refers to the morning sun shining on the
façades of the houses opposite. It must also have been far enough
away from the station in Marylebone Road for Alexander Holder
(*The Adventure of the Beryl Coronet*) to consider taking a cab there.

Watson's references to a 'bow' window are confusing. When

the houses were built in the eighteenth century, all of them had tall, narrow sash windows. There is no record of any of them being bow-shaped. Nor is there any evidence either in nineteenth-century photographs or other documentation that a bow window was installed in any of the houses prior to Holmes' and Watson's time. As the properties were leasehold, it is doubtful if the ground landlord, the Portland estate, would have allowed such an alteration to the fabric of the building.

It is also significant that in Watson's initial description of the sitting-room in *A Study in Scarlet*, recording his first visit to the lodgings, he refers only to 'two broad windows'. There is no reference to a bow window until much later in the *The Adventure of the Beryl Coronet*, published in May 1892, and *The Adventure of the Mazarin Stone*, published in October 1921, by which time not only was Holmes' fame as a consulting detective already established but also Watson's as his chronicler.

It is possible Watson introduced the bow window as a deliberate ploy to throw curious readers off the scent in case they came looking for 221B Baker Street. It would have been embarrassing for Holmes' clients, many of whom were important and influential people, to find sightseers gathered outside the house.

Alternatively, Watson may be referring to the arched brick soffit, or inner curve, to the semi-circular head of the window opening.

SELECTED BIBLIOGRAPHY

As the bibliography of Sherlock Holmes is so extensive, only principal sources are quoted. For all other unattributed sources within the book, readers are referred either to the complete annotated edition of the Holmes' novels and short stories, edited by William S. Baring-Gould, or to D. Martin Dakin's *A Sherlock Holmes Commentary*.

ARONSON, THEO, *The Kaisers* (Cassell, London 1971)

ASH, CAY VAN, *Ten Years Beyond Baker Street* (Futura Publications, London. 1985)

BREND, GAVIN, *My dear Holmes: A Study in Sherlock.* (George Allen and Unwin Ltd. London. 1951)

CHESNEY, KELLOW, *The Victorian Underworld.* (Temple Smith. London, 1970)

CLAMMER, DAVID, *The Victorian Army in Photographs.* (David and Charles, Newton Abbot, 1975)

DAKIN, D. MARTIN, *A Sherlock Holmes Commentary.* (David and Charles. Newton Abbot. 1972)

DOYLE, SIR ARTHUR CONAN, *The Sherlock Holmes' Novels and Short Stories: Complete Annotated Edition*: editor WILLIAM S. BARING-GOULD, (Wings Books, New Jersey 1992) Oxford Edition: General Editor OWEN DUDLEY EDWARDS, (Oxford University Press 1993).

FARWELL, BYRON, *Armies of the Raj.* (Viking. London. 1990)

FULBROOK, MARY, *A Concise History of Germany.* (Cambridge University Press. 1990)

HAINING, PETER (editor), *A Sherlock Holmes Compendium.* (W. H. Allen London. 1980)

HALL, TREVOR H., *Sherlock Holmes and his Creator.* (Duckworth, London. 1978)

HARDWICK, MICHAEL, *The Complete Guide to Sherlock Holmes.* (Weidenfeld and Nicolson, London. 1986)

HARRISON, MICHAEL, *In the Footsteps of Sherlock Holmes*. (David and Charles. Newton Abbot. 1971)

HARRISON, MICHAEL, *London by Gaslight 1861–1901*. (Gasogene Press Ltd. Iowa. 1963)

HARRISON, MICHAEL, *The London of Sherlock Holmes*. (David and Charles. Newton Abbot. 1972)

HARRISON, MICHAEL, *Immortal Sleuth*. (Gasogene Press Ltd. Iowa, 1983)

HOWARD, MICHAEL AND FORD, PETER, *The True History of the Elephant Man*. (Alison and Busby. London. 1980)

KEATING, H. R. F., *Sherlock Holmes: The Man and his World*. (Thames and Hudson, London. 1979)

KELLY'S STREET DIRECTORIES FOR 1881, 1882, 1894.

KIPLING, RUDYARD, *A Choice of Kipling's Verse by T.S. Eliot*. (Faber and Faber. London. 1961)

LAFFIN, JOHN, *Surgeons in the Field*. (J. M. Dent and Sons Ltd. London. 1970)

LANE, PETER, *Success in British History 1760–1914*. (John Murray. London. 1978)

MAGNUS, PHILIP, *King Edward VII*. (John Murray. London. 1977)

MASSIE, ROBERT K., *Dreadnought: Britain, Germany and the Coming of the Great War*. (Jonathan Cape. London. 1992)

MAYHEW, HENRY, *London Labour and London Poor. Vol. 11*. (Dover Publications Inc. New York. 1968)

NEAL, COLONEL J. B., *The History of the Royal Army Medical College*. (Privately Printed)

NEEL, ALEXANDRA DAVID, *My Journey to Lhasa*. Virago Press. London. 1969.

NEW ENCYCLOPAEDIA BRITANNICA,(Encyclopaedia Britannica Inc. Chicago. 1993)

PARK, ORLANDO, *The Sherlock Holmes Encyclopaedia*. (Citadel Press. New Jersey. 1981)

PASCOE'S *London Guide and Directory 1880–1881*

PECK, ANDREW JAY, *The Date Being? . . . A Compendium of Chronological Data*. (Privately Printed in a limited edition)

PETERSON, JEANNE M., *The Medical Profession in Mid-Victorian London*. (University of California Press. 1978)

PIERCY, ROHASE, *My Dearest Holmes*. (GMP Publications Ltd. London 1988)

RICHARDS, DENIS AND HUNT, J. W., *An Illustrated History of Modern Britain 1783–1964*. (Longmans. London. 1965)

SAYERS, DOROTHY L., *Unpopular Opinions*. (Victor Gollancz Ltd. London. 1946)

SHREFFLER, PHILIP A, (editor): *Sherlock Holmes by Gaslight. Highlights from the First Four Decades of the Baker Street Journal.'* (Fordham University Press. New York 1989.) Articles by: ANDERSON, POUL, *A Treatise on the Binomial Theorem* (pp. 272–278); HUBER, CHRISTINE L., *The Sherlock Holmes Blood Test.* (pp. 95–101) SHREFFLER, PHILIP A., *Moriarty: A Life Study.* (pp. 263–271)

SINGER, ANDRE, *Lords of the Khyber: The Story of the North-West Frontier.* (Faber and Faber. London. 1984)

STARRETT, VINCENT, *The Private Life of Sherlock Holmes.* (George Allen and Unwin Ltd. London. 1961)

STORR, ANTHONY, *The School of Genius.* (Andre Deutsch. London, 1988)

STORR, ANTHONY, *Churchill's Black Dog and Other Phenomena of the Human Mind.* (Collins. London. 1989)

TAYLOR, A. J. P., *The First World War: An Illustrated History.* (George Rainbird Ltd. London. 1963)

TRACY, JACK, *The Encyclopaedia Sherlockiana.* (New English Library. London. 1977)

VINEY, CHARLES, *Sherlock Holmes in London.* (Phoebe Phillips Editions. London. 1989)

WAGNER, GILLIAN, *Barnardo.* (Weidenfeld and Nicolson. London. 1979)

WINTER, GORDON, *Past Positive: London's Social History Recorded in Photographs.* (Chatto and Windus. London. 1971)

WOODHAM-SMITH, CECIL MRS, *Florence Nightingale.* (Constable. London. 1954)

YEO, GEOFFREY, *Images of Bart's. An Illustrated History of St Bartholomew's Hospital in the City of London.* (Historical Publications Ltd in Association with the Archives Department of St Bartholomew's Hospital. London. 1992)

ZEISLER, ERNEST BLOOMFIELD (DR), *Baker Street Chronology.* (Alexander J. Isaacs. Chicago. 1953)